Ultimate Freedom

Praises for *Ultimate Freedom*

Vickie and Mia put success, leadership and freedom within the reach of anyone willing to look behind the curtain. Be open to their fresh ideas, implement a few and watch the magic unfold.

—**Rajesh Setty:** Serial Entrepreneur, Author & Teacher, www.RajeshSetty.com

True life stories from the authors provide the foundational insight for guiding anyone down the path of understanding life better and then incorporating more powerful ways to turn passions into profits in order to build the life of their dreams. A remarkable work.

— **Linda Stirling:** International Bestselling Author & Owner,
www.thepublishingauthority.com

An energy drink for the mind! Vickie and Mia offer an honest and direct approach to finally living life on your own terms; stunningly simple ways to understand your power and embrace confidence in who you are. A long-time purveyor of influence, I couldn't put it down.

— **Lori Ruff:** Forbes Top 25 Social Media Power Influencer,
Brand Influencer & Strategist, www.LoriRuff.com

If you want to know the secrets to *Ultimate Freedom* there's nobody better than Vickie and Mia to reveal them. They redefine how you can better understand the world around you to have it all. Powerful and potent; this is a must-read for anyone who wants to decipher the code to claim total success and independence today.

— **Martin Wales:** Author, Media & Radio Personality for Microsoft
& Entrepreneur Magazine, www.MartinWales.com

I believe everyone is seeking freedom. Vickie and Mia not only understand freedom like few people do, they have broken down the process so anyone can claim the freedom they desire and deserve. If you are ready to live life on your on terms, this is truly a must-read book.

— **Terri Levine:** Chief Heartrepreneur™, International Bestselling Author
of *Turbocharge How To Transform Your Business as a Heartrepreneur*™,
www.heartrepreneur.com

Powerful and candid! The authors redefine how we understand the world around us, sharing with us the secrets to having real liberty. This is a must-read for anyone who wants to unlock and claim real success and freedom.

— **Scott Stevens:** Meteorologist, Atmospheric Researcher & Star of the Documentary *Why in the World are They Spraying?*

Unlock the freedoms lying dormant within you! Vickie and Mia show you how to resist the powers that suppress your freedom. Practical and energetic guidance in one book; this is what is at stake, and what your Ultimate Freedom is for—your life.

— **Declan Dunn:** CEO & Speaker, www.SimplyResponsive.com

Truthful and direct! Vickie Helm & Mia Bolte give you the field guide to having it all and creating the life of your dreams. If you value success and freedom, this book is for you.

— **Joel Comm**: New York Times Best-Selling Author

In this candid and thoughtful book on the meaning of Ultimate Freedom, readers will discover several myths of freedom and why they haven't yet achieved Ultimate Freedom in their lives followed by the exact steps it takes to get there. Relying on wisdom from Benjamin Franklin and other leaders through today, readers learn how critical thinking, combined with responsibility and making your passion work for you have a powerful momentum that lead to Ultimate Freedom. This is a must-read book for anyone who desires to feel and live their lives fully free.

— **Felicia J. Slattery:** #1 Best Selling Author of *Kill The Elevator Speech: Stop Selling, Start Connecting,* Communication Consultant & Business Speaking Coach

More than ever we need to value our freedom. These two change makers provide insight into how they've done it and how you can too. It's all before you right now, take it in and stake your claim.

— **Brian G Johnson:** Best Selling Author of *Trust Funnel* & Brian G Johnson TV

Ultimate Freedom

UNLOCK *the* SECRETS
to a Life *of* Passion,
Purpose, *and* Prosperity

Vickie Helm & Mia Bolte

New York

Ultimate Freedom
UNLOCK *the* SECRETS *to a* Life *of* Passion, Purpose, *and* Prosperity

© 2017 Vickie Helm & Mia Bolte

All rights reserved. No portion of this book may be reproduced, stored in a retrieval system, or transmitted in any form or by any means—electronic, mechanical, photocopy, recording, scanning, or other,—except for brief quotations in critical reviews or articles, without the prior written permission of the publisher.

Published in New York, New York, by Morgan James Publishing. Morgan James and The Entrepreneurial Publisher are trademarks of Morgan James, LLC. www.MorganJamesPublishing.com

The Morgan James Speakers Group can bring authors to your live event. For more information or to book an event visit The Morgan James Speakers Group at www.TheMorganJamesSpeakersGroup.com.

Shelfie

A **free** eBook edition is available
with the purchase of this print book.

CLEARLY PRINT YOUR NAME ABOVE IN UPPER CASE

Instructions to claim your free eBook edition:
1. Download the Shelfie app for Android or iOS
2. Write your name in **UPPER CASE** above
3. Use the Shelfie app to submit a photo
4. Download your eBook to any device

ISBN 978-1-63047-986-2 paperback
ISBN 978-1-63047-987-9 eBook
ISBN 978-1-63047-988-6 hardcover
Library of Congress Control Number:
2016911794

Cover Design by:
Rachel Lopez
www.r2cdesign.com

Interior Design by:
Bonnie Bushman
The Whole Caboodle Graphic Design

In an effort to support local communities, raise awareness and funds, Morgan James Publishing donates a percentage of all book sales for the life of each book to Habitat for Humanity Peninsula and Greater Williamsburg.

Get involved today! Visit
www.MorganJamesBuilds.com

For Rene M. White
Thank you for your example of living free.
—Vickie

With love and appreciation for my teachers,
from North Dakota to Nepal,
who have expanded my mind and softened my heart.
—Mia

Table of Contents

Acknowledgments

Mia Bolte: There is a circle of good women who led me down highway 285 to Crestone, Colorado, where I fatefully met the beginnings of this book. Thank you Paki, Judith, Linda, Mary, and Sharon for holding the vision of success and cheering for me each step of the way. Mukara, Brenda, Gillian, and Kate—for always being right there with me, I am deeply grateful.

Not a bit of this would be on the page without my excellent business partner and dear friend Vickie. Look what's come out of a little meeting near the Sangre de Cristos. How lucky!

Vickie Helm: As I begin to reflect on this project, I am reminded of the celebrated basketball player who, in the last seconds, makes a three-point jump shot and wins the game. The fans cheer, the coaches congratulate, and the basketball player gets to happily celebrate the win. But the truth is that it is always a team effort. The player is just the hero everyone sees. What most people don't recognize is the multitude of behind-the-scenes heroes supporting and sacrificing so she has time to practice, hone, and work undisturbed to gain maximum skill.

I have so many hidden heroes and loyal friends, coaches and co-workers who have supported this project that I find myself feeling an overwhelming amount of gratitude. For the first time, I include my Facebook friends in this list. Many of you I haven't even met in person, and your support has made this journey so much easier.

To my spouse, Robin Helm, my mom, and extended family, my love for you and your love for me is my reason why. To the Invincibles, Don Gifford, Scott Stevens, Craig Tomaski, Alberto Olivas, and Robin Helm, thank you for your kindness and willingness to work my hours, do my jobs, and allow me the space to create this book. You are the kindest, most supportive business partners anyone could ask for. Donny, thank you for cooking meals for us and keeping us healthy and fed.

To my editors, Angie Kiesling and Marcia Ford at The Editorial Attic, as well as Robin Helm, thank you for your humor, skill, and work ethic. You make us sound good. To Ken McArthur and Joel Comm, your generous friendship and coaching has made all the difference in the world, and I am so thankful for you both. David Hancock, thank you for working with us in such an integris manner. Your success is my success.

To my fellow author and friend Paki Wright, there are no words to tell you how grateful I am for that little introduction. It changed my life.

To Mia Bolte: "Shambhala vision teaches that in the face of the world's great problems, we can be heroic and kind at the same time." — Chögyam Trungpa, *Shambhala: The Sacred Path of the Warrior*. Thank you for walking this part of the journey with me and modeling your wonderful example of warriorship. May all that we do benefit all sentient beings.

Foreword

By Ken McArthur

Freedom—it's something we all take for granted until it's taken away from us, either suddenly or little by little. Freedom to map out the life we choose, freedom to pursue happiness, freedom to control our time and money . . . even the freedom to live without fear of harm.

I thought I knew about freedom after my family took a trip to Meridian, Mississippi, in the fateful summer of 1964.

I remember my Aunt Mil pointing out the lunch counter in a department store where young high school students had handed out leaflets protesting the fact that blacks were not allowed to eat at the lunch counters.

Andrew Goodman had grown up on Manhattan's Upper West Side, in an intellectual and politically active Jewish family, and attended the progressive Walden School. At Queens College, he had become interested in both acting and anthropology. He was sent to Mississippi after undergoing activist training in Ohio.

On the day he was killed, Goodman sent his parents a postcard from the town from which, later that night, the sheriff would dispatch him and his colleagues to their deaths. Apparently intending to calm any fears they had about his mission, or maybe just referring to the local activists who received him, he wrote:

Dear Mom and Dad, I have arrived safely in Meridian, Miss. This is a wonderful town … and our reception was very good. All my love, Andy.

In 1964 in Meridian, Mississippi, not everyone is a racist, but many people feel their way of life is under attack, and speaking up against fear and hatred is tough.

On June 21, Michael Schwerner, Andrew Goodman, and James Chaney are killed by a Ku Klux Klan lynch mob near Meridian, Mississippi. The three young civil rights workers were working to register black voters in Mississippi, thus inciting the ire of the local Klan. The deaths of Schwerner and Goodman, white Northerners and members of the Congress of Racial Equality (CORE), caused a national outrage.

The three young men were chased in their car, abducted, shot at close range, and buried in an earthen dam by members of the local White Knights of the Ku Klux Klan, the Neshoba County Sheriff's Office, and the Philadelphia, Mississippi, Police Department.

Although the crime was initially classed and investigated as a missing persons case, the civil rights workers' car was not found until three days after their disappearance, and their bodies discovered forty-four days after their abduction and murder. The disappearance and feared murders of these activists sparked national outrage and a massive federal investigation led by the Federal Bureau of Investigation, and filed as Mississippi Burning (MIBURN). After the state government refused to prosecute, the United States federal government charged eighteen individuals with civil rights violations in 1967. Seven were convicted and received relatively minor sentences for their actions.

It was right after the murders when I traveled to Meridian with my family.

My father was raised there, and it was my first experience with racial issues because I was raised in a tiny community on the western slope of the Colorado Rockies—a place where everyone seemed to be the same and race was far from everyone's mind.

That wasn't the case in Meridian.

I vividly remember seeing the separate drinking fountains and wondering how my father came out of that town without any hint of prejudice in his being.

Interestingly, when I asked my father the question—much later when he was about to celebrate his ninety-second birthday—he told me he didn't think he ever had overcome prejudice. He told me when he went to army boot camp that he was shocked by a fellow trainee who was black because he washed himself down with rubbing alcohol each day and he couldn't believe he was so clean.

Sometimes even our inner life isn't so free.

But it was in September of 1970 at Fort Dix, New Jersey, when I finally got the freedom message drilled into my soul.

The country was deep in the mess of the Vietnam War and I was experiencing my own boot camp agonies. Running mile after mile. Endless pushups. But it wasn't the physical pain that got to me. It was an inner pain, because it wasn't long before I realized the truth.

A private in boot camp was owned by the army.

Life isn't free when someone else makes the decision about whether you personally kill someone.

My personal freedom was gone.

It's a fact. Freedom isn't guaranteed.

Freedom is our lifeblood.

That's what makes this book so important to you personally.

You don't have to have your freedom taken away to learn its true value.

As Vickie and Mia will tell you, "The gift of having the Ultimate Freedom is more than a state of mind; it's an action and a way of life, not a guarantee. Freedom is not a right. It is something you claim and develop. It offers an opportunity to enjoy your life to the fullest."

This book gives you those key treasures, but only if you claim and develop your Ultimate Freedom.

You have the freedom right now to choose to make that happen.

All you have to do is keep reading.

Ken McArthur
http://kenmcarthur.com/
Author of *IMPACT: How to Get Noticed, Motivate Millions and Make a Difference in a Noisy World*

Introduction

The only way to deal with an unfree world is to become so absolutely free that your very existence is an act of rebellion.
—Albert Camus

I got up that morning and did what I had always done. I got dressed, grabbed a cup of coffee, got on the bus with a book in hand, read, and sipped coffee until I hit the downtown bus station. From there I would put the book away, get off the bus, and walk the five blocks from the station to the Total Tower building in downtown Denver to begin my long day of work.

I worked under contract in the accounting department for a property management company. It was supposed to be a two-month gig, but it had turned into a year. As I pushed the elevator button, I thought, *I do not like accounting; in fact, I hate it, but it pays the bills. I am grateful that I have a job that pays the bills.* I was hoping my moment of gratitude would help my Monday morning "bummed out to be going to work again" mood.

As I was pushing the elevator button, I felt my heart sink. Then my mind jumped in with another affirmation trying to cheer me up. Even so, I would be spending the day not living the life I wanted to live but living the life I thought I had to live in order to make ends meet.

I had all the responsibilities of an adult: house, car, student loans, and Visa payments; electricity, water, and gas bills; and the children's dance, piano, and karate lessons—all of this had to be paid each month. Responsibilities are part of the life of an adult. Do you have this too? Do you have an adult life that is filled with responsibilities? If so, you are not living the life you want and dream of; instead, it is the life you think you have to live in order to provide well for your family and be a responsible adult.

There are many reasons we live routine lives rather than what we truly desire. We can easily forget about our dreams and make excuses that seem important. These reasonable excuses become lies that we tell ourselves and believe. When we use the "responsibilities" excuse, we do not have to apply our focus or our attention to anything except maintaining the status quo.

Can you see how being so responsible could be an obstacle to knowing, honoring, and pursuing your dreams? What a convenient excuse. We lie to ourselves because our real goals and dreams require us to work at them and to become completely free—free enough to pursue them. For many people, real freedom is scary and uncertain.

Real freedom is a response and an ability. It is our inalienable right to pursue our liberty. What does the Constitution say? "We hold these truths to be self-evident, that all men are created equal, that they are endowed by their creator with certain unalienable rights, that among these are life, liberty, and the pursuit of happiness." Most people don't understand this statement. Instead, they think freedom is an inalienable right.

They think they have the right to freedom because it is written in the Constitution. So they yell in public, "I know my rights. I'm an American. I am guaranteed my rights." This is where things begin to fall apart. Once you believe this, you start protecting your rights rather than pursuing your freedom. This is a cause of confusion for many people and why they don't have the life and freedom they want. The truth is that pursuing your dream of freedom is the only way to protect your rights. If you are not pursuing the life, liberty, or happiness you dream about, you are not free.

Furthermore, your behavior puts your children and their future at risk. Why? Because they do not believe what you tell them. They follow your behavior, not your words. They will follow in your footsteps because they will learn the mindset and actions you modeled for them. If you tell them to pursue their dreams and you don't do the same, they won't know *how* to pursue their dreams. They need your best example. If you are a paycheck slave, chances are your children will be too.

If you think freedom is an inalienable right rather than something you pursue, so will they. They will not know how to pursue life, liberty, or happiness. Your children will learn how to give the most valuable part of their life and liberty to someone else, because they see you doing it.

They also will not realize they are not free if they see freedom as a right instead of the pursuit that it is—and the same will be true of their children. This is how a generation loses its freedom. In America we have been losing our freedoms for generations at a rapid pace.

You probably have heard the saying "Freedom is not free." Most people connect this phrase with the sacrifice our military service men and women make. The truth is, it is easier for people to pretend to protect a right than it is to actually pursue their freedom.

Our military personnel courageously sacrifice so much—sometimes their lives—to protect your right to pursue your own life, liberty, and happiness. Right now, it's not your job to defend the Constitution; that's what our military does. It's your job to pursue and claim the advantages and liberty that our Constitution provides. Our armed forces make the ultimate sacrifice to allow you to have the life you dream of, for yourself and your loved ones. By honoring the gifts of freedom, brought to you by our service men and women, you protect the Constitution and truly honor the sacrifice they make for you.

Freedom takes work, and it is not free. It takes planning and an understanding of what freedom really is by learning about history. This is how I found what I call the Ultimate Freedom. Once I unlocked the secrets, I realized it is the key to creating the life of my dreams and living truly free. Those who choose to claim their Ultimate Freedom can enjoy a level of success, wealth, and liberty that others will never experience. Unlock this freedom, and you will be able to claim your birthright—and your descendants will be able to claim theirs.

Ultimate Freedom is more than a state of mind; it's an action and a way of life, not a guarantee. Freedom is not a right. It is something you claim and develop. It offers an opportunity to enjoy your life to the fullest.

In this book, you will learn to unlock your ultimate freedom and have more time, money, success, and deeper relationships. This book will show you how to claim your freedom right now by understanding how to use it for yourself. For me, learning to claim and honor my freedom is the single greatest legacy I can leave for my descendants. Understanding genuine freedom is one of the greatest journeys and life experiences you can give yourself and your family.

Unlocking your Ultimate Freedom gives you wisdom, discernment, and equanimity in your soul. It is a powerful tool to bring success, keep stress levels down, and create a happy life full of incredible relationships and experiences.

I consider pursuing freedom to be the most important opportunity and gift that I will ever possess. I will lay down my life to protect, grow, and cultivate more freedom for myself, and I will not need to shed any blood or fire a bullet from a gun to do it.

It is with this intent that I share with you the secrets to unlocking your ultimate freedom and developing real, lasting liberty. But freedom is often marketed to the masses with a level of patriotism that is media driven and has its own agenda.

In World War II, soldiers died to protect freedom. Serving was considered a patriotic duty. Although I think it was important for that to happen under those circumstances, freedom is not about loving your country. It's deeper than that. It's about loving a way of living, being, and thinking. It is an action-driven state of being that is available to everyone. In fact, when you are truly free, your very existence is a peaceful act of rebellion.

When freedom is not about patriotism, it becomes about pursuing your own deepest kind of truth. Ultimate Freedom is defining and living your best life. It's about seeing and pursuing opportunities and exploring choices. It's having discernment and critical-thinking skills. It's about exploring spirituality without retribution from someone or something else. Freedom's foundation requires evaluation, creativity, and action.

I learned the importance of freedom from my stepfather (whom I call Dad), Lloyd Lovelace, and my "uncle," Allen Kuhn—not because they were freedom fighters or rich entrepreneurs but because they made their living illegally. Allen Kuhn was a jewel thief. Five decades ago, Allen Kuhn and his partner, Jack Murphy (aka "Murph the Surf"), were young, good-looking beach boys who gave swimming lessons at Miami Beach hotels. They also had a profitable second occupation—as jewel thieves.

In 1964, tired of preying on wealthy divorcées and tourists, my uncle Allen and Murph the Surf drove to Manhattan and pulled off the most audacious jewel heist of the last half-century. Climbing up the stone walls of the American Museum of Natural History, they broke in through a window and stole priceless gems from the J.P. Morgan jewel collection: the Star of India sapphire, the DeLong Star Ruby, and fistfuls of diamonds and emeralds.

My uncle told me the museum alarms did not sound because no one had changed the batteries in the system. No one thought anyone would try to break into the building. They got into the building easily due to a poor maintenance schedule. Because the alarms did not go off, my uncle and Murph got in and out of the building without incident.

My dad met Allen Kuhn in prison, where they became best friends. He is thus my Uncle Allen because he is my dad's best friend for life. My father was one of the first men to extract THC from marijuana plants. He sold it for about $10,000 a dram, which in 1968 was big money. He got busted and went to jail for eighteen months for having a joint in his pocket. That's where he met Uncle Allen.

Although what they did was illegal, how they thought and how they viewed the world was the genius that was passed on to me. After they got out of prison, Dad and Uncle Allen would spend a lot of holidays and dinner parties entertaining us with stories about smuggling weed, diamond heists, and other jewelry thefts.

These stories were often funny and suspenseful since the two men frequently lived on the edge of getting busted. We heard about how they used their ingenuity to avoid a snag with the authorities. What I noticed is how they studied humanity and its habits. When my uncle stole the Star of India, the federal officials only had a suspicion that he was their man. They had no actual proof. They tore his place apart looking for the jewels, but he had hidden them well because he had studied the habits of humanity.

My dad and Uncle Allen were outstanding observers, and consequently they noticed the habits people formed and were able to commit their crimes unnoticed, even in broad daylight. When I asked Uncle Allen where he had hidden the jewels, he said they were in the ceiling of the hotel hallway. My uncle said, "People never look up; they just don't look up, and that includes the feds."

The story of my uncle and Murph is told in the movie *Murph the Surf.* I don't condone my father's and uncle's actions, but they taught me a lot about developing good observation, awareness, and discernment skills, which I was able to apply to the process of creating the Ultimate Freedom.

You often hear people talk about wanting to be free. People run from seminar to seminar and from process group to process group trying to free themselves of their thoughts, afflictions, and pain, not realizing how deep their passion and longing for freedom really is.

When I found the Ultimate Freedom, I realized freedom is a multi-layered process that you develop. Because most people don't know it is a process, they usually work on a single aspect of the Ultimate Freedom for the rest of their lives, thinking that once they sort out that single aspect of freedom, they will be happy and fulfilled. Because it is a process, working on one aspect of it won't work. You need all of it to succeed. This has been the issue with claiming your Ultimate Freedom. People have suffered without knowing why because they only pursued one aspect of the process.

In this book we share with you the secrets to unlocking the Ultimate Freedom, and you'll discover how to claim and develop a life of passion, purpose, and prosperity. Throughout this book our real-life stories are woven into chapters, and even though some of the chapters start with "I" our intention is to help you see how both of us have learned and produced the Ultimate Freedom. We promise to communicate in easy-to-understand terms and share with you the secrets to building and protecting your freedom. Your task is to evaluate and apply the material so you too will experience greater freedom.

Let freedom ring.

Vickie Helm and Mia Bolte

PART ONE

If destruction be our lot, we must ourselves be its author and finisher. As a nation of freemen, we must live through all time or die by suicide.
—Abraham Lincoln

Chapter 1

Unlocking the Ultimate Freedom

A hero is someone who understands the responsibility that comes with his freedom.

—Bob Dylan

I t's never an easy decision, and it wasn't for this woman either. She felt scared to leave and stuck without choices. Hers was a dangerous decision that had to be planned carefully for the safety of everyone involved. She sat at the kitchen table, crying her eyes out, frustrated and scared, wondering what her next move was going to be. She didn't have much of an education and had been a stay-at-home mom for ten years, with no real work experience.

In that era, leaving her husband meant losing everything—all her money, all her things, a lot of friends, respect from others and even family—but mostly it meant being alone with no one to help or even talk to. She had nowhere to turn because turning to others would have put them in jeopardy as well. She was sobbing and feeling helpless, wondering how to free herself and escape from her abusive husband, when I suddenly bounced into the house looking for my mother so I could tell her about my happy day at school.

I peered into the kitchen and was shocked to see my mother hunched over our kitchen table, weeping so hard she didn't even look up at me. She had her head in her hands, and her shoulders shook uncontrollably as she sobbed out loud.

I dropped everything in my hands, ran to my mother, and threw my arms around her, hugging her and patting her back as I tried to comfort her. She knelt on the floor and hugged me back, but she was crying so hard that she couldn't respond to me in that moment. She was letting all her tears go.

I kept asking her, "Momma, what's wrong? Momma, what's wrong? Momma, what's wrong?" I had never seen her cry so hard and so much. I was worried and afraid; her sobs sounded like those of a woman who had snapped. I hugged her as we rocked each other on the kitchen floor until all her tears had emptied out.

I asked her again, "Momma, what's wrong?" I could tell by her disheveled hair and the red welts on her small body that my father had something to do with this.

She picked me up and set me on the kitchen counter so we could see each other eye to eye. She looked at me in a way that I had never seen her look before.

"Vickie, I want you to listen to me very carefully," she said, her eyes filled with tears.

Something in me sensed the seriousness of what she was about to say.

"Vickie, never ever let yourself get stuck. Never let anyone keep you stuck, not for money, not for security, not for anything. Always take care of yourself. Never let yourself get stuck with someone you don't want to be with."

Although I didn't completely understand all of what she meant, I understood the core message she was sharing and it became a defining moment for me. I could feel the importance of those words settle into my bones, my heart, and my soul. It was as if those words echoed through every part of my being. I would never forget my mother's words that day, because even at six years old I knew my mother was stuck, enslaved by an abusive man's wishes. She had no freedom or easy way out.

My mother had snapped because of the loss of her freedom, and now she would have to fight hard to get it back. We made a pact that day. I would never let myself get stuck, and she would get us out of the abusive hellhole we were living in. There was no turning back for her. We both knew it was time to break free.

This meant living in fear of my father finding us and threatening her—and us—with more violence. But when you have suffered as much as she did, you are willing to do just about anything to get out of a bad situation and seek a new life. Tired of the abuse and knowing she would have to hide out with three young girls, my mother took the bold step of leaving my violent father.

She had to plan carefully to sneak out before he got wind of what was happening, and then we would hide out for a while until he calmed down or forgot about us. She couldn't pack any of our clothing or toys or do anything that would tip my father off that she intended to leave him. This was in the 1960s, when there were no strong laws protecting women. There were no safe houses or women's shelters.

The morning of her independence day, she took $500 from the bank and left my father with the remaining $10,000 that was in the account. She threw a bunch of our clothes in laundry baskets, tossed them in the car, and never looked back.

Although I did not have a name for it then, this is how I began the search that led me to the Ultimate Freedom. At first it was because those words my mother spoke echoed through my brain and infused themselves into everything. I did all I could to remain unstuck and be as free as I possibly could. But because I did not have any understanding of what real freedom was, as an adult I often stumbled and fell before I recognized my misperception and delusion.

Like many other people, I was thinking of freedom as a right. This is where I started to get confused, and without realizing it I silently sabotaged myself and my efforts. Eighteenth-century British statesman Edmund Burke once wrote, "But what is liberty without wisdom, and without virtue? It is the greatest of all possible evils; for it is folly, vice, and madness, without tuition or restraint." I understood this because I was succumbing to this madness and folly. When you think of freedom as a right and not as something you pursue, this madness begins to take over without you even knowing it, and it becomes your silent saboteur.

I thought I was free but I was actually becoming a madwoman. "None are more hopelessly enslaved than those who falsely believe they are free," wrote German author Johann Wolfgang von Goethe in 1809. The kind of madness I experienced will enslave you if you don't understand what the Ultimate Freedom actually is. You will think you're free when you're not. Instead, you are enslaved to the passions of the mind and the whims of others' wishes without even knowing it. You harm yourself by confusing enslavement with freedom.

Because I didn't understand what being free really meant, I thought freedom was about being a renegade and getting my way all the time. Freedom meant "sticking it to the man." I didn't see this behavior as unethical or unfair because I was screwing over the mythical man who screwed me over. What a convenient excuse.

Confusing freedom with this growing madness meant making sure no one had any power over me. It also meant being able to do whatever I wanted, whenever I wanted—sometimes in a way that hurt other people or proved to others that I would buck authority. I could walk off a job when things weren't going my way. I confused having the Ultimate Freedom with having no feelings for myself or anyone else. I did not see freedom as simply an inner ability to authentically feel my own fragility.

I wore many masks and disguises that made it look as if I were free, but actually I wasn't. Things that projected success and freedom—like career, money, lifestyle, and possessions—were my favorite disguises, so as not to let anyone see the real me. Believe it or not, I really thought I was free. The truth was that I was trapped in my desire to remain hidden and inauthentic because I thought it was helpful in some way. But I was just spinning my wheels.

When you prop yourself up with material or emotional masks, you reach a dead end where there is no freedom. Instead, you are stuck and don't realize it. Masks can be heavy and burdensome because they rule your decision-making process and detract from your natural ability to be discerning. Masks keep you from facing who you have become, what your life has become, and what you will need to do to change.

I had to learn that freedom wasn't a narcissistic, self-indulgent mindset that thinks, "You can't tell me what to do. I'll do whatever I want. I'll drink what I want, smoke what I want, eat whatever I want, as much as I want. I'm a free person. I'm an adult. You have no authority over me." This is confusing freedom with self-abuse, something I did and a lot of people do every day.

For many years I confused freedom with being sexually free and not being tied down to any one person. It meant playing the field. Committing to a relationship looked like being stuck with the same person, so cheating was acceptable behavior. I could do whatever I wanted with whomever I wanted, whenever I wanted to, because this is what I thought sexual freedom was.

I also confused freedom with entitlement. I either wanted someone to do some unpleasant task for me or simply didn't want to do anything that was hard. If something wasn't easy and I would have to use some ingenuity or navigate a huge learning curve, I felt stuck, and when I felt stuck, I would often quit. I had confused freedom with things feeling or being easy.

If things were not easy, then I did not see the freedom within them. I couldn't see that "hard or easy" wasn't even truth or reality. Instead, it had to feel easy. So I became a chronic quitter, and this threatened my self-esteem and eventual success. I'd have meltdowns and arguments with loved ones because I wanted to avoid anything that was hard. I wanted to have control of everything.

Freedom is not having power or control over something or someone. People who believe this often resort to violence. Real freedom is not the power to dominate another in order to always get your way. It's not about being verbally abusive, manipulative, or unkind while believing it is your right to free speech that allows you to speak to another human being with anything less than the dignity you would want in return.

Someone who is truly free is never at war with themselves or the world but is resourceful and peaceful. I began understanding freedom a little more as I read something that Nelson Mandela wrote: "For to be free is not merely to cast off one's chains, but to live in a way that respects and enhances the freedom of others."

It took me a while to learn that real freedom was not about having a superior intellect either. Being smart does not make you free, nor does knowing Jesus,

Buddha, or Krishna. Freedom is an action, not a religion or concept. Knowing about religious leaders or what they teach does nothing for you unless you take an action and apply it to yourself.

So the action I chose to take was to search for the truth, because all the teachers I just mentioned told me that the truth would set me free. My finding the Ultimate Freedom began when I started to look for the truth as if it were hidden in a cave or on a mountaintop in Nepal. Okay, I thought it was hidden in a bookstore in the self-help section, so I went there and read voraciously.

I began researching and nailing down where the confusion started, and after some thirty years of investigation and learning where and how we mistake manipulation for real freedom, I found the secret to unlocking the Ultimate Freedom.

Some of history's greatest teachers give us clear direction about how to achieve the Ultimate Freedom. Buddha said this: "Work out your own salvation. Do not depend on others."

Jesus said, "You, my brothers and sisters, were called to live in freedom. But do not use your freedom to satisfy your sinful nature. Instead, use your freedom to serve one another in love" (Galatians 5:13 NLT).

Krishna said, "Free from anger and selfish desire, unified in mind, those who follow the path of yoga and realize the Self are established forever in that supreme state."

These teachings made it clear to me that if I wanted to have the Ultimate Freedom I had to claim it for myself, knowing I had the calling to be free within me, and so do you. The confusion over freedom is that many people think it is only one thing, such as financial freedom, and those who work only on a single type of freedom expect this to end all their ills and give them a sense of the Ultimate Freedom. Then when they become financially free, they can't figure out why they are still miserable.

Why does this happen? Because they have addressed only one aspect of freedom. Over the years I have identified six key areas of freedom that produce the Ultimate Freedom. When you address and embrace all six of these keys, you have an opportunity to experience an extraordinary life full of passion, purpose, and prosperity. This Ultimate Freedom becomes your life and who you are in every moment.

Some people who live(d) the ultimate freedom are Oprah Winfrey, Eckhart Tolle, Byron Katie, Jack Canfield, Richard Branson, Mother Teresa, Martin Luther King Jr., and Lisa Nichols. In fact, Lisa Nichols has an affirmation to express her Ultimate Freedom: She says, "I have nothing to hide, nothing to protect, nothing to prove, and nothing to defend." When you ponder this, you will realize that this is the Ultimate Freedom. This is the opportunity and gift of your birthright.

We promise to deliver this Ultimate Freedom process in easy-to-understand terms and share with you the secrets to claiming it and growing it. We will share the biggest roadblocks to freedom and how to move around them effortlessly to create the ultimate freedom for yourself and your family.

To clearly understand the Ultimate Freedom, it helps to see it like the Constitution and its amendments, in that your Ultimate Freedom includes six amendments to freedom, which when claimed and lived well will give you the Ultimate Freedom. Let's look at those six parts. Later chapters will explore these in-depth, but for now they are:

The right to pursue:

- Financial freedom
- Emotional freedom
- Spiritual freedom
- Time freedom
- Social freedom
- Creative freedom

These are the six freedoms that everyone, from your boss, to marketers, to advertisers, to bankers, and so forth, must fight in order to own you or entrap you into indentured service to them. If they have usurped any of these freedoms from you, they own your mind, your money, and your choices. They will tell you how to do everything, and if you are not living in real freedom you will comply.

When they own you, they will tell you how to think, where to live, what school your kids will go to, what neighborhood you will live in, how you will vote, what you will buy, what your yearly income will be, how much debt you will have, who your friends will be, whether you can buy a house, how much credit you qualify for, what vacations you will have, when you can go on vacation and how often you can go, what kind of car you will drive, what clothes you will wear, where you will shop, and essentially how you will live.

I know—it was hard for me to believe this at first too. However, let's see how this happens by taking a quick look at the importance of financial freedom. The average college-educated American made roughly $50,000 a year in 2016. Your income is your quality of life. It's usually income from a job, and it determines your ability to do everything I mentioned in the previous paragraph. You have a boss. He will tell you what time you must be at work, how long you must stay, and what you will be doing. At some workplaces, he will tell you when you can go to lunch or when you can go to the bathroom.

Your boss will also tell you when you can go on vacation and for how long. You won't be taking your family on an expensive vacation, and you won't be sending your kids to private schools because neither will be in your budget. This is living an enslaved life because all of it is owned and controlled by someone else, with your permission, of course. And if you're anything like I was, you are angry at this system, which is being sold to you as having the American Dream and the Ultimate Freedom.

Yes, I believed the marketing and the packaging too. Get good grades so you can get into a good college. When you get your degree, you will be able to get a good job and make good money. But just the debt from going to a university, whether good or crappy, will imprison you for decades, and debt is the number-one killer of freedom.

This education package is not freedom, and they don't want you to know what the real secret to freedom is. They want you to believe freedom is having lots of cash, but cash isn't freedom either. Cash gives you more choices, but they want you to believe that having lots of currency is freedom. But the only real freedom and capital that creates wealth is human capital.

Humans have brains full of ideas, inventions, discernment, and solutions; currency does not. It only provides a medium of exchange. Becoming rich is a result of applying human capital to ideas, inventions, and solutions that create products sold to other humans for currency. You either do that for yourself or do it for someone else, but essentially that is the process.

Using the Ultimate Freedom, you learn that you—not currency—are the wealth and the riches. When you trade time for money, you're selling your most important asset: you. Consider this when you think about large corporations where no one is really accountable. They don't want you to stop believing that money or their bottom line is more important than you are. They want you to continue believing them because it helps them make more money.

Benjamin Franklin once said, "The Constitution only gives people the right to pursue happiness. You have to catch it yourself." This is an important part of the secret to the Ultimate Freedom. The Constitution only gives you the right to pursue freedom. Most people pursue what they think will bring them freedom (money, career, power, popularity) but end up in confusion and enslavement without knowing it, never finding the real process that will give them the ultimate freedom.

I uncovered the Ultimate Freedom process accidentally. I was sifting through my confusion to find the truth that would set me free. At first it felt as if I just kept running in circles. Nelson Mandela once said, "There is no easy walk to freedom anywhere, and many of us will have to pass through the valley of the shadow of death again and again before we reach the mountaintop of our desires." This was me. I just kept circling the valley of death over and over again before I found the Ultimate Freedom.

Where I found myself most often tripped up was in my own thinking and its misperceptions. To uncover the Ultimate Freedom, I would have to invite a different point of view. I would have to engage with a different form of discernment. I would have to look at the pitfalls to freedom.

Chapter 2

The Pitfalls to Freedom

No one has proof that I know of, that a higher power exists; yet a major portion of the world believes in it and relies on it in faith, in trust, in what that is. Where is the science in that? And yet you have incredible belief in that.

—Sandra Bullock

W e were both safely strapped into the vehicle. I turned on the lights and sirens and began the chase. I was driving faster than I ever had before. My partner grabbed the radio mic, and I could hear the scratchy sound of the talk button.

"We are in pursuit of a four-door blue sedan with Colorado plate 404 X-RAY, ADAM, HENRY, eastbound Highway 7, over." The dispatcher came back with, "Copy County 24, in pursuit of a blue four-door sedan eastbound Highway 7, license plate 404 X-Ray, Adam, Henry, do you need assistance?" My partner replied, "Negative, we do not need assistance at this time, will advise." The dispatcher came back and replied, "Copy, negative no assistance at this time, will advise, keep this channel clear and open, no other traffic at this time."

I felt anxious as adrenaline pumped into my blood and rushed through my veins. I thought I was driving fast when suddenly I heard my partner yell, "VICKIE, DON'T LOOK AT THE SPEEDOMETER, THAT'S NOT WHERE THE BAD GUY IS! Look around you. Feel the car on the road, don't look at your speed. Don't look at the lines on the road. Look at what's happening! Step on it, you can go faster, punch it, he's getting away! Feel the police car move. There is plenty of power left, punch it!"

I hit the gas and felt the car work its magic. I was thankful my partner was coaching me and yelling directions as we chased the bad guy. Because I could feel the adrenaline rushing through me and I felt uneasy, I had looked at the speedometer and taken my eyes off the road while we were racing at about 100 miles per hour. That felt risky, even around the police training racetrack at the top of a mountain in Golden, Colorado.

I could hear the tires squealing around the turns and the engines roaring. I started to lose focus on what was happening outside because my thoughts had alerted my internal senses that there was a potential for danger. My partner brought me back to what was happening in real time. I became aware again as I pursued the car in front of me. This was practice, and I loved being on the racetrack. It was also fun. You practice to hone your skills so that you're prepared when the chase is real.

What's important to know about this is that having a mind full of beliefs is like having a complete tool chest that helps you create your abilities, outcomes, and life. Your current beliefs are the creation tools that give you your current life experiences and your level of freedom. Your beliefs are indicators of where your attention is focused and what your point of view is.

For example, if you believe you are smart, you will find learning easier than if you believe you are stupid. Your attention and focus is on one of two things: you are smart (therefore it's easy), or you are stupid (therefore it's harder.) If you believe you are stupid, that does not mean you are incapable of learning. It just means your belief will make it a slower process.

In my case, because I suddenly believed the chase was dangerous, I began to slow the vehicle down to return to a comfort zone. Instead of staying present and aware of what was happening, and maintaining the right speed for the pursuit, I wanted to feel safe because this would calm my mind down and lower my feelings of fear.

My partner yelled at me to wake me up and help me retrain my mind. Nothing was dangerous about that high-speed chase except what I was telling myself. It was creating my reality—and quickly. I was letting the bad guys get away instead of changing my point of view about it being dangerous. But that change is where we begin to unlock the Ultimate Freedom.

We often let our goals and dreams go because of what we are telling ourselves and not because of what is actually happening. We slow down and move into our comfort zone instead of stepping on the gas and giving it our all simply because we want to feel safe and lower our feelings of fear. This is how most of us have learned to command our mind and its neurotic thinking. We allow our unchallenged thoughts to rule our actions and outcomes, hoping this will soothe uncomfortable feelings we don't want to feel.

When we tell ourselves something disempowering, we lose our freedom to discern or take action. Whatever you tell yourself in the moment, you instantly become. It's the same for the belief that you are either left-brained or right-brained, linear or artistic. Beliefs tell your brain, your body, and the universe who you are and what you are capable of.

There are essentially only two types of beliefs, either a fixed universal belief or a flexible belief. A fixed universal belief is a belief that is generally agreed upon, usually backed by some sort of scientific evidence. We have universal laws as a result. For example, not breathing under water or gravity are fixed universal beliefs. No matter where you are in the world, people believe the law of gravity exists and they know they will drown if they try to breathe while submerged.

Whether you are in Australia or America, if you throw a ball off a cliff it falls downward. Whether you are in Australia or America, if you dive off a cliff, you will fall downward until you hit the water, but you must come up for air. These beliefs are universally accepted. Even so, we have developed solutions to break through these fixed beliefs. We have space shuttles, crafts and rockets that defy gravity and land on the moon or launch satellites into space and diving gear that helps us breathe underwater.

To break through a fixed universal belief requires an understanding of the universal law and then the creative energy and innovative thinking to accomplish it. Thus the Wright brothers gave us airplanes that fly in spite of gravity. Cornelis Drebbel gave us the submarine, which allows us to explore underwater despite our natural inability to breathe air while submerged. The belief is fixed unless a solution is found. A simple change in point of view won't work.

The second type is a flexible belief. It doesn't need a solution. Instead it needs a simple shift in perspective and some practice. A flexible belief is neither right nor wrong, true nor false. It is subject to change, depending on an individual's point of view. It does not have universal agreement, only the believer's agreement.

A flexible belief is malleable and can be influenced by attention, knowledge, or point of view. In the human experience a flexible belief can either empower or impair an individual's abilities by his point of view, focus, and attention. This is what creates and influences his abilities and experiences, and thus his outcomes.

Roger Bannister challenged the belief that if you ran faster than a four-minute mile your heart would explode. He broke the four-minute mile record in 1954, with minimal training while practicing as a junior doctor. He later became a neurologist.

Why is this important? Now the four-minute mile is the standard. The belief shifted when he shattered the record. He held the record for only forty-six days before it was broken again, which gave this belief a new perspective and response from others. It shifted the consciousness of humanity and what people thought was possible. Bannister was able to challenge this flexible belief on his own because of his knowledge base. As a doctor, he was convinced his heart would not explode, and besides, he could monitor it.

Because he was a doctor, he would know if his heart was failing. He used his medical knowledge and other skillsets to empower his abilities and alter his point of view.

This is an important aspect of knowing whether a belief is a fixed universal or flexible belief. A fixed universal belief usually requires an invention or innovation, while a flexible belief requires a simple shift in your actions, attention, knowledge, or point of view. Either way, breaking through a fixed or flexible belief system is how we shift our consciousness as well as that of humanity. Over time it produces greater and deeper levels of freedom. This is part of the Ultimate Freedom. The process shifts and awakens consciousness.

To shift your point of view or create a solution, you must know whether a belief is fixed or flexible and invent a solution or practice to hone your skills. This requires you to be willing to engage with a new belief. Solutions or new thinking can be applied to all beliefs. You simply continue to hone your skills until you are competent or until you find a solution. This only requires that you focus on a solution or a new point of view.

This is how you develop new skills that create new outcomes. This is the beginning of understanding the Ultimate Freedom. Freedom doesn't see problems or challenges. It asks questions and evaluates situations: "What am I telling myself about this flexible or fixed belief, and how is that affecting my outcomes?" Then it asks, "What needs to change, my point of view or my solution or both?"

Success happens when opportunity meets preparation. This means you are willing to get over yourself and your desire to be right. It happens when you move into discernment and evaluation. Shifting into being open creates mindfulness, confidence, and wisdom. Being right creates a false sense of self-esteem and other unhealthy reactionary behavior. Unlocking the process requires evaluation and discernment, not unhealthy emotional reaction.

We lose much of our freedom and many of our abilities when we are children since we are so influenced by our pliable beliefs and the huge amount of data that is constantly flowing into the mind. When we are children, we don't have actual discernment because discernment comes with experience. It's something you develop over time. But neuroscientists, marketers, advertisers, media, religions, and governments all know the power of training your mind at a young age by instilling flexible beliefs and having you believe they are truthful fixed beliefs.

The mind is greatly affected when your malleable beliefs can be triggered by a sound or a sight. For example, my young mind learned that speeding in a car was against the law and dangerous. It learned that the lines on the highway or road were to be obeyed to avoid traffic accidents.

To be a safe police officer I had to retrain my beliefs about being present and mindful when I was engaged in a high-speed chase instead of relying on past knowledge of road laws and speed limits. This was the first training that enabled me to realize that in order to have the Ultimate Freedom, I had to become more aware of my surroundings and circumstances.

Belief systems of all kinds put your awareness to rest. When you lose your awareness, you lose everything else and are easily manipulated simply because you are not paying attention. You live the status quo and habitual patterns that you learned in the past. This is why you need to determine whether a belief is flexible or fixed. Challenging a malleable belief system gave me greater freedom, abilities, and mindfulness and thus more freedom and success in my life.

If you want to unlock your Ultimate Freedom, you need to ask yourself if your malleable belief systems are impairing or empowering your potential to experience the Ultimate Freedom.

Chapter 3

Lies and Freedom Myths

Freedom is what you do with what's been done to you.
—Jean-Paul Sartre

I t didn't take me but a couple of seconds to figure out they were fake coins. I looked through the loupe and then placed the coin under the microscope and looked again. Slowly shaking my head, I didn't have the heart to tell the client that he had been conned into purchasing counterfeit Trade Dollars (a type of early American coin).

I thumbed through the pile of coins and slid the box of coins back to him.

"I'm sorry, these are all counterfeit coins."

"No way, I paid $300 for each of these seventeen Trade Dollars," he said.

"I'm so sorry, they are all fake."

He looked at me in desperation. "There is no way they are all fake. I bought them from a guy selling coins in New York City, and look, they have the mint mark on them and everything. I don't think you know what you are doing. You're trying to rip me off. I know they are not fake!"

I understood how painful it must have been to discover that he was conned out of all that money. I breathed in and began to speak when he interrupted me.

"The guy who sold me these coins was an honest guy. He told me his wife had cancer, and he needed to sell the coins to help pay for her treatment. I saw his wife; she *is* sick with cancer. He told me that each coin was worth $600. He showed me online that each coin was worth $600, and he would sell them to me for $300 each and I could double my money by selling them to a coin dealer, and that's why I brought them here to you. I saw it on the Internet with my own eyes. These coins look exactly like the ones I saw on the Internet. I knew this guy! These coins are not fake!"

I spoke as compassionately as I could. "I'm certain you knew the guy who sold you these coins. I am certain he was being honest with you, and I am just wondering, if he knew you could make more money selling them to a reputable coin dealer, why did he sell them to you for half price? Why didn't he sell them to a reputable coin dealer himself and make all the money, especially since his wife was so sick?"

There was a long moment of silence as I let him ponder the questions I had just asked him. Then I picked up one of the coins from the box. I put it squarely under the light for both of us to see.

"The issue isn't just the mint mark on the coin," I said. "There are so many other things you could look at on this coin that make it an obvious fake, but the real issue you may want to look at is the date on the coin."

It was a clearly marked 1872 CC (the mint mark of the Carson City, Nevada, mint) sitting in the middle just above the word "Trade Dollar."

He took the coin, looked at it closely, looked up at me a second, and then back at the coin and asked, "Yeah, what about it?"

"No Trade Dollars were ever produced in 1872, from any mint, anywhere in the United States," I said. "That is how I know it's a fake."

The room was quiet. I handed him a coin book so he could verify the information for himself. I sat with him as he let the shock and pain of betrayal sink in. I watched him as he came face to face with his own ignorance. He looked at me and asked, "Now what do I do?"

My heart sank because there was nothing I could do to help him.

His desire to believe the story the man told him stopped him from doing any research or having discernment and asking the man the right questions. Having authentic freedom means having discernment and evaluating a situation from an inner place of wisdom.

This is what made Benjamin Franklin so beloved. He understood the process of unlocking freedom. He valued liberty and protected it with his intellect and his heart. He recognized the value of hard work, self-evaluation, and wisdom. He left a message from his personal freedom code: "How few there are who have courage enough to own their faults, or resolution enough to mend them." He believed that in order to be truly free, we must have the courage to evaluate our own faults and capabilities.

The second step is having the willingness and courage to own your faults and capabilities. When you examine and retrain those aspects of yourself that surrender your freedom to something or someone else, you are unlocking this code. It is the willingness and courage to stake your claim to freedom and develop it that actually sets you free.

In order to develop real freedom, we need to discern how freedom is sold to us every day and understand the lies and myths surrounding that. Like the man who bought the counterfeit coins, we often want to believe these lies and myths. We need to examine why we like to believe these lies and how we can free ourselves from their delusional grip.

There are eight great lies and myths that rob us of our freedom, and before you can unlock the Ultimate Freedom and not be tripped up by those lies and myths, it will benefit you to know them. Here they are, in no particular order:

Myth No. 1: Freedom Is Your Birthright

This is partially true and partially misleading. It implies that you get the Ultimate Freedom at birth just because you were born. It misleads some people into thinking there is nothing else they have to do to obtain the Ultimate Freedom. They expect that their birthright promises them the lifestyle they want simply by virtue of their birthplace.

However, just like learning to walk, you must learn to become free. And just like walking, it takes awareness, practice, and a willingness to stake your claim to freedom. The more accurate statement is that freedom is an opportunity bestowed on you at your birth (in certain countries). It's similar to education. You have the opportunity for a good education, but how you use that opportunity determines how good or bad your education will be.

If you learn to read fast and well, that is great—unless you never pick up another book after high school. Then it doesn't matter how fast and well you read. The skill of reading is beneficial only when you practice and implement it. You may create a belief that reading doesn't actually help change your life.

Yet the power of reading, applied in the right setting (as you're doing now), will help you develop the Ultimate Freedom. We are living in an era of full disclosure. There are no more hidden texts. Everything you want to learn, every ancient text and code, is available on the Internet and in books at the lowest cost in history. The tools for learning are readily available.

Secret texts and powerful knowledge can only be assimilated through some form of learning. It is not a birthright; it's an opportunity to apply reading skills to gain the Ultimate Freedom.

Myth No. 2: Freedom as a Marketing Tool

Freedom as a marketing tool is sold to get you to buy a plethora of products and services that you don't need. Because many people don't have a sense of what freedom is, they are often seduced by the words "free" and "freedom," and they want freedom without having any discernment. They want everything from getting free from their job, to the "free to be me" self-help memes, to free downloads on the Internet. We love free.

The word "free" entices many people into spending thousands of dollars on products or services that don't really create freedom for anyone but the seller.

When you do not understand what freedom is for you, you buy what freedom is for others, and that may or may not unlock your own Ultimate Freedom. Because freedom is used as a marketing tool, if you don't know the Ultimate

Freedom, you can be easily misled, swindled, or manipulated by pitches that sound smart and are delivered by honest-sounding folks.

Isn't that what happened in our mortgage debacle? People didn't research or evaluate the contracts. People wanted to believe in the honesty of the guy selling the mortgage to them, just as my counterfeit coin client did. In the end, millions of families lost everything and did not know what to do.

Freedom is not something you buy. It is something you claim and develop. Freedom is an ability that produces a way of life, not a product or service for purchase. Many people who see the word "free" instantly lose discernment because they love the word so much. One example is this: 500 million people installed a free flashlight app on their smartphones, but when it is turned on it can access all the personal and private data on the phones. An April 21, 2015, ABC News video warns us about those free smartphone apps: http://abcnews. go.com/Technology/warning-free-smartphone-apps/story?id=30484903

Why would a flashlight app need private and personal data? A piece of malware in an app sets you up to be a victim of a cybercrime. Can this be in any app? You bet it can, and because cyber criminals understand our love for something free, they can put malware in any app and send it out for free in order to gain access to your passwords and other privacy settings.

Myth No. 3: Convenience as Freedom

One of the biggest lies and myths about freedom has been sold to so many people it has become a flexible belief disguised as a fixed belief. It is the "convenience as freedom" belief. Our lives have become absurdly convenient. We now have confused freedom with being a form of convenience, and it has become an unhealthy addiction in our society. Most of us think instant gratification is a form of freedom.

The more convenient our lives become, the more we crave more convenience—faster computers, phones, service, meals, and more. People are addicted to a certain level of convenience in exchange for their freedom, simply because they are confused about what the two really are.

Convenience, like belief systems, also keeps our awareness at bay. It helps us fall asleep in our lives and move like sheeple. It makes us believe that if things are not easy, something is wrong. This is not true. Evaluating freedom as something you should conveniently feel instead of an action you take creates this confusion and leads you to folly and madness.

Freedom is not a convenience, like a microwave or a fast-food burger; it's an ability. This is why many people don't have the Ultimate Freedom—they are addicted to things being easy. People who are addicted to convenience will quit before they even start to succeed because they confuse freedom with convenience. They will think, "This is not easy," and either quit or check out mentally because they don't like the pain they feel when things seem hard.

Today many people are desperate for instant gratification and addicted to it as a form of freedom. They believe that freedom is the ability to see what they want manifested quickly and easily without too much work on their part. This kind of thinking surrounds multilevel marketing (MLM) opportunities. People join an MLM with the notion that they can earn millions of dollars without too much work. They quit when they find out that it is not as easy as they first imagined.

This instant-gratification type of thinking and action has manipulated us into several generations' worth of debt, simply because most instant gratification requires a debt instrument, like a lease, credit card, or loan, in order to obtain it. We have been sold this "convenience as freedom" so often now that we don't even notice we have been seduced into the fixed belief that living beyond our means is a normal way of life.

This is the unspoken enslavement you get when you exchange your freedom for convenience. Perhaps you're beginning to see how one myth weaves into the next. This is how corporations and others are usurping your freedom. They get by with it because of this addiction to convenience.

It's not just things that we want to be convenient. We want our religions and spiritual beliefs to be easy too. People are sold counterfeit spiritual truths about prosperity and wealth; just concentrate on what you want and suddenly it will appear, without a process or an action. People are swindled out of the real spiritual freedom they seek because they believe religious freedom and affluence is a convenience that comes by simply feeling positive and happy about money.

The pursuit of fast and easy fixes is a multitrillion-dollar industry that's growing. People would rather pop a pill than eat nutritious food. We have bought and sold the flexible belief that freedom means that life must be easy at all times. We are told that the ordinary things in life should be outsourced or delegated, from cooking our meals to everything that a virtual assistant offers. This way, more time is available for you to enjoy other activities that you think are easy or fun.

We have subjected several generations to this addiction without realizing it. We have taught future generations to loathe having a work life that commands more than four hours a week and to work as little as possible to achieve success. So people expect the overnight success story because it is convenient, but it comes at the expense of their real ability to achieve what they want and have their Ultimate Freedom.

We have programmed future generations to detest inconvenience in such a way that they don't identify or even realize that they have lost their freedom, only the loss of convenience. Our addiction to this process does not allow us to see how we are generational slaves to one of the subtlest and most addictive forms of oppression ever created, because it is now ingrained in our society.

We lose discernment, freedom, wealth, and evaluation skills because we are addicted to instant gratification. Convenience is nothing more than counterfeit freedom. I hope you are asking yourself, "What do I do now?"

Myth 4: Government Protection as Freedom

In his freedom ethics, Benjamin Franklin said, "They who can give up essential liberty to obtain a little temporary safety deserve neither liberty nor safety." Since 9/11, we have allowed our freedoms to be chipped away at in order to feel safe. Right now, fear of terrorism is so strong in the world that it is consuming our discernment and reason at an alarming rate.

Because of this, our government establishes new regulations and laws to protect us and make us feel as if we are a safer society. However, this has slowly eroded our rights, liberties, and personal freedoms. Edward Snowden's act of releasing top-secret government documents revealed our complete lack of privacy. We now know our government has been lying to us and spying on the world. Living in a surveillance world is not freedom. Yes, we were relieved that surveillance cameras captured images of the suspects in the Boston Marathon bombings, but being constantly spied on is not freedom and being overly regulated is not freedom.

As we give up more and more of our personal freedoms to the government in order to feel safe and secure, our protectors will eventually and quietly become our captors because we have given them that opportunity. We are living in a security-at-any-cost society. Few people are stopping to ask how this is affecting our freedom, both long term and short term.

If you're in prison, you're much safer from the outside world but you have a lot less freedom. Would you voluntarily incarcerate yourself? This is essentially what we are slowly doing. And yes, I think some security is important, but I also believe that the dangers are often exaggerated to encourage cooperation or submission.

The point is, giving up your rights does not guarantee that you're more secure. We can give up many freedoms and still become victims of terrorist attacks and cybercrimes. Samuel Adams said, "The liberties of our country, the freedom of our civil constitution, are worth defending against all hazards: and it is our duty to defend them against all attacks." Many of these new regulations are attacking your liberties.

In the June 2016 issue of *Forbes*, Editor-in-Chief Steve Forbes writes, "Two ominous trends threaten us. One is the monstrous growth of the regulatory state, whereby 'independent agencies,' such as the EPA and the FCC are creating countless rules that carry the force of law. Another weapon of oppression is the criminalization of a torrential number of what were once civil violations. A typical example: It is now a federal crime to walk a dog on federal lands with a leash that's longer than 6 feet. Violators can be sentenced up to six months in prison. No one knows for sure how many federal laws there are these days that can trip up—and imprison—the unwary citizen. There are some 300,000 criminal offenses listed in the 80,000 page Code of Federal Regulations. Right now if Uncle Sam wants to get you he can."

We are not paying attention to how our freedom is eroding. When will we notice how inconvenient this is? Defending freedom does not require a violent act. Defending liberty is a critical-thinking act. Will we use force if we have to? Sure—a peaceful force. Defending something does not always mean using guns and bombs. It can be a cooperative, peaceful alliance and act. Mahatma Gandhi defended and won India's freedom in this manner.

Myth 5: Social Proof as Freedom

We have confused social proof with freedom. Wikipedia describes social proof as "a psychological phenomenon where people assume the actions of others reflect the correct behavior for a given situation. It is driven by the assumption that the surrounding people possess more knowledge about the situation."

This indicates that we have forgotten how to think for ourselves. Instead of using our own critical thinking, we look to experts, celebrities, and the wisdom of the crowds to tell us what to do, what to buy, and what is important to us. Social proof is about taking someone else's word for it instead of evaluating what's best for us and our situation.

Some people seem to love to give their decision-making power over to someone else. In a thirty-second commercial, the Burger King CEO shakes hands with rapper P. Diddy and says, "Diddy, as CEO we need a campaign to tell people BK is open late." Then Diddy looks pensive for a second and says, "Tell 'em Diddy says BK is open late." The CEO replies, "Huh, that's it?" Diddy looks over his sunglasses because he knows the BK CEO doesn't believe him. Diddy walks over to his TV and flips it on to see people screaming and running with excitement into BK. https://www.youtube.com/watch?v=sIV7g_HQXEw

This is the power of the celebrity influence. It is now over the top, but social proof is not freedom. Having and using your critical-thinking skills is freedom.

Even our decision makers are taking someone else's word for it and rushing bills through Congress. This is legislation that affects you.

In his movie *9/11* Michael Moore noted that when the USA Patriot Act was in this process, it wasn't available to the public and was barely made available to members of Congress. Many representatives voted for it without even reading what was in it. They used social proofs and the wisdom of the crowds to pass it. This is not at all intelligent because it doesn't protect or defend your constitutional freedoms. It's a form of politics as a convenience.

The Patriot Act was only one item through which social proof was touted as offering us protection from evil forces. If you want to learn something from the Patriot Act as a case study on social proof, then look at the stimulus bill, the housing legislation bailing out Freddie Mac and Fannie Mae. It shows how over the years Congress has pushed through important bills without providing the time for lawmakers to read them. It didn't matter which party was in the majority.

When even our legislators rely on the wisdom of the crowds, they set a precedent that says social proof is an acceptable way to freedom. This is how we become susceptible and dupable to other violations of our freedom that use the social-proof method. This is not true freedom, and you will not find it inside the Ultimate Freedom process. If you are driven by the assumption that other people possess more information about the situation than you do, you will easily be taken advantage of.

Myth 6: The HIPPO Lie as Freedom

We often give our power and freedom away to authority figures without thinking about what we are doing. Priests, teachers, pharmaceutical companies, gurus, cult leaders, doctors—all can get HIPPO syndrome (Highest-Paid Person's Opinion). The power of authority over us without our discernment or evaluation can lead to us being manipulated. The tradeoff is often about giving power away for validation.

It's easy to have someone tell us what to do or give us expert advice, and sometimes this is a good thing. However, "experts" are making a fortune sharing expensive, irrelevant advice because some people believe the most expensive to be the best. This *may* be true for cars or appliances, but certainly not for advisers.

Research shows that clients perceive the value of a therapist based upon their hourly rate. The client views the difference in price range as a reflection of the therapist's expertise and skill level. They believe that the most expensive therapist is better than the least expensive.

Look at the big oil companies as an example. Their top experts tell us how safe their oilrigs are and back that up with their findings—and yet our oceans, skies, and rivers are polluted by pipeline failure. Monsanto, the agrochemical company, sprays toxic chemicals over crops, while pharmaceutical companies produce harmful medications. All along people accept what they do without doing any research or insisting upon accountability if something goes wrong.

No matter how much money a company pays out in compensation, if the pollution is irreversible, that money won't mean much. On March 11, 2011, the Fukushima Daiichi Nuclear Power Plant was hit by a huge tsunami that resulted from a 9.0 earthquake in Japan. Reactors overheated, causing explosions.

Although that power plant is now being decommissioned, the damage was done. The radioactive materials have been dispersed into the air and into our oceans. It doesn't matter how much money Tepco, its parent company, pays out; it cannot reverse the damage done.

We often rely on experts telling us what to do instead of evaluating and researching our options for ourselves. Philosopher Julian Baggini said: "People should not expect the state to protect them from fraudsters. If we do, we get into the habit of neglecting our own powers of intellectual discernment."

Myth 7: The Acceptance of Lies

If there is one thing that politics, governments, the media, and advertising agencies have done, it is make us numb to lying. Their lies have deadened our natural revulsion for lying. We have learned to lie to ourselves and see it as the truth.

How can we teach our kids that we should respect an honest person when a legitimate whistleblower is made to look like a criminal? That's what happened to Snowden after he revealed that our government had been spying on us and lying about it.

Politicians stare right into the camera and lie by omission or manipulate statistics to further their party's agenda. There are so many advantages to being honest, but there must be a lot of advantages to dishonesty as well, given how often our elected leaders display that character trait. And workplace lies happen just as often.

"It wasn't me."

"I forgot."

"I didn't get your text."

"I didn't get that email."

"I don't know."

"I can't be at work today because I'm sick."

Dishonesty has nearly become the standard now. People lie to themselves as a habit. We have forgotten that trust is a powerful tool for building wealth and freedom. Oprah Winfrey is still one of the most trusted people in the world. She can sell millions of units of anything with just her approval, simply because people trust her.

The power and freedom of honesty has been forgotten. As Benjamin Franklin said, "Honesty is the best policy." Short and sweet, being honest is freedom. If you cannot be honest, especially with yourself, you are enslaved by your fears, doubts, and insecurities. Abolitionist Frederick Douglass said, "The life of the nation is secure only while the nation is honest, truthful, and virtuous."

People lie, hoping that it gives them an advantage over something or someone. When you do this, a part of you does not believe in yourself or your abilities. Isn't that why one of the number-one ways to lie is on a resume?

Real freedom requires truth and honesty, especially with ourselves. This is where the truth will set you free. "To thine own self be true"—another line from Shakespeare—is part of having the Ultimate Freedom.

Myth 8: No Worries—the Government Has an Emergency System in Place

We have come to rely on our government to provide for us during emergencies or hard times. We have been trained to look to our government as the go-to resource in difficult times. Because of this, we have forgotten how to rely on ourselves or come together within our local communities.

One of the worst myths most people believe is that the government has systems in place for unseen emergencies. We think that somehow they will call out the National Guard, and they will rescue us from any emergency.

However, as we have seen in events like the aftermath of Hurricane Katrina, our government is slow to react and often does not know what to do during catastrophes. Our governmental response on September 11, 2001, was equally slow. The immediate response to the 9/11 attacks of dozens of senior US Air

Force officials at the Pentagon—who were together in a meeting when the attacks began—appears to have been far from what we might reasonably expect, considering the serious and unprecedented crisis the officials had to deal with and the Air Force's key role in responding to it. *Evidence suggests that after the first plane crash at the World Trade Center was reported on television, there was a delay of over ten minutes before the officials' meeting was interrupted and they were alerted to the incident. The subsequent response of the officials appears to have been slow and lacking urgency.*

Journalist and *New York Times* bestselling author Ted Koppel, in his book *Lights Out: A Cyberattack, a Nation Unprepared, Surviving the Aftermath*, explains how unprepared our government really is. He writes, "The Department of Homeland Security has no plans beyond those designed to deal with the aftermath of natural disasters." After watching the response to Katrina and Sandy, I'd say this doesn't inspire confidence.

Having the Ultimate Freedom means never relying on the government to help you through a crisis. This is not freedom. Learning how to be as self-reliant as you can creates freedom.

Those are the eight myths that stop you from accessing the Ultimate Freedom. Having the courage to look at how you use or believe these myths will help you unlock the Ultimate Freedom. Sigmund Freud once said, "Most people do not really want freedom because freedom involves responsibility, and most people are frightened of responsibility."

If you truly want to have the ultimate freedom, it will benefit you to understand your personal pitfalls and what myths and lies you believe about freedom. It will benefit you to do as Ben Franklin did and "have courage enough to own your faults, and resolution enough to mend them." Without this, you will be manipulated by the great conspiracy theory, which we'll discuss next.

Chapter 4

The Great Conspiracy Theory

The most courageous act is still to think for yourself. Aloud.
—Coco Chanel

In 1970 Marshall Applewhite claimed he had a vision during a near-death experience. During his recovery, he and his nurse, Bonnie Nettles, discussed mysticism and concluded they were the divine messengers mentioned in Revelation 11:3: "And I will appoint my two witnesses, and they will prophesy for 1,260 days, clothed in sackcloth." They were convinced this was their assignment.

Together they opened a bookstore and teaching center to spread their message. They believed a spaceship would follow in the wake of the long-awaited visibility of a comet. In order to board this preordained spacecraft, they would have to let go of their human bodies. Applewhite and Nettles told their followers they would be visited by extraterrestrials, who would provide them with new bodies.

Initially Applewhite said that he and his followers would physically ascend to a spaceship, where their bodies would be transformed. Later he came to believe their bodies were mere containers of their souls, which would be placed into new bodies. They called their cult Heaven's Gate.

In the early 1990s the group made an effort to publicize their doctrine. In 1996 they learned of the approach of the comet Hale Bopp and rumors of an accompanying spaceship. They concluded that this vessel would take them on board for a journey to another planet. Believing their souls would ascend to the spaceship and be given new bodies, the group members committed mass suicide.

They all drank a lethal cocktail of cyanide, arsenic, phenobarbital, pineapple juice, and vodka. They dressed in similar black attire and tennis shoes, with armbands that read "Heaven's Gate Away Team."

This is a glaring example of the power of persuasion on an unfree mind. It shows how a cult leader can control the mind and actions of a follower, even to do something as drastic as kill oneself. Many people wonder how Applewhite was so powerful that he could persuade people to abandon their lives and follow him into the abyss of his delusion.

But we need to ask ourselves how we might be doing something similar— much less dramatic, but still harmful. How are we abandoning ourselves and following something without looking closely at it? Many people do not believe they are being influenced by sources that are hoping to control their choices. Are you being led into an abyss of delusion?

Do you often feel powerless to change your circumstances? The conspiracy theory holds sway over people who don't examine what convinced them to abandon themselves and follow modern-day cult leaders in disguise.

This is how cult leader Warren Jeffs, the notorious polygamist and self-proclaimed prophet of the Fundamentalist Church of Jesus Christ of Latter-Day Saints, got away with sexually assaulting children for years, until he was picked up by authorities.

This is also how the Catholic Church was able to hide the sexual abuse of children. Those may seem to be extreme cases, but similar occurrences happened in Mexico, the UK, Belgium, France, Australia, and Germany. When you don't own your mind or have discernment, someone else does.

Most people enjoy validation and belonging so much that they will give up their freedom and discernment in exchange for the temporary feeling of support from someone they value. People need support. Thus, they want authority figures to approve of them and their choices.

Unhealthy support systems are often why other people can make us feel impaired. We are looking outside of ourselves to feel cared about. When our need for this is strong, we can be easily manipulated by someone else's agenda.

When you do this, you may lose your critical-thinking skills. Big Brother, pseudo gurus, and cult leaders want to control your critical-thinking skills because it makes more money for them. When people lose their ability to discern, they are at risk of becoming sheeple. Big Brother—the symbol of a totalitarian state—does not want you to feel comfortable listening to your inner intelligence or be able to think broadly and clearly.

Taking in new information that runs counter to a current belief system is challenging. If you are not paying attention to what you think, you will be duped by someone else's agenda. This can cause cognitive dissonance—a term used in modern psychology to describe the feeling of discomfort that arises from being confronted with two or more conflicting ideas, beliefs, or values.

This suggests that we have an inner drive to hold on to each of our beloved, albeit limiting, beliefs and attitudes. (Remember the idea of fixed beliefs?) We avoid the discomfort and instability that accompany new ideas, regardless of whether or not those ideas are backed by evidence and sound logic.

Instead we follow what the media, our leaders, and other authority figures tell us. Why do we always believe mainstream media and big companies without consideration of what they are telling us? Why do we hold their information to be true, without question? We need to learn to think for ourselves. We must go beyond Fox News and NPR and educate ourselves on the larger reality, one that is less influenced by government information and manipulated media outlets.

In an article by the *Huffington Post*, Rabbi Shmuly Yanklowitz wrote, "Researchers have shown that most students today are weak in critical thinking skills. They do poorly on simple logical reasoning tests. Only 6 percent of graduating high school seniors can make informed, critical judgments about written text. This problem applies to both reading and writing. Only 15 percent of 12th graders demonstrate proficiency to write well-organized essays that consist of clear arguments."

If we are to avoid getting sucked into delusion, what Yanklowitz calls "the abilities to both generate and critique arguments—are crucial elements in decision-making." Removing this critical-thinking ability results in a loss of discernment regarding almost any matter. Thinking critically doesn't sound very sexy or fun, and yet without it we are giving away the life we really want to be living. Being able to employ rationality could mean the difference between life and death, happiness and misery, health and sickness, wealth and poverty, and slavery and freedom.

Being able to think strategically and objectively is a vital tool to be used alongside more direct, intuitive gut feelings. Critical thinking joins both the heart and mind. Most people are never taught how to think well. Further, you may not know how to examine your current thinking habits and what they are producing for you. Instead you rely on groupthink, allowing others to tell you what you should consider and whom you should believe. We deceive ourselves into believing we think rationally.

The Ultimate Freedom process encourages you to think critically and understand how you wish to act on information in a way that is both responsible and effective. Then you can be transformed from a passive member of society into an action-oriented, awake, and mindful global citizen.

In this era, critical thinking is one of the most important skillsets to have, because of the vast amount of information we have access to. Distinguishing between fact and opinion, between what is credible and what is only intended to forward a dishonest agenda, is crucial to creating an action plan tailored to your true values, wishes, and personal beliefs.

Twenty-first-century information comes to us from many sources, including blogs, YouTube, newspapers, Facebook posts, podcasts, TV and radio shows, and so forth. The issue with current-day information is that we also have more misinformation than ever before. American poet and feminist Adrienne Rich said, "Responsibility to yourself means refusing to let others do your thinking, talking, and naming for you; it means learning to respect and use your own brains and instincts; hence, grappling with hard work."

In order to unlock the Ultimate Freedom, it will benefit you to follow in Ben Franklin's footsteps and take your responsibility as a citizen seriously—question authority, especially your own. Is there a conspiracy to have mass control of everyone's mind and have us lose critical-thinking skills? I believe so. That is how people are led to agree with corrupt governmental and corporate actions, including going to war.

These are well-crafted plans sponsored by some of the largest media companies. We went to war with Iraq based on the media and government convincing us of the existence of weapons of mass destruction—weapons that did not exist.

Our founding fathers faced huge challenges in creating the Bill of Rights. It needed to be applicable not only for that time but also for the future of our nation. One major challenge was creating the foundation for a free society without knowing the future—and the unbelievable technological advances that were to come. Who would have thought we would need to explicitly prohibit the government from engaging in mind control?

One item that promises our protection from the government is the fourth article in the Bill of Rights, which states, "The right of the people to be secure in their persons, houses, papers, and effects, against unreasonable searches and seizures, shall not be violated, and no warrants shall issue, but upon probable cause, supported by oath or affirmation, and particularly describing the place to be searched, and the persons or things to be seized."

Yet propaganda techniques have been usurping critical-thinking skills for generations. As early as 1928, psychologist Edward Bernays's book *Propaganda* alerted us to "the conscious and intelligent manipulation of the organized habits and opinions of the masses is an important element in democratic society. Those who manipulate this unseen mechanism of society constitute an invisible government which is the true ruling power of our country." This is how media and big companies have influenced our government and our reasoning. Propaganda may not be as obvious as actions of the Heaven's Gate group, and yet it does exist in subtler and more harmful ways today.

As technology advances, mind-control techniques are becoming more sophisticated. Over time the government and corporate media have funded mind scientists for the continued discovery of how the human brain functions, learns, retains information, and behaves. We are being manipulated by this breakthrough science, which could be used in any way, positive or negative. Effective brainwashing techniques are used by the most successful propaganda networks and advertisers. When you watch TV they can have constant access to your mind.

In order to think for yourself again, it will be important for you to shut off the TV and read a book. Oh wait, you *are* reading a book. Congratulations. You are being responsible for your freedom.

Chapter 5

The Freedom of Thinking

Education is not the learning of fact, but the training of the mind to think.
—Albert Einstein

Thinking is free. A person can never be hindered from thinking whatever he wishes, because thoughts are still private. You can quietly talk to yourself and have any thought you wish. But there is little training to help us learn how to think beneficially and healthfully.

What many people don't know is that you may think in a disempowering manner without even knowing it—and still believe that how you think is good enough. Many people do not pay attention to how they have learned to think or what they are actually saying when they talk to themselves. Consequently, people have not learned *how* to think but instead have learned *what* to think via lexical entrainment (The phenomenon in conversational linguistics of one person adopting the reference terms of another--usually a person in a teaching or leadership mode.).

Most people do not believe their thinking habits are marginal or controlled by someone or something else. Most people have no idea their thinking process is not their own or that by allowing someone else to do their thinking for them, they have lost trust in themselves. We are losing critical evaluation skills every day. Most people don't really know how to evaluate that. But let me show you how your ability to think and discern are being usurped.

The reality is that we now have many computer algorithms that select information for us based on a variety of data we share on social sites. Thus, millions of people think they have found their soul mate based on an algorithmic line of code placed on a dating site that matches them to a mate. Dating sites like Match.com do the thinking for them. They do not even notice how the power of fate or destiny fades when they hand over their love life to an algorithm. In fact, many people aren't even aware that an algorithm guided their decision in choosing a mate. They just give away their critical thinking and powers of discernment to a sequence of code and don't notice how disempowering that is.

Whom we date and fall in love with is such an important aspect of our human experience that it seems there should be more divine intervention and human interaction and fewer computer algorithms involved in the process. Yet more and more these days we evaluate choices that a computer spits out for us instead of relying on our own awareness and inner feelings as guides. This is simple yet powerful evidence for how we are losing our critical-thinking skills to apps and programs designed to make falling in love and finding a mate both convenient and painless. We quietly tell ourselves that we are not capable of finding Mr. or Ms. Right with our own discernment.

In his article "What Big Data Will Never Explain," magazine editor Leon Wieseltier writes, "With the help of big data, we will no longer regard our world as a string of happenings that we explain as natural and social phenomena, but as a universe comprised essentially of information . . . . In some ways the technology is transforming us into brilliant fools. We are renouncing some of our primary human experiences."

Apps are being created to help people choose what to wear based on what their date would approve of and what would make a strong impression. The apps determine this by scouring the data provided by the date on their social network sites. If you can't be yourself, exactly who is showing up for the date—you or the algorithm?

We are subtly losing our discernment to the convenience of having something else think and make choices for us. If we dig even deeper, we can see that we have a deep distrust in our innate ability to think for ourselves and guide ourselves. Ralph Waldo Emerson said, "Trust thyself: every heart vibrates to that iron string." Your discernment and critical-thinking skills fade with every choice you hand over to an algorithm. What is unfortunate about this unhealthy habit is that the loss of critical-thinking skills will rob you of your ability to unlock the Ultimate Freedom.

Every day we have to rely on the way we think. Our current thinking abilities have produced our current environment, lifestyle, and friendships. Many people don't pay attention to their thinking habits or how they are being reshaped by algorithms. They do not notice what the real issue is or look inside themselves to see how their destructive thoughts are shaping their realities.

Neither do they notice how choices are being denied them as they allow something else to think for them or provide them with alternatives. The unlucky thing about this approach is that we still are using our old unhealthy thinking to evaluate our new external world. Often we end up with the same results over and over again because we are provided with the same choices over and over again by algorithms. This is dangerous to real freedom.

The true price of freedom is the ability to have discernment and critical-thinking skills. The forefathers of our democratic society were critical thinkers of the highest order. They valued liberty and all its expressions. They understood that without these basic freedoms, a democratic society would not emerge or last.

The power in our Constitution and the Ultimate Freedom code lies in the manifestation of our forefathers' critical-thinking skills. We would not have the Constitution or Bill of Rights without the foundation of their ability to evaluate and think critically.

Without this profound level of thoughtfulness, liberty would not have persisted. If you do not have this ability, it will be very hard for you to produce the kind of freedom, meaning, and wealth that you desire.

Developing and honing my critical-thinking skills is how I moved from having a life of madness and folly to finding the Ultimate Freedom. At first I misunderstood what critical thinking meant. I thought it meant criticizing my own or others' habits. I believed it was about finding fault and then trying to fix the fault. I confused critical thinking with criticizing myself or others.

How do you know if you have unhealthy thinking habits? Check to see if you are prone to complaining, judging, and condemning others. People who do this apply this behavior first to themselves and then to others. In today's world we call them "haters." These are people who feel better about themselves if they can pass judgment on another. It gives them temporary self-esteem to feel as if they are better than someone else.

A large part of having healthy critical-thinking skills is allowing the wisdom and expression of heart-centered analysis to be present. The Constitution was developed with the type of thinking skills that still make it relevant today for everyone. It will still be relevant another two hundred years from now because of its well-thought-out foundation.

Using the Ultimate Freedom doesn't work in groups in which people are motivated by self-interest or have competitive natures. If the ego is leading, there is no critical thinking. If people are only interested in what is advantageous to them rather than what is beneficial to the group, you won't see critical-thinking skills in action. Our forefathers viewed the creation of the Constitution with an eye for cooperative, democratic and mutually beneficial collaboration. This is how our forefathers demonstrated their thinking about liberty and having the Ultimate Freedom.

Skilled critical thinkers learn how to evaluate all sides of an issue and are good listeners, open to new ideas and new information. They embrace new solutions and directions that benefit everyone, not just their limited self-interests.

When liberty was created along with our Constitution, people did not live in a culture in which minds are consumed by advertising, marketing, sex, violence, fear-based media, corporate greed, video games, aggression, unhealthy food, and

TV. Today's media reflects our Western values, what our minds are preoccupied with, and where we are going. Every day we are losing our fundamental ability to use and choose our freedom because we have allowed our minds to be usurped and programmed. We no longer know how to think critically.

Unlocking the Ultimate Freedom requires the same type of critical-thinking skills our forefathers valued and used in creating the Constitution. Critical thinking is a holistic approach to thinking. It builds confidence, inner trust, and strong relationships, as well as authentic self-esteem. It empowers your abilities to succeed and creates a feeling of well-being.

There are six critical-thinking skills that support us in having the Ultimate Freedom.

Critical-thinking Skill No. 1: Reason

My Field Training Officer (FTO) and I had been dispatched to a local McDonald's where a very drunk woman was lying on the floor because she was too intoxicated to lift herself into a booth. Shortly after we arrived, my lieutenant showed up on the call. Once a senior officer shows up, they are in charge, so my job was to stand down and be in a supporting role.

The woman was so drunk she couldn't even stand up. My lieutenant knelt down beside her and asked what her name was. She just looked at us and rolled her eyes, but she was obviously so drunk she couldn't put a sentence together. My first thought was, *We need to take her to a detox center and let her sober up.* I watched the senior officer try to communicate with her.

"Ma'am, can you tell me your name? What's your name, ma'am?"

But this woman was so trashed she could only look up at us with a wobbly head and murmur incoherent sounds that made me chuckle. We couldn't make out anything she was trying to say because she was obviously intoxicated well past her tolerance point. My arrogant mind wondered how she could get the bottle to her lips, being that drunk.

The lieutenant noticed a nice purse on a nearby table. He asked the woman, who was now trying to get up off the floor, "Ma'am, is this your purse?" He said it a little bit louder, hoping to communicate with her. "Ma'am, is this your purse?" She couldn't even reply. He stopped everything he was doing and tried to help her sit up on the floor.

My lieutenant appeared frustrated as he looked up at me.

"Sir, would you like me to take her to a detox center?" I asked. But in my head I was laughing at her and thinking, *Wow, how much did you have to drink?*

He shook his head, as if to give him a little more time to find out her name and where she lived.

He grabbed the purse off the table, brought it down by her, and opened it up.

"Ma'am, is this your purse?" he asked again. He riffled through it and found a photo ID that proved without a doubt that we had this woman's purse. While looking through the purse, he also found several candy bars and a tube of some kind of goo. He opened the tube, put some goo on his finger, and put it in her mouth.

Then he asked me to call an ambulance. I was confused but did as he wished. I figured he thought she may have had alcohol poisoning. He showed the inside of the purse to me and said, "See, look at this—she has so many candy bars in her purse." I didn't know what to reply. I thought, *She's a drunk, and of course she eats unhealthy.*

He put everything back in her purse and kneeled on the floor again.

"Can you tell me your name?" he asked again.

This time she was suddenly sober enough to tell him her name. I was amazed that she could make a coherent sound. I thought we could move her to a detox center at that point because she could talk and possibly did not have alcohol poisoning.

My lieutenant was now carefully helping this woman sit in a chair. He squatted down to ask her if she was feeling better. She was looking better but was still drunk and wobbly. He kept watching her to make sure she did not fall on the floor again.

"Do you have diabetes?" he asked.

She nodded. Then she muttered the words, "I've been raped."

"What?"

"I've been raped."

By then the ambulance had arrived and the EMTs were taking over. My lieutenant told the EMTs, "I think she's in diabetic shock and has been assaulted."

Because of the color of her dress, the bloodstains were well disguised. But once I shifted my point of view about her, those stains were clearly visible. The EMTs loaded her into the ambulance and drove away to the hospital.

I was feeling horrible because I realized that I had been judging this woman instead of doing what my lieutenant was doing—using his reasoning skills to evaluate the situation and find out what was really happening. My judgmental attitude blocked me from noticing the bloodstains on her dress, as well as other evidence.

When you are judging, you lose mindfulness, awareness, and critical-thinking skills. You lose the ability to evaluate something with any clarity. This woman had gone into diabetic shock, and someone saw an occasion to assault a defenseless woman, leaving her to fend for herself. Her diabetic shock kept getting worse until she reached that McDonald's and could no longer function.

When you use critical-reasoning skills, you draw inferences or conclusions that are supported or justified by evidence. I was using my ego, and my lieutenant was using his critical-thinking skills. I realized that if he had not shown up and I had been in charge of the call, she could have died at a detox center because my ego could not get over itself. I kept thinking that I was right—that she was stupid drunk.

I kept validating my ego with unhealthy thoughts like, *I'm a cop; I know what's going on here. She has no respect for herself, getting that drunk.* I felt powerful wearing that uniform. I felt as if she had no power and was less important than me. She was just a drunk person lying on a floor.

I wanted to be right and feel important more than I wanted to find out what the truth was. Do you know how much our society is addicted to this judgmental mindset today? So many people want to be right and feel important instead of finding out what the truth is. But only the truth will set you free; self-importance will not. This is the hidden madness and folly that blocks our ability to think well. In my mind I was important, and that made everything or everyone else wrong. Or at the very least, they needed my permission to act. That woman could have died because of my sense of self-importance.

Having the Ultimate Freedom tells us that all men are created equal, yet many people still have a flexible belief in a hierarchical order of humanity. Our unhealthy thinking leads us to believe that we are better than, less than, or equal to someone else. We play with this flexible belief and use it to support our poor self-esteem. Instead we could be using our reasoning skills.

When we think someone is better than we are, we give that person authority over us. When we think someone is lesser, we give ourselves authority over them. When someone is equal to us, we call them a peer. When we hold this flexible belief as truth, we may treat people differently based on our perceived position of better than, less than, or equal to. When we play this game, it is hard to get over wanting to be right and important. This will rob you of a great deal of freedom and success.

Authentic reasoning doesn't ask who or what is right or wrong, or who is better than or less than. It knows everyone is equal. It deduces from gathered information. It produces a rationale that gives a conclusion based on evidence and facts.

My lieutenant gave me my performance evaluation on the way to the hospital to take a report from the woman and return her purse to her. I was frightened because I knew I had screwed up badly.

It was quiet at first, and then my lieutenant asked me, "What did you observe?"

I sheepishly reported that I saw her inability to make a sentence and thought she was drunk because she couldn't stand up.

"Is that all the evidence you gathered and acquired? Did you smell alcohol on her?"

"No, sir," I said.

"If she was as drunk as you pronounced her to be, do you think you would have smelled alcohol on her clothing or breath?"

Now I was feeling like a jerk and had determined that I sucked at my job. I looked at the floor of the car.

"Yes, sir, it would seem reasonable that as drunk as I thought she was, I would have easily smelled alcohol on her," I said.

My lieutenant was silent as he let me sit in my mistake until it penetrated my heart, mind, and soul. He knew I was feeling bad about the situation.

"Vickie, there is a difference between gathering facts and general speculation. There is a difference between what you know and what you think you know. Many officers get tripped up on what they think they know because they think their statements or speculations are facts, simply because they are a police officer. Remember, we gather evidence and facts, not statements of speculation or pronouncement."

"Yes, sir," I replied.

I would never do that again. I didn't get written up or chastised. Instead he let me feel the pain and embarrassment of my egocentric actions and my arrogant thinking. This was a defining moment for me. It forced me to look at how I was sabotaging my life by confusing judging others with evaluating a situation.

One of the most sacred parts of the Ultimate Freedom is found in the Fifth Amendment to the Constitution:

"No person shall be held to answer for a capital, or otherwise infamous crime, unless on a presentment or indictment of a Grand Jury, except in cases arising in the land or naval forces, or in the militia, when in actual service in time of war or public danger; nor shall any person be subject for the same offense to be twice put in jeopardy of life or limb, nor shall be compelled in any criminal case to be a witness against himself, **nor be deprived of life, liberty, or property, without due process of law;** nor shall private property be taken for public use without just compensation."

Nowhere in that amendment did it say "or the court of Vickie's opinion and Vickie's judgments." It took a nanosecond for me to judge and pronounce another person as guilty. That quicksilver response removed my ability to observe, reason, or discern. Critical thinking is an evaluative thinking process that uses reasoning and fact gathering to assess the validity of something. This can be applied to any statement, argument, research, news story, or situation.

Critical-thinking Skill No. 2: Feeling and Compassion

It was a hot summer night in California, the kind of night when it is still 90 degrees outside at midnight. I lived in Fair Oaks and was working at Jimboy's Tacos, which I liked a lot. I had just graduated from high school and was waiting for my milestone eighteenth birthday, which was about six weeks away.

One night my favorite manager and I were closing the store. She was in her early thirties and married with two sons. She was bright and fun to work with; we got along well. It was time to take out the garbage, as I did every night at closing. The manager had just put some extra cash into the safe, and we were listening to loud music and laughing while we were working.

I opened the back door to the restaurant to take the trash to the Dumpster and was confronted by a man wearing a blue bandana. He was only slightly taller than I am but had a big muscular frame. He mumbled as he pushed something into my stomach, saying what sounded like "Take ou yo dashes."

Our music was so loud that I didn't understand him.

"What?" I called out as I looked down to see a big revolver pressed against me. I noticed the bullets in the cylinder and realized this was really a loaded gun. I looked up at him again, but this time I was aware of what was happening. The fear pounding through me pulsed like a fire hose at full blast. I was shocked, wide awake, and fully conscious. I couldn't scream or speak, but I became fully aware of everything. He repeated himself, only this time he talked much louder.

"Take off your glasses!" he yelled.

I quickly reached up and pulled off my glasses. I put them on the sink as he pushed his way inside the closed store.

"Who else is here?" he asked.

By the time he said this, my manager was screaming in terror. She threw her hands up in the air and shook. The robber kept the gun pointed at my stomach as he told my manager to lie facedown on the floor. She complied quickly.

He turned to me. "Get me the money," he said.

But something happened to me when he spoke that time. Something I will never forget came over me in that moment.

As I said "yes," I looked at him and saw the intense fear in his eyes and I unexpectedly felt this incredible compassion run through me. He was more scared than I was. I saw his humanity and fragility, but at that young age I couldn't have put words to it.

Suddenly an amazing calm and peaceful loving-kindness enveloped me. I immediately felt a forgiveness and authentic love as I had never felt before. I didn't see him as good or bad, right or wrong. I just saw the pain in his eyes and his inner conflict. I had never felt like this before, but compassion for him had overtaken me. All of this happened in a flash, but it felt as if it were happening in slow motion.

Suddenly and magically I was able to listen to an inner voice I had never heard before. It was speaking to me as if it were a guardian angel. I could plainly hear something wordlessly guiding me. I had become quiet enough inside to hear it.

I heard, "He doesn't want to hurt you, Vickie, he just wants the money." I stopped listening to the robber and began listening to this unseen presence that was guiding me. I complied with what it told me to do or say without realizing my inner calm and peacefulness also had produced a type of love that I think the robber noticed. It was calming for him too.

The unseen presence spoke again. "Don't give him both drawers full of money. Give him the drawer with the least amount of money, which is the second drawer. He won't notice that there are two drawers." I appeared to be doing what the robber wanted, but instead I did what the unseen inner intelligence was telling me. Quickly I opened the drawer that the manager had just removed the excess cash from and put the money in a bag, which I then handed him.

He told me to lie facedown on the floor. Then he pulled my manager up. She too had calmed down a bit. I was feeling compassionate and utterly at peace. I knew in my bones that this man did not want to hurt us. He ordered her to go to the safe and get the money out. She did so, but he did not believe that she had given him all the money because it was just a tiny bag of money.

"All of it, put all the money in the bag!" he said.

"I did—I put all the money in the bag."

He still didn't believe her, and he became more agitated and pointed the gun at her.

"Put all the money in the bag, now!"

The robber hesitated to look in the floor safe where she had placed the money because he would be exposed to a big window where passersby would be able to see him.

"I did. I put all the money in the bag," she said.

He did not believe her, and again he became more aggressive. This time that unseen presence let me know what to say.

"Tell him to go look in the safe. Do it now—tell him to go look in the safe."

I popped my head up off the floor and spoke to him as if he were my friend. I was not scared.

"Dude, go look in the safe. She's telling the truth—go see for yourself."

Something came over him. He began to trust me.

"Go look in the safe. You'll see there is no more money," I said again.

I don't know what happened, but he began to see me as an ally. He took my advice, stayed low, leapt behind a counter section where no one would see him from the window, and looked into the floor safe.

To his satisfaction, he saw no more cash. He ordered my manager to lie facedown on the floor next to me, and he fled out the back door into the night. Later that evening I couldn't sleep, not because of trauma, but because I still felt so calm, awake, loving, and peaceful. Instead of sleeping, I sat in a park feeling the joy of the swing underneath me, the heat of summer, and the encounter I had just experienced.

For the first time, I tapped into an unseen intelligence and presence that resided in me. I wanted to meet it more often. From then on, I knew that feeling compassion and listening to that inward voice were the keys to accessing this guidance and deeper freedom. The robbery shocked me into becoming instantly more aware. I realized later that when situations appear to offer a choice between life or death, this gift becomes more readily available. However, when you unlock this gift without it being life or death, it becomes part of your Ultimate Freedom.

People often tap into this sound and unseen intelligence in an emergency. I wanted to learn how to access it without it being a crisis. This silent intelligence knew exactly what I should do and showed me that compassion and genuine kindness are tools we can use when we listen. We must listen not only with the mind but also with the heart. When we have become so routine and unaware, we must be jolted out of our usual way of thinking before we can listen to the subtler messages or messengers.

Because we access this part of our thinking capabilities only when we are in an emergency, every bit of access to our capabilities shows up. But then when the crisis is over, we let the gift go. Why do we do this? Why don't we listen to this silent intelligence more often than we do our minds? The silent intelligence has your Ultimate Freedom at heart.

Having feelings of compassion helps your mind move beyond the dualistic thinking of right or wrong. Instead, compassion creates kindness, and this produces right action in the moment. Authentic kindness is a game changer. It didn't matter that he was robbing me. In my case, feeling kind and peaceful was the right action, so that the robber began to calm down, and we could avoid a possible violent situation.

Compassion is the ability to comprehend the emotional state of another person and respond to their suffering in a way that creates connection between you and them. It opens up trust and allows love to be present. It instantly grounds us.

Compassion is often seen as a sign of weakness by people who confuse it with feeling sorry for someone. Feeling sorry for someone is more like pity. It expresses a negative evaluation of the bad situation of others—someone's horrible plight, story, or circumstance. Pity joins them in their misery, all the while thinking there is not much they can do about it. Feeling sorry for someone can end up with us being scammed, while compassion involves discernment and boundaries.

Compassion is also an inner expression of intelligence, and it involves action. It includes a willingness to become personally involved in the situation. Feeling sorry does not. Compassion helps others by giving them the gift of feeling understood when they are conflicted or deeply distressed. It calms them and lets them feel safe with you.

This is why the robber began to see me as an ally and not someone he was robbing. I could see the fear, conflict, and distress in his eyes. Authentic compassion, which is a form of love, tempered that situation and kept everyone safe.

Compassion is a loving response that unleashes your inner silent intelligence, because compassion is a deeper form of critical thinking. It doesn't use words to speak to you. Instead it uses a type of presence or sound to speak. Compassion is a wordless action that is felt by the one receiving it.

Authentic compassion carries a power to connect and transform a situation based on the receiver feeling your authentic love. Because love is the most powerful form of intelligence, it is a critical aspect of unlocking authentic freedom. This intelligence shows itself in many forms, compassion being one of them.

Critical-thinking Skill No. 3: Mindfulness

It was a beautiful sunny day, and the mountains were shining their many earth-toned colors. The wildflowers swayed through the fields and were touched by a breeze that kept us from overheating during our uphill climb. We were hiking at a gentle pace, and I was enjoying the beauty of it all: the stream, leaves, and fresh air. It filled me with joy, calm, and relaxation.

We were hiking at a steady pace because we knew we had a long distance to go and had to reserve our energy for going back down. My hiking buddy and I were quiet. In this kind of beauty, silence seemed to be part of the experience.

The trail we were on was clean and wide at first. As we got higher, the trail seemed to get narrower and was not as easily recognizable. Soon we were well past the switchback trails and had to carefully maneuver through some shale and other rocks. I could feel myself get nervous as I hiked higher and saw the distance to the ground should I fall.

I have always been afraid of heights. Everyone I know always wants to try and be my hero and help me get over this fear. I've stood with friends nervously looking over steep cliffs or driven over high, narrow mountain passes hoping to get rid of my fear of heights. My hiking buddy was no different; she knew I was afraid, but she was not very tolerant of my fear. She felt no need to help me get over my fear as we hiked.

When we reached the part of the hike where I would have to climb to the summit, I wanted to go back instead of hiking the narrow trail to the top, because that meant walking by cliffs with deep drops. The thought of it was so scary that I would have rather gone back down than face that fear.

Of course that pissed off my hiking buddy. She was not happy with me and turned around to look me in the eye. With an angry, disgusted look in her eyes, she said, "See, that's your problem, Vickie. You're so worried about what might happen that you aren't looking at what *is* happening. How do you know if anything is going to happen at all! Has anything happened to us yet?"

I looked at her and started to answer no, but she was clearly frustrated. She put her hands up and said no for me. Then she went off on me. "You aren't afraid to climb to the top, that's not what you're afraid of. You are afraid of the conversation you're having with yourself while you're climbing to the summit, and I'll prove it to you."

I interrupted her, saying, "Okay, okay...chill out, I get it. I'm afraid of heights, and you want to go to the summit."

"Well, don't you?" she asked. "Isn't there a part of you that would like to finish this hike and actually enjoy it, without feeling afraid or panicked?"

I thought that was an interesting question. No one ever asked me that before. As I thought about it, I realized that I did indeed want to experience hiking to that 13,500-foot summit and not be tied in knots of fear while doing it. Was that even possible for me? I looked at her. "Yes, I would love to experience that," I said.

She looked at me with both hope and disgust and said, "Great, pick up your pack and let's go, now! Don't think about it, let's begin now!"

I could feel the fear well up in me. My nervousness and stress levels went through the roof as I flung my day pack on my shoulders.

My friend could tell that I was feeling my fear.

"Shut up! Stop listening to yourself. What is happening right now? Are we safe? Is anyone hurt? Are we in any danger?"

"No," I replied.

"Great, then take another step forward."

I followed her directions again and took a step.

This time she spoke more gently. "Stop listening to yourself. What is happening right now? Are we safe? Is anyone hurt? Are we in any danger?"

Again I said, "No."

Then like clockwork she said, "Great! Then take another step."

My hiking buddy was aware that I was telling myself something that made the fear come up in the first place. She understood that I was thinking about how I could die by falling and not thinking about the fact that I wasn't falling. I had visualized slipping and dying. I could feel my fear of death by falling, and I was never fully present to what was actually happening. No wonder I was scared of heights—look at what I was telling myself! Wouldn't you be scared of heights too if you were telling yourself the same thing I was?

As we continued to the summit, every few minutes she would ask me, "What's happening now? Are we safe? Is anyone hurt?" My reply was the same each time: "No." Pretty soon I was noticing what was scaring the crap out of me. It wasn't what was happening in the moment; instead it was what I was saying to myself. I had flexible beliefs about heights being dangerous and my falling and dying.

Mindfulness is the ability to command your attention, presence, and point of view. It is you taking charge of being present in the world. It's the practice of noticing, observing, and witnessing what is actually happening here and now in the present moment. It is being curious about what is going on. It is knowing the difference between what you are saying to yourself that is creating a reaction and what you are observing in the moment that evokes no emotional response.

When my hiking buddy taught me the difference between what I was saying to myself and what was happening, I suddenly had more choices because I had more command of what I chose to focus on. I could observe what we were doing rather than listen to the scary story I was telling myself. It became easier for me to command my own point of view on what was occurring.

When we got nearer to the summit, I had to say to myself over and over again, *Shut up, Vickie! Stop listening to yourself. What is happening right now? Are we safe? Is anyone hurt? Are we in any danger? Great, then take another step.* At first it felt like a battle in my mind because I noticed I really wanted to believe the story I was telling myself rather than pay attention.

This is where you have to get over yourself. You must be willing to witness your mind in action and then be willing to tame it by being the adult and not allowing it to have its tantrums by telling you scary stories that are false. When you practice mindfulness, over time you will find you have more confidence in yourself and more abilities showing up for you, because you are no longer capping your capacity with untrue stories about what you can and can't do.

Mindfulness is the gateway to having authentic discernment. It engages your inner silent intelligence along with your outer reasoning. This promotes more clarity because critical thinking isn't just using your brain function. It is also the ability to assess the moment, allowing your inner silent intelligence to respond and your other skills to create the actions necessary for what is happening in the moment.

Using mindfulness during my ascent up the mountain helped me unlock and use my freedom more fully. You must be able to command your mind if you want to command your outcomes. As I was hiking, I was moving slowly but peacefully, and before I knew it I was drinking in the view—and my transformation, as I literally drank some water at the summit.

Critical-thinking Skill No. 4: Discernment

We were days from launching our new product when my business partner died. I was in shock and had no idea what to do. I didn't know how to replace him. I couldn't believe the timing of his death. Because I couldn't handle such a big project alone, I just put the launch and the entire project into neutral as I considered my options.

I was so scared, and I was also grieving, hurt, and angry all at once. I thought, *If the divine wants you to do something, it shouldn't be this hard. It's not supposed to be this painful or scary, is it?* Weeks went by, and even long after his funeral I had no answers to my prayers. I kept waiting for a sign or an answer from the heavens, but there seemed to be no reply.

I wasn't going to take a $46,000 loss and throw a project away because my partner had died. But I couldn't have just any business partner either. I didn't need the best business partner. I needed the right business partner. Despite my praying and pleading with the divine, I was feeling abandoned by the universe, and this pissed me off. I felt as if I was getting the silent treatment.

I was angry at God and thought it was about time God and I had a talk. So I drove out into the middle of nowhere and got out of my vehicle. I was angry and crying, shouting to the heavens, *You and I had a deal, man. You told me that I had the power and right to transform my outside world into anything I desired by serving my calling. What kind of bullshit is this? You can take anyone you want at any time, so you thought it was smart to take my business partner four days before we were supposed to launch?*

I yelled, cried, and screamed until I was sweating, breathing heavily, and too exhausted to yell anymore. Somehow it felt good to let out all the fear, anger, and frustration. I did feel a little calmer. Suddenly I thought, *Maybe instead of complaining about what happened, what would happen if I asked for what I do want?* This gave me the space and opportunity to get clear about the type of business partner I did want.

So I made a list of what I wanted in a business partner. I wanted someone who has integrity, is as good if not better than I am at what I do, is spiritually awake, is honest to the core even if it hurts me, is accountable, is good with people, likes travel, believes as I do, knows the Ultimate Freedom, loves the work so much they don't see it as work, feels a calling to serve humanity, loves our company's mission and branding and is committed to it wholeheartedly, is fun and funny and smart as all get-out yet also kind, has a backbone and healthy boundaries, and is worth going to the mat for and will go to the mat for me.

I wanted someone I admired, not someone who just admired me. I wanted a partner who had all of the above and complemented my skillsets too. I didn't want a vice president, I wanted a co-CEO, someone who is not afraid to make decisions and lead with me, not under me. I didn't just write it down on paper, I stood outside and yelled it out to the universe and made it my prayer, my declaration, my intention to attract this magical person to me. I put the universe on notice: "Find me this perfect person and send them my way now! Please."

Again, weeks went by and nothing. I had even forgotten I was looking for this magical person when I walked into a restaurant to have dinner with some friends I was developing a new business with. We happened to walk by a table where a client of mine was having dinner with two friends.

We were surprised to see each other. We hugged and started in with the small talk. Then she turned to introduce me to her two friends.

"Come here, Vickie, this is someone I have been trying to introduce you to for a long time now. I've told her what you do and thought you two could talk," she said.

I didn't want to take on another client because I was busy and already had a waiting list.

A small hand reached out over the table, and at first I did not hear her name. I asked her to repeat it. And because I wanted to remember her name, I said it aloud several times until I could remember.

"Mia, Mia, Mia, Mia, Mia, it's nice to meet you, Mia, I like your name."

"You need to schedule an appointment someday for both of you," my friend said.

I started to turn and walk away from the table. Suddenly that silent intelligence told me to turn back around and schedule a time right then. Naturally, I complied.

I scheduled the appointment for the next day, and when Mia came into my office I liked her instantly. There was something about the light coming from Mia's eyes that made her stand out. I liked what she was about, so even though my schedule was absolutely full, I'd squeeze her in if she wanted my business development services. I left her to make the decision, and she could call me if she wished. A little over a week later she called and set an appointment to work with me. For some reason, when that brief conversation was done I felt something happen to my soul. It was as if my soul was saying, *Pay attention, Vickie.*

After the very first appointment with Mia, I knew she was the person I had requested from the universe. I knew in my heart, in my gut, in my soul that she was the person who was to work with me. But I was not sleeping at night because I was ruminating over my client policies. I had a set of "supposed to be like this and look like this" rules running through my head and Mia did not fit into them. I started listening to my thinking surrounding the rules and not my inner discernment and this created struggle.

How do we know when we are doing this? Well, when your mind begins to argue with what is and what you think it should be, you are not being mindful or discerning. I could feel my discernment kicking in, but then my mind would say, *You don't turn clients into business partners.* That was like therapists who sleep with their clients. If you are the consultant, you have a fiduciary responsibility to your client's wishes, not to your agenda. And yet I knew without a doubt that we were supposed to be business partners.

It was obvious to my discernment, but getting it past my thinking agenda was another thing altogether. Mia had it all. She taught at two universities, had had a consulting and counseling practice for as long as I had, and was well-respected in her industry and by her peers. She was a great speaker and educator. She was innovative and creative. The writing was all over the wall in big letters, but I was stuck in my unhealthy thinking.

Mindfulness is the magic connection between the material world and the infinite world. You cannot hear the infinite world without it. Unlocking the Ultimate Freedom unites these two worlds to create discernment. The Dalai Lama said, "The ultimate authority must rest with the individual's own reason and critical analysis." This is the core of developing discernment inside the Ultimate Freedom.

It was a no-brainer for the universe, but I had to overcome my unhealthy thinking habits. Mia was very good at challenging them in a way that did not put her agenda on my lap. Our conversations were brilliant, intense, and honest. There was an ease in working together, and the more I learned about her the more I couldn't sleep at night because I was fighting what I knew, what the silent intelligence was telling me to do, and what I honestly wanted to do too. I did this in order to follow the rules I had followed for some seventeen years, without ever violating them.

When your mind has an agenda and you think things are supposed to go a certain way, you lose discernment and mindfulness. Instead you create struggle for yourself. Lucky for me, Mia is really smart and intuitive. She could tell something was not being said. After watching me struggle for about four weeks, she gently confronted me. I finally told her that I was battling my discernment in order to follow my rules of conduct, but that I really wanted her to be my business partner and not a client.

She honored my struggle and would not interrupt my process. She let me have my own meltdown over following either my discernment or my rules of business conduct. She held space for me to work through that without adding her opinion or influence to the mix. To this day I do not know what she actually wanted to have happen, but she is my business partner, and that's perfect.

There is a grand illusion that I have fallen victim to so many times—perceiving reality from my past learning or unhealthy thinking instead of from my mindfulness and discernment in the present moment. Christian author Lewis B. Smedes once said, "Seeing reality for what it is, is what we call discernment. The work of discernment is very hard."

Discernment is work because it requires you to understand your individuality and your values. Many religious systems or personal development styles love the "one size fits all" systems that most often don't work. My rules about clients not becoming business partners were about me having one-size-fits-all situations, circumstances, and conditions; thus I could not see or did not want to see that my prayers had been answered, and there she was right in front of me. I wanted to follow the rules. Mindfulness is the precursor to having discernment. Mindfulness brings you to the here and now.

Authentic freedom comes from a response inside you that is mindfully here and now. It knows everything and everyone has an individual path. It knows what will benefit us most because the infinite's hand created the opportunity in the first place. It already knows that what is good for you may not be good for another. When you can command your attention to consistently talk with and follow the infinite within you, then you will have developed mindfulness and discernment.

Discernment allows us not to be swayed by the one-size-fits-all trap. Freedom and discernment go hand in hand. The freer we become, the more we are able to access the Ultimate Freedom in a wise and discerning way.

When making decisions, we are nearly always biased in some way by a flexible, malleable belief that we think is fixed. In my case it was my client rules. We can often have some emotional investment in this flexible belief and thus try to ignore the real truth. Having discernment allows us to move from our judgmental nature into neutral and not be swayed by our desires or our emotional investments.

Having discernment is a great way to release our ego and arrogance. We no longer care if we are right or wrong; instead we are invested in connection with the truth of the moment. When this happens, it allows us to become indifferent and disinterested in our biases, unnecessary rules, and emotions long enough so that we can objectively weigh our greatest opportunities and options. This provides more success as you claim more freedom. I think faith is the small mustard seed of opportunities that require you to trust your inner truth and knowings. This is having discernment.

Critical-thinking Skill No. 5: Being Nonjudgmental

I was seated in my criminal investigations training class looking over crime scene photos. At first the nature of this class appeared to be about examining blood splatter and other tools of crime scene investigation. I was actually looking forward to this class because to me investigations are interesting. It's like putting the puzzle pieces together to find out what happened. Somehow you would think this is a cut-and-dried technique, but it's not.

No matter what crime scene photo the instructor put on the overhead, we all kept getting the scenario wrong. The detective was actually teaching us rookie cops to think through the crime scene rather than react. So of course there were a lot of curve-ball pictures that were often gross. He would say, "Tell me what happened at this scene."

The picture would show up on the overhead and we would begin studying it. His goal was to help us observe instead of judge. This exercise helped us look at our own shortcomings based on race, religion, beliefs, and training. Most people don't think they make judgments that hinder their success, and yet most people do.

It's not always fun to look at your shortcomings, but I never forgot what he told me. He said, "Having a nonjudgmental stance is a skill." People confuse good judgment with what they see. It's not about what you see. It's about what you don't see, because you are fixed in your belief about what you do see.

We became certain of what we saw in the crime scene photos based on our judgments. No one passed a picture-slide test; he knew we were being judgmental. He pointed out over and over again how we believed what we thought we saw. We failed to look past what was familiar to us.

And this is the trap of being judgmental and what robs us of freedom. We only see what is familiar to us. In the movie *What the Bleep Do We Know?*, Candace Pert, author of *Molecules of Emotion*, says, "We match patterns that already exist within ourselves through conditioning. So a wonderful story that I believe is true is that when the Indians, the Native American Indians on the Caribbean islands, first saw Columbus's ships approaching, they couldn't see them at all. Because it was so unlike anything they had ever seen before, they couldn't see it."

Because our brains like to recognize and categorize data, we can make snap judgments without actually seeing something that is so unlike anything we have ever seen before. We are conditioned to placing judgments on our observations. The power of taking a nonjudgmental stance is to give ourselves more opportunities by viewing the same old things but opening ourselves to thinking about them in a different way.

You can see this process of nonjudgmental transformation in the evolution of phones. We don't even call them phones anymore. They are devices capable of several forms of communication—text, video, writing, or speaking. If the inventor had just looked at the phone without a nonjudgmental view of it as something else, the phone would not have evolved into a device that has many options for communicating.

In order to see the potential of something or someone, you must view it in a different way. This includes yourself. The power of this type of critical thinking is that it allows you to have a different view of yourself—once you get over your attachment to who you currently see yourself as and judge yourself to be.

Critical thinking requires analysis that is open to observing without judging so you can make a more multifaceted observation. Don't just view yourself as a phone because it is familiar. What other gifts can you add to the device of *you*, simply because you no longer see yourself as just a phone?

When you are attached to who you say you are, it is not very freeing. People love labels without realizing they are creating a crime scene. Once you label yourself, you have assassinated any other part of you that could be more empowering. We match patterns that already exist within ourselves through conditioning. The way to move out of this is to ask yourself a more powerful question.

Critical-thinking Skill No. 6:
The Ability to Ask Powerful Questions

Voltaire said, "Judge a man by his questions rather than by his answers." This is how I do an interview inside my current consulting firm. I don't give a crap about your resume or where you went to school. I want to know if you can look at a computer screen and see a different question that allows you access to a site or can protect my client's site better.

I want to listen to the conversation we are having during an interview and ask questions in a different way. I know there are typical interview questions, and then there are curiosity questions about the company, mission, expectations, and long-range plans. The questions you ask tell me more about you than the questions I ask during an interview.

What will I get to learn by working for your company? Is there authenticity, interest, and passion in your questions? Is there creativity in your questions? The ability to ask effective questions, whether of yourself or another, can be one of the most powerful, transformative tools for critical thinking.

Becoming good at asking a question is also one of the first steps to having skillful means. Skillful means, which is simply a thoughtful response rather than a reaction to a situation, are a mark of someone who is emotionally intelligent and embraces the Ultimate Freedom. It is an action that is both wise and compassionate. (We will discuss skillful means in the next section.)

When using the Ultimate Freedom, asking powerful questions will create stronger relationships and more meaningful exchanges. This approach allows more options and choices as the receiver becomes more interested in you as they answer your questions. It will help you become a trusted thought leader.

Why is this skillset so powerful? Because asking questions is how we unearth more or new information that produces opportunities, understanding, or connection. This skillset opens us up and enables us to have a vaster view on the topic we are asking questions about. You let a person explore their inner world more easily when you ask authentically. Questions engage the communicating parties and help us dig deeper into an issue so as to have a strong outcome. Questions improve performance and outcomes because they challenge the status quo.

Author Thomas Berger said, "The art and science of asking questions is the source of all knowledge." The key to asking powerful questions is to do it with dignity, authenticity, and respect. Belittling someone or showing how smart you are by asking a question just shows the world that you secretly dislike yourself. Those who are truly free do not engage another in a disrespectful manner. Those who engage the Ultimate Freedom love humanity and don't feel as if they are "more than" or "less than"; they know they are equal to everyone else.

When you ask a question from a place of dignity and respect, it changes the resonance of the conversation even if the parties are mad at each other. Inquire, don't interrogate. Thoughtful questions are a powerful tool for learning more and nurturing understanding and cooperation. No one likes to be interrogated!

As with any other communication tool, be aware of your own intention in asking the question. If your intention is to learn more rather than attack someone else's ideas, you create trust and empower both parties. If you are hoping to manipulate someone with your questions, then you are still attacking them. Also, the tone of your voice, your body language, and your word choice all create the environment where you can either empower or impair the situation. When questions are asked with kindness and authenticity, you will have much more success.

The person hearing an authentic question will rise to meet you in a place of respect. There are techniques to asking questions that can help you establish this vessel of dignity; however, you must be authentic for it to have power. When you practice questioning yourself, you will get good at commanding your outcomes, and you will be more self-directed.

Many personal-development programs cover the process of asking self-directed questions to assist you in exploring your inner landscape. As the Greek philosopher Socrates said, "The unexamined life is not worth living." This is often the most avoided area of the Ultimate Freedom. Yet if you don't ask yourself, how will you "Know thyself"?—another ancient Greek saying. When you "know thyself," you will have the clarity you are looking for that allows you to create thyself and the life and freedom thyself wants.

People in Western cultures will do just about anything to avoid being quiet and focusing inward. They also tend to avoid using self-reflective or self-directed questions. Silence can be unsettling in our busy, noisy culture. Yet contemplation and mindfulness create the rich ground that yields insightful questions and responses.

Meditation trains us to sharpen our observations and listening skills and helps us learn to listen to others more skillfully. Self-reflective and self-directed questions help create skillful means and are a key code in reshaping our character in a way that moves us into the Ultimate Freedom.

PART TWO

Character is like a tree and reputation like a shadow. The shadow is what we think of it; the tree is the real thing.
—Abraham Lincoln

Chapter 6

Reshaping Character

The closer you come to knowing that you alone create the world of your experience, the more vital it becomes for you to discover just who is doing the creating.

—Eric Micha'el Leventhal

I was twenty-six years old when my older sister told me she was pregnant. I was super excited. I didn't have any kids of my own, and this would be my first niece or nephew and my parents' first grandchild. It seemed like forever waiting for that little guy to be born, but she finally went into labor and delivered my nephew. I know everyone has defining moments in their life, and for me one of them was the first time I held little Dustin Yager in my arms. It changed me forever.

Holding him for the first time reshaped my character instantly. It suddenly was important for me to be there for him and provide as many opportunities for him as I could. I promised him that I would never leave him and would always be there for him. I wasn't his mother, but I knew I was one of his guardians for the first part of his earthly journey.

I suddenly cared about his quality of life and worked to buy him things and take him places. I wanted to be the aunt he was proud of and could come to in times of trouble. I wanted to be a good example and role model for him. I quit smoking and stopped drinking alcohol. I was protective of what he was exposed to on TV and in the world, and this was helping my own mind too.

This happened effortlessly. At the time, I didn't notice how my thinking had changed. I just noticed how my love had changed. I thought I had found something that deepened my feeling of love. Children often unearth a deeper level of love that we may not have accessed without a child in our lives. But the hidden truth I found was that this level of loving already existed within me before Dustin was born.

His birth simply helped me reshape my attitude toward love and my understanding of it, allowing more of what was already in me to come out. What I learned was that my love is dependent on my state of being. It didn't matter what he became, whether he was über successful or not. I would love him simply because I love. Reshaping your character is about allowing your greatness to come out.

I learned that my character could easily be reshaped. It happens quickly when you have a deep love or yearning inside you. Real freedom is about reshaping your current programming into something that you want to let out—not become but let out what is already in you—and this reshapes your character.

So many of us cannot engage with the Ultimate Freedom because of what I call a misunderstanding of self. We are unaware of who and what we are, as well as the enormous power that we have to shape or reshape or form or reform our lives. We have been programmed into a certain style of living and thinking. We don't actually own our minds and thoughts.

Because our minds are not our own, many of our choices are not our own. Many of us depend on the five senses to decide who we are. We judge ourselves based on the prevailing social memes or marketing standards of the time set by advertisers and promoters who establish the fashion and lifestyle for today. Many people don't actually know who they are. How can you have freedom without knowing who you are? The answer is that you can't.

We spend a lot of time and money trying to make ourselves over to fit into these parameters. We follow workout regimes, diet fads, and even go so far as to have surgery to add or remove a part of ourselves that doesn't fit these artificial standards.

Character is defined as the sum of all our beliefs, attitudes, and personal traits that allow personal behavior to arise. It represents what you think is possible for yourself, and this is your resonance and attractor field (more on that later). Reshaping your character is not an outside task; you must be willing to reshape it.

The character of an individual is made up of the mental and moral qualities unique to that individual, as well as learned behavior from your lineage and other authority figures. It is the character of that person that determines the thoughts, feelings, words, actions, and reactions that dominate the person's life.

Character is one of the most important aspects of the Ultimate Freedom because it is what others will read or sense from you without words. Your character is your personal vibe. Every person carries a resonance or vibration about them. You hear people saying it in slang terms: "He's laid- back," "She's high-strung," "She's a hoot," "He's a player." These are some of the ways we use words to describe personal resonance and character.

Many, if not most, people have a BS detector. Manipulative and dishonest people want you to distrust your BS detector and believe what they are telling you. All along, your BS detector—if it's working properly—is having an energetic conversation with the world. This is how resonance speaks. It doesn't use words, but it does have a sound and a current, and it leads to an energetic discussion.

Your BS detector feels the resonance, current, and sound and tells you whether you like hanging out with a certain group or not. It is the sensor that matches your vibratory resonance to people who feel good to you in the moment. You call them friends; when your character and resonance change, you get new friends. Your character is what determines your resonance. What shifts your resonance, sound, and current is your level of inner freedom, your mindset and mindfulness.

People either feel your authenticity or they feel your inauthenticity. One will bring you influence and the Ultimate Freedom, and the other will not. This begins with integrity and being true and honest with yourself and a transformation of your mind. When you understand the Ultimate Freedom, you will shift your character and reshape your outcomes. As you begin to reshape your character, you change your resonance, and this begins the process of bringing more of the Ultimate Freedom to you.

To enter this level of freedom, start by becoming aware of who you are and what your resonance is saying to the world. How do you see yourself? You will learn how to move, shift your character, and connect to a more aware and mindful sound, current, and resonance through contemplation, learning the laws of the universe, and then beginning to apply these laws. This is part of the Ultimate Freedom.

Bob Procter, author, speaker, a star of *The Secret,* and a master of the Ultimate Freedom, calls this "The Law of Vibration." He says,

"The Law of Attraction is secondary to the Law of Vibration. Everything moves, nothing rests. It's all energy at a different rate of vibration. Your body is a different molecular structure at a very high speed of vibration. Your brain is an electronic switching station. Your brain does not think, instead you think with your brain, and there's a difference. As you activate brain cells, you set up a vibration in your body. Vibration is something that must be understood if you're going to take control of your health, relationship, if you want to become wealthy, and if you want to really master the art of selling, vibration is an essential. You've got to understand it. **The vibration you are in is going to dictate what you attract in your life**. The laws that govern our being, the laws that govern the universe, how do we get in harmony with the law? Everything will come to you when you get in harmony with it."

Vibration is essential to understand. This is why the Law of Attraction is secondary to the Law of Vibration. Using the Ultimate Freedom, the Law of Resonance or Vibration allows others to feel your intention and want to work with you, do business with you, listen to you, or be involved with you. People have good BS detectors, and what a BS detector senses is the sound, current, and vibration of your character, intention, and authenticity.

People with the Ultimate Freedom give off a vibration or resonance that others want and want to be in contact with. This is how advertisers and marketers know what and how to pitch you a product. They are trying to sell you a product that you hope enhances your resonance and vibration through material status. Advertisers know that you want to have a powerful resonance. People usually aspire to a higher vibrancy than they currently have. Everything evolves, including us.

People go into debt trying to buy their way into the Ultimate Freedom without realizing this is what they want. But real freedom can't be bought. Real freedom is an action of your character that is woven through everything you do, and your resonance shows it. The process unlocks, reshapes, and raises and opens your vibrancy, resonance, sound, and current. It shifts and awakens your consciousness.

It doesn't matter how much status you buy or how much success you achieve; you will not fool people whose BS detectors are strong. Success and material possessions do not equal freedom. Even if you have the latest and the greatest, that does not buy you the Ultimate Freedom. The only way to access this level of freedom is to reshape your character. This is how authentic freedom becomes an aspect of your character and not an inauthentic aspect of your past programming.

While you are reshaping your character, your ego will take a backseat and your discernment will begin to take the driver's seat. You will notice the difference in your flexible beliefs and be able to let them go more easily. You will become more mindful and begin to sound different, feel different—more empowered— and your vibe will shift, reshaping your character and life.

At first you will be concentrating on intellectual humility. You'll begin to notice that you can admit you are wrong without it affecting you. You'll begin to notice when you refuse to admit you are wrong, even in the face of glaring evidence that you are in fact wrong, and you will begin to question why this is hard for you. This is reshaping your character because you are asking different questions.

You'll notice when you become defensive. When another person tries to point out a deficiency in your work or your thinking, you will not be as reactive. This is a powerful aspect of the Ultimate Freedom.

You'll notice when your intellectual arrogance keeps you from learning—for example, when you say to yourself, *I know this*, or *I already know*. Or *I know more than anyone else about this topic*. When you reshape your character, these ego-driven defenses will no longer rule you, and the shift in your resonance will set you free in a way that will blow your success rate through the roof.

When you dispose of your own arrogance because you value your freedom more than arrogance, you will begin to empower your life more than you can even imagine. Your resonance will change effortlessly. This is when skillful means meets opportunity. When you use skillful means, you use discernment.

Let's say two different students come to me telling me they are late with their work and want an extension. My response to the student who is perpetually late, disorganized, and lacking consideration for classmates is likely to be different from that to the student who is always timely, prepared, and easy to work with. You may think both should be treated in the same way. Application of skillful means says not necessarily. An extension for one student may be a gift, while to the other it's feedback and encouragement to continue work habits that won't be acceptable in the workplace.

The idea of skillful means comes from eastern Buddhist traditions. In the Lotus Sutra (a collection of Mahayana texts) the Buddha uses skillful means based on his all-knowing eye that accurately discerns the capacities of different beings and the teachings that would benefit them. In Christianity, it would be using the wisdom of Solomon to discern the truth in the moment.

The idea behind both of these texts is the spiritual awakening or deepening of mindfulness to raise awareness and thus reshape your character, which raises your resonance and thus shifts your outcomes.

In his bestselling book *Power vs. Force,* author Dr. David R. Hawkins uses a "Map of Consciousness" to show a scale of awakening to resonance. He says, "Each level of consciousness represents an energy field dominance as a consequence of its concordant 'attractor field,' which acts similarly to magnetic or gravitational fields. This is your resonance field. The future attracts us, like filings to a magnet."

Dr. Viktor E. Frankel said, "Are you going to react or respond? You will attract to you whatever you are in harmonious vibration with. Between stimulus and response there is a space. In that space is our power to choose our response. In our response lies our growth and our freedom."

One purpose of spiritual freedom is to unleash the potential that reshapes your character and becomes your new resonance and your new reality. You cannot buy your way into this, you cannot think your way into this, you cannot fashion your way into this, you cannot fame your way into a higher resonance; you must become this resonance in order to become this reality.

This is what Albert Einstein meant when he said, "Everything is energy and that's all there is to it. Match the frequency of the reality you want and you cannot help but get that reality. It can be no other way. This is not philosophy. This is physics." This is the Ultimate Freedom, and it takes courage to step into it and reshape, reform, and rethink your life.

Chapter 7

The Statue of Responsibility

I recommend that the Statue of Liberty on the East Coast be supplemented by a Statue of Responsibility on the West Coast.
—Viktor E. Frankl

My stepfather had a very good system for giving us our allowance. Everyone started off with $2 allowance each week (hey, this was a lot in the late '60s). You were assigned chores on a list that was always up on the wall in the kitchen. Your name would be entered next to the chore you were to do. If you did not do your chore, another member of the family could do it, and a nickel from your total would move to their total. You would have $1.95 and the other person would have $2.05 in allowance due to them.

So if it was my turn to do the dishes and I did not want to do them, my sister could do them, and I would have a nickel deducted from my total and added to my sister's total. At the end of a week, we would line up for payday. If you did more work, you got more money; if you did less work, you got less money.

I realize that through this system my dad was hoping to teach us about having a work ethic and responsibility. My dad was very managerial about the process of giving us our allowance. He would look up and down the list, use a calculator to add everything up, and then pay us our wages. He always held a poker face and never praised or belittled you. He just paid you.

I can remember being the last one in line on one payday in particular. When my father looked up and down the list, he reviewed it with the eye of a manager. He used the calculator, looked at the total, reached into the money supply, and placed a shiny new nickel in my hand. I continued to hold my hand open, waiting for the next part of the money to drop into it. He looked at me, puzzled, and said, "That's it."

I also looked perplexed, so he went over the list of chores with me. That's right, I got one nickel. Because it took forty nickels to make $2, that meant I had not done thirty-nine chores that week. This was my first lesson in self-responsibility. Throughout the years, my father and I would have a good laugh about that allowance day. I was amazed at how I thought I could do very little and be rewarded with lots of allowance money. Carl Jung said, "People will do anything, no matter how absurd, to avoid facing their own souls." And in the area of self-responsibility, many people don't want to face their own souls.

Friedrich Nietzsche said, "Freedom is the will to be responsible to ourselves." When you're a teenager, there are some words that authority figures say that make your eyes roll, like accountability, discipline, or responsibility. These words make some people cringe.

Some people—those who have managed to get by so far without having to be very responsible—avoid those words, because at first the thought of assuming responsibility can be painful to them, but after you have reshaped your character, you will settle for nothing less—not because you are disciplined but because this is who you have become. It will feel good and purposeful to be responsible.

At first this is not as easy as you would think because it means detoxing yourself from ingrained habits resulting from the media and your upbringing. This is where you get to explore how to reshape, reform, and rethink your life in order to have the Ultimate Freedom by shifting your resonance.

There is no shortcut to having the Ultimate Freedom. You must reclaim your mind, discernment, and actions. By reclaiming your life, you not only gain more control over what happens, but you also begin to reshape your character into knowing that you can do more. You will feel a new level of excellence grow inside you, and you will want to be more responsible because it feels better than your past. Suddenly your authentic self-esteem begins to take hold.

Your resonance will rise, and unexpectedly your attractor field will pull toward you more of what you want. You will start to see that not only is this possible, but also it will be manifested. This shifts your resonance and deepens your freedom.

Your inner resistance to the words accountability, discipline, and responsibility start melting away as you begin to enjoy authentic self-love and the new resonance around you. Taking action will become a natural state of being because your thoughts have changed around it. Even when you fail, you will no longer react to it as you have in the past. You realize that you get to choose your behavior and you choose your consequences. This is a necessary step toward authentic freedom.

This is shifting your resonance and not chasing a dream. How many people do you know who create resolutions every January because they have a dream of something they want to achieve? Maybe even you have a dream to achieve something so badly you can feel it in your gut—and it keeps you up at night.

Even though millions of people dare to dream of creating something new in their lives every January, by the end of the year many people would not be able to say they had achieved their dream or goal for that year, let alone for a lifetime. Why is that? Because chasing a dream is a marketing ploy that many people, including me, fall for.

Learning how to chase your dreams is a trillion-dollar industry that I too have been suckered into. What good is it to have the right to freedom if you do not know how to claim it, unlock it, or create it? Remember, you cannot buy your way into the Ultimate Freedom. If this is what you're doing, this mindset is stifling all of your opportunities and possibilities.

Taking action and being accountable helps to reshape your character; this reshapes you and your outcomes. It reshapes your future because it helps you become more innovative in your thinking, giving you more access to inner hidden devices that help you communicate in a more holistic, multifaceted way, giving you more "response ability" and more success.

In his book *Smart Cuts*, Shane Snow writes, "In a piece called 'The Common Denominator of Success,' Albert Ian Grey said that "What successful people do is they form the habit of doing the things that unsuccessful people don't like to do." And he says what motivates them is that successful people are motivated by the desire for pleasing results. Failures are influenced by the desire for pleasing methods and are inclined to be satisfied with such results as can be obtained by doing things they like to do."

The difference between someone who enjoys responsibility and someone who doesn't is the "results vs. method" process. Making the change is simply a switch in perspective or point of view. Looking for the fastest and easiest way to do something and get the greatest outcome is the method approach. When you use the method process, you most likely will look for the most convenient method.

However, if you can ask yourself a more powerful question that removes the method and requests the results you would like, you will move into the response ability technique. This may require you to become more mindful or have a breakthrough that results in an "aha!" response and deepens your understanding of your own capabilities—or it may require that you learn and hone a new skill.

Seeing responsibility and accountability as the powerful tools of transformation that they are deepens our self-confidence and expands our opportunities. When you begin to enjoy how you feel being responsible and accountable, you will have flipped a switch inside your resonance that allows you access to a deeper purpose within you. It helps you enjoy the results vs. the method. It makes this switch inside you without you even knowing it.

This happens effortlessly because having real purpose requires a deeper connection to self and the silent intelligence within you. It shifts your resonance to a higher attractor field. It is this private conversation among you, the silent intelligence, and your current level of freedom that will help you remain engaged with and responsible to that deeper connection and purpose. Your confidence will no longer be knocked over because it is not hooked to unhealthy ego, beliefs, or methods.

When you have authentic confidence, you will not look for convenient shortcuts and methods. Instead you will evaluate the results you want to create, and you will work with them. Does this mean you will not run into hardship? No. Remember, I lost my business partner four days before our launch.

Yes, I did have a meltdown. I cried. I spent sleepless nights wondering what to do. I went out into the middle of nowhere and screamed at the universe and the silent intelligence. What I did not do was camp out in my meltdown forever and use it as an excuse for not completing my divinely given project.

Instead, I asked a more powerful question. What would happen if I actually asked for a new business partner and outlined what I wanted? When you become responsible, you don't camp out in problems or weak methods. You add a new skillset and innovate until you enjoy your results.

Chapter 8

Smart People

A man must be big enough to admit his mistakes, smart enough to profit from them, and strong enough to correct them.
—John C. Maxwell

I n the late '80s and early '90s, many innovations started with the word "smart," used in phrases like smart choice, smart watches, and smart investing. These marketers and advertisers were trying to introduce a new product or service to a market of status-quo thinkers and get them to try it by making them feel they made an intelligent choice.

They played on the consumer's love of intelligence. Marketers introduced Smart Balance Butter Spread or Smart Choice frozen foods brand to make you feel smart about your choices. Weight Watchers has the Smart Ones brand. People love to be seen as having good judgment, and this includes making smart purchases.

Then the SMART meme evolved and turned into a goal-setting acronym developed by George Doran and used to describe a technique for setting strong objectives: Specific, Measurable, Assignable, Realistic, and Time-related. This is the SMART goal-setting system.

Now we use the word "smart" to describe the functionality of an innovation. This is the era of smart design, which often describes the capabilities of our technology. Thus we have smartphones and smart cars. Smart design is about an innovation's abilities and not how clever you are in your choices or goal setting. We have smartphones, smart products, and smart sensors that do tasks and think for us. We can shut off our house lights while sipping a Starbucks far away in another town.

In all of these evolutions, we can see that there has been a lateral-thinking redesign and change in definition of the meme "Smart." Lateral thinking is solving problems through an indirect and creative approach. It uses critical-thinking skills such as reasoning to deliberately look at how you can innovate, disrupt, and transform traditional models by using smart lateral thinking. This lateral thinking also creates simplicity.

Bestselling author Shane Snow says, "Lateral thinking doesn't replace hard work; it eliminates unnecessary cycles." This is the power of having smart lateral-thinking habits that create more simplicity. If we look at the change from postal mail service to email, we can observe simplicity in action. Email eliminated the cycle of buying stamps and moving mail by automobiles. Email made communication faster, easier, and cheaper. This is an example of the simplicity of lateral thinking. This is one of the skillsets that is most valuable today because we are rethinking, retraining, and reinventing everything about out world.

The whole world is evolving into a smart lateral-thinking process. We are now living in the smart era. The world is looking at traditional models of doing business, living, and relating, and eliminating any unnecessary cycles or intermediaries. In the new era of smart lateral-thinking and smart design, there are plenty of opportunities for anyone to use lateral thinking to innovate, disrupt, and transform any industry. This is why there are so many new billionaires.

You don't need to have a big sum of money in savings to become a millionaire or billionaire. You don't need to be the smartest person. It took Andrew Mason only two and a half years to become a billionaire after he started Groupon. The company offers percentage-off deals for consumers and helps cities promote restaurants and stores. Coupons are not a new business, but how the coupon is sold is new. It's a smart, lateral way of thinking and serving both the seller and the buyer.

If you like a deal, you purchase an electronic coupon directly from Groupon using your credit card or PayPal account. You print the coupon (or save it on your smartphone), take it to the restaurant or store, and redeem it for much more than the value you paid. This is the power of using smart lateral thinking in business. It's about using your creativity to create a new service from an existing industry.

Another example is Zappos Shoes. In this online success story, CEO Tony Hsieh looked at the shoe industry and reinvented customer service, but his real claim to fame is his leadership. Hsieh uses the Holacracy work experience. It is a new way of running an organization that removes power from a management hierarchy (intermediaries) and distributes it across clear roles, which can then be executed autonomously and without a micromanaging boss. This is a smart lateral-thinking style in the workplace and has made Hsieh a well-loved CEO and very wealthy.

Living in the smart era means being creative, agile, and flexible because innovations are happening faster than they ever have before. It takes new thinking and different questions to break through and transform anything. A smart lateral-thinking but small company with just a couple of partners can slaughter a traditional behemoth company overnight and reshape an entire industry in no time.

Look what Uber, Zip car, apps, Airbnb, YouTube, cloud-based storage, social media, Bitcoin, and Travelocity have done. These are smart lateral-thinking companies. They innovated, disrupted, and transformed how we do business, live, and work. They eliminate unnecessary cycles of debt and spending because they have reinvented how something is done. We now have smart lateral thinking that has moved us into the share economy, where what you own can be rented to others. This is reshaping how we do so many things, and it is allowing a smarter lateral design to transform the world and how we make money.

More importantly, smart lateral thinking is also transforming human consciousness. Traditional or standard models of thinking come with outdated stereotypes that are being innovated, disrupted, and transformed throughout the world. For example, our values related to ownership are shifting. The share economy has grown from this values shift.

It is no longer a success symbol to own a car when you can share one by calling Uber or using a Zip car. More people are realizing that ownership for the sake of ego is costly and damaging to the environment. They prefer to save money by sharing a car rather than owning one.

Even how we view smart people has changed. Now when we describe smart people we don't necessarily think about academic ability. Instead, many people think about innovative and creative abilities. We have reshaped our definition of smart yet again. Now smart people are those who challenge the status quo by thinking differently. There is an openness to this type of thinking. It requires a person to look at things with an eye toward how it can change to benefit everyone.

This smart lateral thinking is reshaping our future and its outcomes. Freedom evolves as consciousness evolves. Freedom is not an unchanging, immovable object. This is also the basis of our company Smart Group Firm. We help people and companies innovate, disrupt, and transform their businesses and lives: http://www.smartgroupfirm.com

Smart lateral thinking challenges the status quo by using imaginative, creative approaches. This is the new intelligence. It's not always about good grades. It's now about thinking in ways that challenge our current circumstances and state of affairs. An inventive mind is the new smart; rote memorization and test results are the old school mentality. Having an inventive mind means learning how to go around obstacles to shed a new light on an old belief, then making a smart lateral creation that transforms it.

When Benjamin Franklin was in his teens, he worked in his brother's printing shop. Ben's brother James would not publish anything his brother wrote because he thought sixteen-year-old Ben was too young to have anything important or profound to say to the readers of his paper.

Benjamin became frustrated with his brother's opinion of him, and he decided to create the persona of a middle-aged widow named Silence Dogood. Once every two weeks, Benjamin would leave a letter under the door of his brother's printing shop—fourteen letters total, all of which were published in his brother's paper. The letters became very popular, and eventually James discovered that all fourteen letters had been written by Benjamin.

Unfortunately, this angered James. Benjamin left his apprenticeship without permission, which in those days you just did not do. Young Ben had to make a lateral-thinking move to get his work recognized and valued. This did anger the establishment, but that eventually shifted and shattered the flexible beliefs regarding age and capabilities.

In our modern era, this is the power of the Internet and tools like YouTube. If you can't get that record deal, you simply do what Justin Bieber or Tori Kelly did, and you start creating your own audience without the help of the major record companies. Did this anger the establishment at first? Yes, but then smart people go past the obstacle and choose to innovate, disrupt, and transform their opportunities. This is how Bitcoin is going to affect our global currency wars and old financial systems. When you learn to do this, you have built the Ultimate Freedom into your life.

Say what you want about Justin Bieber, but Bieber has the highest social-networking profile of any other star and is the third most powerful celebrity because he used smart lateral thinking and moved past any perceived obstacles. This can happen now because an array of self-service tools and apps can help us create just about anything we want. When we choose to take advantage of these systems and apply them to what we want to create, that is real freedom.

Our traditional 9-to-5 workdays are being innovated, disrupted, and transformed. Was this initially popular? No. People don't like being laid off or seeing their job shipped overseas. Old thinking says that someone stole your job.

Smart lateral thinking says that the routine of working at the office is dying. Entrepreneurship and project-based assignments are the new working style. Working from home, whether for a big company or for yourself, is the lateral move. Work schedules that enhance your freedom are more readily available. Instead of clocking into the office and having your every move decided for you, your time is yours, as long as the project deadline is met.

This is a great innovation, as you can work during the hours you are the most refreshed and creative—when you do your best work. Some people are not morning people and feel more creative late at night. Others are more creative in the wee hours of the morning. With this new innovation in working hours, you will be able to protect your most creative hours for the project you're working on and won't be forced to be creative during your least creative hours.

In the era of smart lateral thinking, you will have to learn new skills. This means you need to be willing and accountable to learn what it takes to create an income from home. Is this convenient? No, not at first. There is a big learning curve and the absence of the usual paycheck. But pay attention to the results you want and suddenly you will notice the freedom and not the fear or inconvenience. Don't be rigid about using the method you are used to. Make a lateral move and look at how you can innovate, disrupt, and transform your past habits into a more creative work situation that makes you more money.

You can have more time with your family. You can create and control your time, as well as make great money, but you must embrace new thinking. Learning how to have smart lateral thinking requires a flexible, malleable belief system that is willing to unlock the Ultimate Freedom to the results you want.

Rigid thinking is not freedom. For years humankind has been caught in the rigid-thinking trap because of manipulation by religions and the media. But using your old thinking to create a new life won't work.

Albert Einstein's famous quote "We cannot solve our problems with the same thinking we used when we created them" is why it is so important to have smart lateral thinking. How do you know if your thinking is rigid? If you are reactive and not open, you are using an old thinking habit.

Remember when I was hiking with my friend? I was reacting to heights based on an old thinking habit. I was not observing or witnessing what was happening in the moment. Instead I was in my mind, projecting out to the future the possibility of dying while climbing. I was not present at all; instead I was reacting. I would freeze. I had to have the support of someone who could unfreeze my thinking to help me go past my old thinking. The thought of injuring myself or losing my life kept me frozen and prevented me from ascending to the summit.

I had to ask myself new questions to solve my hiking issue. I had to think differently to move forward. This is also how you have to solve the riddle of freedom, by asking a different question that allows you better access to your abilities. In order to ask different questions, you must be open to doing things differently. If I asked a different question but was unwilling to actually climb the mountain, I'd still be stuck.

A new action creates a new experience. If you don't take the new action, you are not free; instead you are imprisoned within your comfort zone, which is an addiction to convenience. This is nothing more than counterfeit freedom. If you are answering your call for more freedom, critical thinking skills and smart lateral thinking mixed with new ideas will give you a fresh look at how to unlock the Ultimate Freedom, which will enable you to unlock the secrets to a life of passion, purpose, and prosperity.

We have been taught how to think in a status quo way and not in an ever-changing, smart lateral way. Too many people believe that change is not good and feel safe and secure when things stay the same. They find change uncomfortable, and thus living in today's world can be scary for them. *Just keep asking yourself, Is everything okay right now? Is anyone hurt? Great, then take another step.*

Chapter 9

Unlocking Momentum, Unlocking Freedom

The momentum of freedom in our world is unmistakable—and it is not carried forward by our power alone. We can trust in that greater power who guides the unfolding of the years.

—George W. Bush

She was on the platform ready to swim her backstroke race. I was drying myself off with a towel because I had just swum a respectable second place in the first group of backstroke swimmers. I loved being on the swim team. Parts of California can be really hot in the summer, and swimming, surfing, and other water sports are how we keep ourselves cool. I also love competing, and this team offered me the camaraderie and excitement of competing. That day we were competing to see who was going to the state finals.

My teammate was excited and nervous. She was in the second group of backstroke swimmers. She got in the water and set herself up in her lane. She whispered to me, "When I come back and do the turn, tell me what place I am in." I nodded. She smiled at me, and suddenly we could hear the referee say, "Swimmers, take your mark."

Boom! The gun went off, and the swimmers were racing to see who was going to the state tournament. My teammate had a great lead and was swimming really well. If she completed the first flip turn well, she could have a strong lead—and that's just what she did. I was excited over her first-place lead. But I knew that at any moment that lead could be shortened by another determined swimmer.

My teammate neared the wall in front of me and did her flip turn. She was pulling a strong backstroke when I held up one finger to signify that she was in first place. She immediately radiated joy, and she suddenly had more power and pulled farther into the lead. She gained more momentum just knowing she was in first place. I was happy too, so I started to yell and cheer her on. The rest of the team saw me so excited that they jumped up to help me cheer her on too.

We were screaming and jumping up and down, waving our hands like maniacs, even though our teammate had given herself a significant lead. No one was going to catch her. She missed the record by two-tenths of a second or something close to that. We all helped her out of the water and hugged her and cheered.

Okay, so she didn't break any records. She wasn't headed for the Olympics. But she did take advantage of her momentum, and this helped her succeed. We all enjoyed a small win together. It boosted our team's confidence, and we had fun celebrating our teammate's accomplishment. It helped the next swimmer want to do better and be better. It helped us all learn to support each other more. This was a small win with a powerful outcome.

She didn't realize she was being carried to greater success by momentum. She just noticed that she had a spectacular race and it resulted in a first-place finish and going to the state finals. She had more energy and more resolve after she knew she was winning. This is how momentum works.

Momentum is a key force to unlocking your Ultimate Freedom and greatness. It is the continuous forward motion of an object without external help. It is also a measure of how hard it is to stop a moving object. Momentum is the product of the object's mass and velocity. In humans it has another aspect—it generates more life force and drive inside the soul.

If an eighteen-wheel truck is coming down a mountain road, it picks up speed. This is momentum. As it continues down the steep road, it will pick up even more speed—not because the driver is intentionally accelerating but because the weight of the vehicle engages with the downward forward motion of gravity, creating momentum, which causes it to move faster.

Now you could try to stop the truck by stepping out in front of it and holding your hands out in hopes of slowing it down. But you will most likely be run over by the truck. The truck becomes unstoppable. This also happens when humans take action. It doesn't need to be huge action, although sometimes that helps.

"By itself, one small win may seem unimportant," wrote Dr. Karl Weick in a 1984 article for *American Psychologist*. "A series of wins at small but significant tasks, however, reveals a pattern that may *attract* allies, deter opponents, and lower resistance to subsequent proposals. Once a small win has been accomplished, *forces* are set in motion that favors another small win." This is how you create momentum.

To me, momentum is like a super power. In emergencies it can turn into superhuman strength where people are suddenly able to do what is believed to be beyond normal—things like a parent lifting a car off their child. And that is the secret to momentum. It gets you to do what is beyond your norm. It gives you a stronger life force and determination to achieve a win.

This helps the small wins to add up and create big wins. Momentum is a force and power that is unlocked inside of you as you create a series of small wins. Doing this begins to reveal what is necessary to access greater passion, purpose, and prosperity.

This also requires that you concentrate on your insides and not on what is happening in other people's insides. Freedom is individual; you don't group-walk into the Ultimate Freedom. Yes, you can be in the company of likeminded people. However, your path to freedom is individual.

So again, what then is freedom? According to its definition, freedom is the power or right to act, speak, or think as one wants without hindrance or restraint. In Western countries, most people have this option. But when you look around the world today, things seem dismal. Stress levels are skyrocketing as the complexity and uncertainty of living in a society of über-fast transformation and constant disruption is upon us.

There is no easy way through this. Our world is changing rapidly, and this causes a lot of stress. For those who don't understand the Ultimate Freedom, this can be confusing and painful. Half of marriages in the US end in divorce, while 60 percent of couples claim to be unhappy in their relationships. Some 80 percent of people are unhappy with their jobs.

When we look at our current level of stress, we can see that technology has lied to us. It promised to make our lives easier and less complicated. It promised us a life where we were going to work less and have more wealth and free time. Instead, it has sped life up to such a degree that we are moving faster and faster and doing more and more. Technology has made many things more convenient, but it has not necessarily made it easier or helped us slow down. We work longer and faster, in some cases doing the job of three people.

We work much more than eight hours a day and at an intensely fast pace. We are under such pressure that our attention spans have shortened and emotional resourcefulness has diminished. In an article for *Scientific American*, Julia Calderone reports that over the last decade the use of antidepressants has shot up due to the anxiety and pressure of just living. Now 8 to 10 percent of the population, or about 35 million people, take an antidepressant.

Millions of people are walking around medicated and trying to quickly accomplish more. We want to get rich quick, eat a quick meal, have a quick word, take a quick look, or ask a quick question. No wonder we are so neurotic. Suicide rates are outrageously high. Suicide occurs every 12.8 minutes, making it the tenth leading cause of death in America. What is happening that is oppressing freedom and the pursuit of happiness in a way that would cause this tragedy? Why do we live amid such speed, pressure, and chaos? Freedom and the right to pursue your happiness are part of what this country was built on, not the stress of a fast-paced life.

You may have a lot of money, but if you don't feel good about your life, then what's the point? What keeps us from slowing down and living our dreams? Why don't people move beyond their psychological roadblocks? A lot of people numb the pain, and even more don't know what to do about the roadblocks in their way. So many people focus on fixing the pain instead of focusing on the action they are meant to take that will set them free.

The Declaration of Independence explicitly mentions three rights that all humans have: life, liberty, and the pursuit of happiness. No one may deny us these gifts, and since they are "unalienable," we can't rightfully forfeit them either.

The pursuit of happiness is not the right to have greater conveniences and more possessions. Instead, it is the right to use your talents to obtain assets and material goods, and to use them as you see fit, as long as you do not injure yourself or another. But how do you pursue happiness? Humans are forward-motion beings; we thrive on momentum because it helps us grow, excel, and achieve. The secret to unlocking freedom is that many people are confused by the difference between speed and momentum. Momentum creates success. Speed confuses success because it is often a result of unhealthy thinking.

Speed in this form is a manmade force that creates chaos because it makes you believe that everything has to happen right now. This is reflected in our addiction to instant gratification. Momentum is engaging with an organic process that unites all universal laws and attractors. Momentum uses timing and flow. Things and projects gain momentum because the timing is understood. This produces an authentic speed, but it is not stressful. Instead it is fun and joyful. It promotes a healthy drive, and encourages abilities within you. Happiness is created because you are engaged with all aspects of your being, momentum, and life force.

When we engage in momentum, we are engaging with the silent intelligence that creates the small wins, which over time creates big wins. When we engage with our minds we enter unhealthy instant gratification speed. We want to go faster and get there sooner. Unhealthy speed creates resentment, anxiety, and stress.

Momentum creates inner joy, feelings of support, and boundless energy. It is often described as being in the zone or feeling the flow. You're aligned with your inner timing, and this is always aligned with universal timing. This helps you grow and creates progress and success. Benjamin Franklin said, "Without continual growth and progress, such words as improvement, achievement, and success have no meaning." The Ultimate Freedom involves continual growth, not continual speed.

To ignite momentum, you need to engage with the "first right action," not the most comfortable action. This is where some people get confused. People want to take the most comfortable action and hope it builds momentum. It won't, because you will be out of alignment with your inner timing, which is showing you the first right action. Often the first right action is the one that scares you most; many people don't want to face that fear, so they take another action that is more familiar and less scary—but it is not the first right action.

As soon as you allow your fear to move you out of the right first action, you have lost momentum. When you move beyond your fear and take the first right action, you have answered the calling inside you, and momentum will engage with you and tell you the next right action.

If you open a business from home and know the first right action is to pick up the phone and talk to people about your services or product—but the fear of doing so leads you to design your logo instead—you have lost momentum, even if the logo gets done.

A nagging voice in your head is telling you what the first right action is. In this case, it is to call someone. When you choose to avoid the first right action, you will sense a negative alignment that shuts off possibilities. It's not the attractor field that is shutting it off; it is you. The attractor field is there to help you take the first right action.

If you know your first right action is to write a book but you tell yourself that the task seems daunting or that you are a horrible writer, and so you avoid the first right action of just writing, you will lose momentum because you are avoiding yourself. Momentum leads and challenges the status quo. It invites you to live in the continual growth and progress Benjamin Franklin spoke about.

Without momentum, how will you break free? You will need this unstoppable force to help you free yourself. Reading this book will not create freedom for you. It is simply designed to help you identify and connect with the things that allow you to claim and unlock the Ultimate Freedom so you can enjoy a life of passion, purpose, and prosperity. Momentum is a key aspect of creating small wins that in turn create forward movement, freedom, and success. Engaging with momentum effortlessly promotes awareness and mindfulness. It gets you there sooner and will reshape you and your success.

When we stop our momentum and turn on the speed, we are no longer engaged in or pursuing freedom. Instead we are pursuing our unhealthy thoughts and addiction to instant manifestation. Most people will quit whatever they are doing when they enter this mode of engagement. This is painful after a while and creates folly and self-sabotage. It results in boredom and resentment that things aren't going your way or fast enough.

Then you begin having the "should" conversations in your head. *It should be easy. I should be better. I should work longer. I should [fill in the blank].* We feel disappointed and begin to look for a convenient way to ease our pain. We turn to food, sex, drink, drugs, TV, and so forth. These actions suppress the speed and your momentum. Then depression sets in because your mind has run off with your momentum and turned it into unhealthy thinking, speed, and self-sabotage.

We react and compare ourselves to others instead of paying attention to our individual journey. We begin to abuse ourselves emotionally, thinking there is something wrong with us because we are not keeping up with the pack. We think, *I am twenty [or thirty, forty, fifty . . .] and I have not gotten where others have. What's wrong with me?*

We react in this manner because we are used to and addicted to instant gratification and convenience. If things take longer than our mind says they "should," we begin to think unhealthy things such as *It's not easy. It's too hard. I'm not good at this.* And then we quit. Once this happens we become disillusioned and fall back into our past. We lose our momentum and life force. No wonder we are depressed; look at what we're saying to ourselves.

Then we start to soothe our pain. We don't notice how this slowly leads into depression. We blame someone or something, and for a moment this helps us ignore the pain we are feeling, but we start to lose ourselves even more when we resort to blame. It drops us deeper into depression.

Since many people have opted for convenience instead of freedom, we don't even notice how the convenience slows momentum down and how boredom shows up. This cycle begins without us knowing it because we are no longer mindful of ourselves.

Momentum involves an inner dialogue between you and your inner silent intelligence. It doesn't ask you to speed up. Instead it requires you to become more mindful and listen to what is the next move for you. It requires you to act, observe, and watch for what your next best move is because this means momentum has begun! When momentum begins, it doesn't always mean moving into overdrive. It means paying attention to your next best move and taking that action. Then complete your next best move. You will begin to have a series of small wins that catapult you forward.

Tony Robbins understands momentum and taking advantage of freedom. He says, "Success comes from taking the initiative and following up—persisting—eloquently expressing the depth of your love." Just change the word "success" to "freedom" and you have my definition of freedom. It eloquently expresses the depths of your love, not going as fast as you can, unless that is the natural expression in the moment.

Freedom comes when you can take the initiative and follow up—persist—in each of the six key areas of freedom. Your authentic love for your work, finances, industry, art, life, self, and so forth is how you engage with momentum and take the next right action. These are all expressions of the Ultimate Freedom.

In order to unlock your freedom, you must be willing to unlock your life, your liberty, and your happiness in such a way that you are expressing freedom by following up. This will create momentum and trigger potentials that reshape your character and life.

Creating momentum is vital in every "people activity." No matter what the activity, whether it's a project, starting a business, competing in a sport, momentum is critical. Why? Momentum moves the project, business, or competition to a point of becoming virtually unstoppable.

Momentum shifts your resonance, and your series of small wins suddenly helps you see that what you thought was impossible is actually possible. This is the transformation that happens when you have small wins that give you momentum and more energy, joy, and success. This is what propels people forward. Small actions equal big results over time.

Momentum starts from small beginnings. J.K. Rowling was fired from a secretarial job because she spent too much time daydreaming about a boy named

Harry Potter. The daydream was the silent intelligence within her asking her to take the first small action and just write the story. When your attention nudges you to pursue one of the six key areas of freedom, it is your cue to follow it.

Rowling took the first small action and began writing a story, not worrying about how big or little it would be, whether it would turn into a movie or not, but just writing to create a story. She immersed herself in the pleasure of writing about Harry Potter. This was the small beginning where momentum started to build because she engaged with her inner nudge to take the first right action.

This is how you unlock your Ultimate Freedom. It's a series of first, right, small, and powerful actions. You must engage with your momentum. This is making the most of where you are in the moment. Momentum requires that you pay attention to what is working in your life. It requires celebrating your successes and little wins. This quietly reshapes your character and shifts your resonance, and suddenly more momentum shows up, more influence shows up, and more credibility sneaks in too.

As you go deeper into your momentum, confidence will show up and you will be having fun as you hone your freedom skills in each area. You will develop a level of excellence and pride with your work. Suddenly your work ethic will grow, and the discipline and precision you feel becomes something you enjoy and take pride in. You learn to honor your abilities and creative nature when it shows up for you. The "shoulding" slows down and disappears as you begin to appreciate your creative expression and your flavor of freedom.

You feel more peace, and thus you become more peaceful. You learn to appreciate others in their authentic freedom expression and can feel happy for them when they succeed. You have more drive and more life force pulsing through you as you see more and more of your freedom showing up for you. You will become more mindful and freer while enjoying your life.

In Part Three we will delve into how to unlock the six areas of freedom. The secret to unlocking them is that you must unlock them at the same time. If you only unlock one, you will only have one code in a series of six, and this does not usually bring happiness or liberty. You will not feel free. Unlocking each area will provide you with the momentum that is required to change your character, shift your resonance, and provide you with the success you dream of having.

This is about becoming more mindful as you develop your small wins and build daily momentum, reshaping your character, and becoming more aware of what is working for you. It is about engaging with your silent intelligence, using your discernment and critical-thinking skills to rethink and unlock your passion, purpose, and prosperity.

Congratulations on getting this far. We are honored by your courage, tenacity, and willingness to enhance your life's journey with a touch of freedom. Here's to your life, liberty, and happiness.

Let's continue.

Chapter 10

Passion, Purpose, and Prosperity

Passion precedes prosperity.

—Andrew Hildreth

I t was Thanksgiving, and my sister had spent nearly four days preparing our holiday dinner. I rarely get to see my sister Edie because she lives in Germany and works all over Europe. My sister is a chef trained in France, and she has all the accomplishments and accolades that a French-trained chef can have. She is also Buddhist, so as she prepares food she prays over it. To her, cooking is a meditation practice.

Mostly, though, hers is the best food you could ever eat. I think she doesn't visit much because when she gets here I show her to the kitchen and ask her to cook. Not much of a vacation, right? For my sister, cooking isn't simply something you mindlessly do because you are hungry. She refuses to engage in this form of cooking. To her cooking is about waking someone up and giving them an experience they will want to be fully present for. She feels that most restaurants don't do that kind of cooking because they want to turn the tables more quickly.

Instead she cooks at Buddhist retreat centers and for dignitaries around the world. She cooks at places where you can have an exceptional experience, for as many as five hundred people at a time. She prides herself on creating the most uplifting dining environment, with the most sumptuous meals that the budget will allow.

To her a meal is an experience that should enliven you and awaken you, because the environment and food do not let you become mindless. All your senses come alive when you enter a dining room that my sister has created. It is elegant, beautiful, and mindfully decorated.

She is precise in everything she chooses, from the table linens to the crystal to the serving trays. Everything is meant for the guests to be transported into a different space and energy. She says, "A proper dining room experience helps your guests stop their mindless thinking and begin observing the beauty around them. This is how they become mindful before you serve them. They will feel the energy and become whatever you create in that room. If it's a folksy table, people will become folksy. If it's elegant, people will become elegant. Ambience is a powerful tool."

When you walk into her dining room, your senses awaken to the beauty that surrounds you. She is a master at creating space. My mother is too, and my sister evidently inherited that gene. I can tell you it certainly hasn't been my strength.

"A beautifully set table is the first part of experiencing dinner," she says. "A beautifully set room and table invites the experiencer to awaken and become mindful. They feel cared for and special. They are then present enough to enjoy the food. No matter how bad their day was, they will begin to experience equanimity and dignity when they sit down for a meal in an uplifting, elegant environment."

This was the experience she had created for me and my twenty-eight guests for Thanksgiving. This was a beautiful gift to me because rarely do people get to have an experienced chef come in and cook a meal that is made just for them with such intense care and awareness. My sister's eye for detail is exquisite; she misses nothing.

For this particular Thanksgiving meal, we ate at a friend's house because he was away and his kitchen was more professional than mine. His house also had a bigger dining area, one that overlooked the Sangre de Cristo Mountains in Southern Colorado. Edie spent four days shopping, chopping, dicing, rinsing, soaking, flavoring, decorating, and preparing a meal fit for kings and queens, constantly being mindful and praying over everything she created. The day of the event, my guests arrived and were amazed by the ambience and setting. You could hear the surprised, excited chatter as wine and hors d'oeuvres were served.

Soon my sister invited us to help ourselves to the feast she had created. When we gathered in the dining area, you could hear the oohs and ahs over how things were laid out on trays. Everyone filled their plates, as you do on this American holiday, and began eating. I happened to look up to see where my sister was because I was so proud of her and wanted to thank her for doing this for us. I found her sitting on the patio looking in.

At first I thought she was hot and tired and was cooling herself off outside with a glass of wine. I figured she would join us when she was ready. But soon I noticed that she was not coming in, and people had gone back for a second serving. Then I thought maybe something was wrong. I slipped out to the patio to see what was up with her.

"Honey, are you okay?" I asked.

"Yeah, yeah . . . sit, sit, you are blocking my view," she said.

I immediately sat next to her to see what it was that she was looking at. She didn't say anything, and neither did I for a few minutes. Then I asked her what exactly she was doing.

"I am studying my work."

"What?" I asked.

"Vickie, when I cook and create a table, it is my passion. The energy of that passion is what is put into the food they eat. My purpose is to share that passion with them through their ingesting my food. It creates upliftedness, equanimity, and prosperity."

We were silent for a moment, and then she continued with a question.

"Why do you think some of the biggest business deals are done in fine restaurants?"

"I don't know. Why?" Actually I thought that was a very interesting question.

"Because when you create an elegant environment, people feel valued; they calm down and feel happy. The people who are there to close the deal trust each other more over a meal together than over a conference room table. They are more likely to come to an agreement and close the deal in an elegant atmosphere and are more likely to spend more money. They are also less likely to cheat or manipulate in an elegant atmosphere; instead of cutthroat businessmen, they become gentlemen."

Hmm, I thought.

She continued. "You see, people have passion, purpose, and prosperity all wrong. They think passion, purpose, and prosperity are something you find and then create, but that's not true. It is something you let out of you while you are creating and is the result of the care and excellence you choose to put into those things. Right now, I am studying how my creation is shifting people's energy, because that is what food and ambience does. Don't worry; I'll be in in a minute," she said.

That conversation changed my life. It showed that I thought passion and purpose were things you found and then could use to create prosperity. Passion and purpose are not things you find; they are essences you let out from within you. Combined, it is the level of excellence you choose as the standard for your talents. It is why people hone their skills—so they can let out their passion, purpose, and prosperity. It is what separates the ordinary from the extraordinary. This passion and purpose can be in anything you create. Prosperity answers your level of passion and purpose.

Violinist Vladimir Horowitz said, "The difference between ordinary and extraordinary is practice." My sister paid a high price to unleash her passion for cooking. When she was younger, she took a lot of teasing when the dish she cooked was subpar, but she didn't let that stop her.

I remember in her late teen years she absentmindedly left a loaf of bread to bake in the oven, and it turned into a dry heavy brick. My stepfather noticed it. That night at dinner he dropped that loaf onto the center of the table, where it landed with a great thud. In a sarcastic, playful voice, he asked who would like a slice of bread, and we all laughed, including Edie. That bread was so dry that we placed it on the Thanksgiving dinner table for many years after. We all thought it was so funny; the thing never even molded.

At Christmas my stepfather would wrap the bread brick and give it to one of us as a joke. Each year we would wonder who was going to get Edie's bread brick that year. Even with all our teasing her about the mistakes she made, she never gave up her passion.

She never said, "Wow, I burned the bread. I should just go be an accountant." Nope, she just kept going and became this amazing chef who understood the power of passion, purpose, and prosperity. Passion helps you persevere and keeps you going because you love becoming excellent at what you are doing. Understanding the dynamics of this changed my success rate overnight. Having a passion for excellence raises the bar above the ordinary and brings more freedom and success.

Passion unleashes openness and curiosity. It carries with it creativity and experimentation. It innovates and transforms. Painting, music, cooking, designing, entrepreneurship, inventing, managing, connecting with people, organizing—whatever your passion is, it invites you to grow in excellence. This builds authentic momentum and purpose—and prosperity, when you discover how to monetize a passion.

My spouse has been in the same career for more than thirty years. She is an occupational therapist at the top of her field. She has worked at the number-one rehabilitation hospital in the country for twenty-plus years and at some of the top hospitals—and some dive nursing homes as well. She has traveled all over the country helping interns get their feet wet in the field.

She has spoken on stages all over the country, in front of hundreds of people, in order to educate doctors and surgeons. She has trained incoming staff to educate them on proper procedures and patient care. She has managed large teams of people and prides herself on turning marginal facilities into competent facilities that have earned a five-star rating by *Newsweek*. She is always among the favorites in her building because her attitude and point of view match her passion.

My spouse is passionate about her level of excellence in every area of her life. Fitness, nutrition, gardening, knitting, education, relationships, hobbies— whatever it is, she lives it passionately. Others admire and emulate her.

In her industry, she has chosen to work with the toughest cases. She specializes in brain and spinal cord injuries, along with dementia patients and aging issues. By the time people come into contact with her, they are usually at the lowest point in their life. Many times she has talked them out of committing suicide and helped them build a new life or helped them find peace before they pass on. She has loved them when everyone else has forgotten them. She has sat with families while they are in their deepest grief in order to help them understand how they can help their loved one live a new life. This is her calling.

She says, "When you are born, there are many people to help you. Nurses, doctors, parents, grandparents, teachers, and mentors. However, when you're old or disabled in some way, you are often forgotten by society and often neglected. My passion is to love the forgotten in the world enough for them to enjoy and rebuild a new life or allow them to pass lovingly and peacefully." My spouse lives her life at a level ten. She has lived a life of passion, purpose, and prosperity in the same career for thirty years. Is it always fun? No. Does she break down and cry when she loses a patient? Yes. Was getting to her level of expertise easy? No.

In order for her to remain at the top of her field, she takes continuing education courses far more than the average therapist does. She studies management skills and reads or listens to books on related topics every day. She is always growing or learning something new about her field or how to improve her skills. She infuses her passion for excellence into everything she does, even when she is just cleaning the house. It is a way of life for us. Passion and purpose is who she has become because she lets them out as the standard way of living.

After listening to my sister and watching my partner, I started to notice my passion for excellence. I realized authentic freedom and success was not just finding something I felt passionate about and doing it at an ordinary level. Instead I would hone my skills and put my passion, purpose, and prosperity into them and develop a level of excellence. This is how you become what you want to attract, and it ignites the silent intelligence within you to help you become successful. This produces confidence, well-being, and freedom. Benjamin Franklin said, "Well done is better than well said." If you look at his hidden message, it is not just about getting things done; it's also about doing them well.

This is the power of letting out your passion, purpose, and prosperity, because what you focus on grows. Our mind creates what we focus on. Success isn't what happens to you when you hit a goal or target. It is who you become and what you let out of you on the way to achieving your targets. Goals are just milestones on the way that help you have a focus. When you live at this level, you are reshaping your character along the way and growing more freedom.

This same understanding of passion, purpose, and prosperity is what built companies like Apple, Virgin, OWN, Microsoft, Tesla, Google, Facebook, Rolls Royce, Fleming, Cartier, and others. Passion is the level of excellence you choose to produce or demonstrate in how you do something. The *New York Times* bestselling author of *Secrets of the Millionaire Mind*, T. Harv Eker, said, "How you do anything is how you do everything." This is looking at your level of passion and excellence or your level of convenience and instant gratification. It's only your love of doing your best work that will raise your bar and your level of prosperity. There is no convenience or instant gratification in this process.

Claiming your passion, purpose, and prosperity is not about conveniently creating a get-rich-quick scheme, because that doesn't exist. It's not walking through your day feeling prosperous and grateful for what you have either. It's about living at a level of first right action and passion that drives your momentum into the direction of excellence. This is imbued into everything you do, so much that you humbly stand out in whatever it is you are doing and you *become* grateful. Gratitude is not a feeling. It's a honed skillset that powers the three Ps.

Oprah Winfrey said, "What you focus on expands, and when you focus on the goodness in your life, you create more of it. Opportunities, relationship, even money flowed my way when I learned to be grateful no matter what happened in my life." The skillset of gratitude supports freedom, passion, purpose, and prosperity and helps you move out of your addictions to convenience and instant gratification.

This is not about being perfect or great at what you do; it's being passionate about the excellence in what you do and your willingness to embrace a steep learning curve until you are great at what you do. I don't necessarily like writing, but I have a passion for getting my message out and sharing it with others. I don't have a degree in journalism, and anyone who knows me knows that I was not a good writer or speller. The writing learning curve was tough for me, but this is the skill I had to learn in order to spread the message I wish to share.

I had to become excellent at the tools of my trade, things like using Microsoft Word, because this is the tool I use to write with. Passion is the level of excellence I choose to bring to those skills I want to use and hone them in order to bring my message, products, brand, and service to market at a purposeful level. Working in this way grows my momentum and confidence as well as my freedom. I am grateful that I pushed myself to live at this level.

Passion is the level of excellence you develop that you put into something. Purpose is thinking about the design and the end user, and prosperity is your investment in yourself in order to reach a level of distinction that provides you with the best remuneration. Singers put in thousands of obsessive hours developing and letting out their passion for singing and honing their craft for the purpose of uplifting us.

A big myth about passion and purpose is that it will garner you fame. What passion produces is credibility, respect, and influence in whatever you are doing, because you have achieved a certain level of excellence. Having this is much more valuable than anything else. Fame is fleeting and not real. You don't even have to be good at something to get fifteen minutes of fame. Passion is the skillset of excellence you choose to become in your life. Having passion isn't boastful; it is humble and willing to make small wins every day until you reach the goal and the greatness you want to experience.

If you have not found your purpose, it is because you are looking outside yourself for something that doesn't exist. People do not have a special purpose; there is no such thing. But you can have a special calling. In fact, you can have more than one special calling. You can bring a sense of purpose to whatever calling you choose to put your attention on. Whatever you choose to put your passion for excellence into becomes purposeful.

Inviting and living at this level of excellence is an act of freedom and is most often not convenient. Raising the bar means becoming more passionate and excellent at what you do, not feeling more purposeful about what you do.

No matter how purposeful you feel, people are still not attracted to marginal products or services. When you buy a new iPhone, it is because they have added new features and the product has become better. Otherwise why would you buy it? It's the same when the product is you. The bar gets set higher every day as companies and innovators try to create something better than their last product.

It's a constantly improving smart world. If you are looking for an easy, convenient freedom, there never was one. Claiming real freedom is about claiming yourself. Your current level of passion, purpose, and prosperity is already producing the lifestyle you are currently enjoying. If you want more, you will become what you need to become in order to have the more that you seek. Oprah Winfrey says, "Doing the best at this moment puts you in the best place for the next moment."

I had to take a good look at what I was doing in my life. I asked myself, *I know I'm good at consulting and writing, but am I passionate and purposeful about it, or am I doing the average kind of consulting and writing? Do I have a "normal or exceptional" consulting and writing practice?* You will need to ask yourself these questions if you want to get to the next level of anything, because the next level is full of people who had to go above "normal" to be at the next level of excellence. The next level always includes more freedom because it is full of people who worked hard and followed and managed their momentum in order to get there.

When you are at the next level, you will meet likeminded people. This is why the people you are relating to represent where you are in your life. It's a good indicator of your level of freedom. You will find likeminded people at every new stage while claiming your Ultimate Freedom. When you want to achieve more independence, it will benefit you to begin to hang out with people who value you and are at that same level of liberty you are looking to claim.

Freedom grows and has stages within a person. It invites momentum, growth, and deeper forward motion. It is an ongoing process that helps you become your best. There is a beginner, intermediate, and advanced level of freedom until you have claimed your ultimate freedom. As you claim and move to the next level, you score more freedom, passion, purpose, and prosperity. How then do you move to the next level of freedom? That's where we are going now.

Chapter 11

Learning to Do What You Think You Can't

Whether you think you can, or you think you can't—you're right.
—Henry Ford

In my early career as an entrepreneur I was having a conversation with a very wealthy man—very successful, very Christian, and very nice. We were having dinner at an upscale restaurant in Dallas. I was attending a convention that I could barely afford to attend, but I made it there anyway. The conference was filled with people who were much more financially successful than I was, and I felt intimidated because they made millions while I made into the high five figures. At that time I had lots of debt. I felt out of place and yet wanted to be there so badly I scrambled to figure out how I could attend.

This gentleman lived near Dallas. We had football in common and talked about that, but I wanted to know how he got to where he was in his life. He looked as if he was in his mid-fifties or early sixties. He had all the signs of wealth—*real* wealth. Sure, he was older than I was, but I figured he began acquiring his wealth when he was the age I was at the time. I wondered what he did. I knew it was something entrepreneurial because everyone at this convention was an entrepreneur.

It took me a while to get the nerve to ask him what he did for a living. But after some small talk and connecting, I asked him his secret to success. Instead of answering, he asked me a question in return.

"Vickie, do you want to be rich?"

No one had ever asked me that question before, but I knew in my heart the answer was "Yes!"

"Great, would you like to know the secret to becoming rich?"

Of course I replied, "Yes, please share that with me!"

Notice that I was not being direct. I was too afraid to ask him what I really wanted to know, which was "How did you become rich?" or "How do you become rich legally?"

Thank goodness he was able to see past my bogus question, and he asked the one question that I needed to ask myself—which was, "Vickie, do you want to be rich?"

I actually had to confront the part of me that wanted to be rich. When I replied "Yes," I was committing and declaring to myself that I wanted to be rich.

The next question he asked me was, "How rich?"

I don't know, I thought. The question stumped me. I just stared at him with that deer-in-the-headlights look.

Because I paused, he continued. "You won't be rich if you don't know what being rich means to you or how much you want."

I had never considered that in all of my thirty-one years.

He looked at me with such kind eyes. He realized that I had never been taught about money. Of course not—my parents made their money illegally. And that may sound interesting as a story, but in real life it sucks. When you make a lot of money illegally, you can't spend it on cool stuff because it tips everyone off that you are doing illegal things. You can't buy that big house or big boat or fancy car. People would begin to wonder how you acquired all that cash since you don't have a job or business. The IRS would wonder how you could afford what you have when you have no legal income.

In order for my father to be protected, he could not live the lifestyle he could afford with his drug money. So being rich at first meant nothing to me. What's the point of having wealth if you can't spend any of it on experiences or things you dream of having? So when he asked me how much I wanted, I realized I simply had never considered this question. What I did want was to make every last dime the legal way. I did not want to do anything illegal. Living in America this actually is possible. You can be as wealthy as you like—make as much money as you want, and do it legally.

Because I only made into the high five figures, I thought a million dollars was a lot of money.

"I think I should start at a million and see where it goes from there," I told him.

His reply stumped me again.

"You will never make it with your attitude. You are not committed yet to that number. Either you want a million dollars or not."

I interrupted him and said more emphatically, "No, no, no—I want a million dollars a year or more. I just think my starting point should be a million a year."

"Great, Vickie. Do you have a notebook? Because I am going to tell you how to make as much money as you want, and you're going to want to write this down."

I quickly opened my briefcase and grabbed a pen and my notepad (hey, it was the '90s, and the iPad had not been invented yet). I pushed my dinner plate back and took notes as he began to share with me the secrets to wealth. I'm going to share them with you now because they have worked for me.

Here is what he said: "Vickie, you have to embrace everything I'm going to tell you and practice it every day until you *become* it. This will make you successful in whatever you choose to do. There are twelve things I have done to make me successful in my life and business, and I do them every day. You will become as wealthy as you want to be when you become good at these twelve things and implement them in your life." Here is what he told me:

1. **Be direct about what you want.** Otherwise you will be a beggar. There is no time for you to be wishy-washy about success and wealth. You have

to know what it is you want out of your life and why you want it. That is
the only way you can commit your precious time to it. If you don't know
what you want, you'll just float through your life accepting whatever is
given to you, and only beggars do that. You'll beg for a job, beg for a
raise, beg for time off, and beg for everything you get.

God didn't intend for you to be a beggar; He intended for you to be
a light in the world. When you pursue your dreams with all your heart,
you'll work like you are on fire, and you'll become a light in the world
because people will notice that you are led by something greater than
your problems and greater than your mind. You will be showing others
what it's like to be led by real faith. When you're on fire, people will want
to watch you burn. They will want to know what you have that makes
you so focused and determined. Only you will know that it's the Holy
Spirit that is keeping the flame inside you lit.

When you know what you want, stop begging, and start working
toward your goals, you're going to hit some bumps in the road. You're
still going to have to be direct about what you want. Do you want help?
Then ask for it. You're going to have to manage your mind. Be direct
about what it is that you want. If you feel down, ask yourself, "Do you
want your goals more than this bump in the road, yes or no?" If you do,
then you're going to have to figure out how to get over that bump in
the road. This is your first taste of real confidence and freedom, which
brings me to point number two.

2. **You gotta learn to fail and stand back up.** Most people don't know
how to stand up after they have been knocked down by life. You have to
understand that success and failure go together. It's not one or the other.
Some products fly off the shelf; others don't. It's just how it is; it's not a
reflection on you. When it comes to success and failure you have to pay
attention to what is working, not who is working or who's to blame. This
is how success leaves clues. You have to study your success clues. Sure, it's
great to read about them, but what are *your* success clues? If you don't
know what they are, how are you going to sell them to others? Failure is
the classroom that makes you great once you learn how to stand back up

and evaluate. Then get on the field and take another turn at bat; give it all you've got, which leads me to point number three.

3. **Don't care about what other people think of you.** Somewhere along the way, someone is going to make fun of what you're doing. They are going to stare at you funny. They are going to make a comment or suggest that it is not wise for you to do what you're doing or chase your dreams. They may even be angry at you and want you to do something different than work as much as you are working.

When you start to have some success, they are going to be envious at first. However, as you gather more success, they are going to want to hang out with you more. As you gather more success, they will begin to drop your name and hope it gets them influence or respect because they know you. When you become influential in your industry, people are going to want to talk with you, work with you, or be around you. You still can't care about what they think. You can't care about whether they think you're a failure or successful. You have to care about whether you are achieving your goals or not. Either you are or not, and what anyone else says is none of your business. Your job is to stay focused and do your job well, which brings me to my next point.

4. **Learn to do what other people hate to do, and do it well.** Vickie, pay attention to this. It is one of the easiest and greatest ways to get wealthy. People hate or are intimidated by doing what they think is hard to do, and they are overwhelmed by having to do it. People are intimidated by or dislike selling, advertising, marketing, business planning, computers, technology of any kind, programming, accounting, finance. Be great at what other people don't like to do and you will be wealthy.

Most people won't even make a business plan when they start a business because they think it's hard and they hate doing it. So they pay someone else thousands of dollars to do it for them. If you embrace these skills and learn to do what others don't like doing and do it well, you will always have work you can charge a lot of money for. You will always be wanted for projects, and you will have had one of the best breakthroughs you could ever have. You move from being unknown to becoming the most valuable player in the business because you can do what others can't. This means you have to learn to do what you think you can't do.

5. **Don't think you are smarter than you are.** Keep your ego in check. Always be open and willing to see another's point of view. Be curious and kind to everyone. Don't let some toxic person run away with your manners, dignity, and reason. Be polite as much as you can, but have boundaries and kindness—this is the most powerful combination.

   If you learn to do what other people hate to do and do it well, but you are a cocky, hotheaded, arrogant jerk, no one will want to work with you or for you. You will not have credibility with your peers, and they will not refer clients to you. Being a jerk is just a big sign on your forehead that says, "I have low self-esteem." True intelligence always leads with dignity and kindness toward others.

   Be willing to learn more and grow more every day. Success is not stationary. It's not a place you arrive at. It's a way of life that you embrace. Success has a constant learning curve, and you must enjoy that lifestyle or learn to enjoy the outcome of having that lifestyle.

6. **Read at least two books a month on business** if you want to remain relevant. Many jobs have continuing education programs, but when you are building wealth and growing a business, you don't have anyone forcing you to take a continuing education class. In order to maintain your success, you will have to provide yourself with your own education. Going to conferences and reading books will help you grow and stay at the top of your industry.

   If you want to lead your industry, you will want to read more than two books a month, maybe more like three or four books a month. Either way self-education will help you improve your skills. Make sure you are reading books that help you improve on skills that other people hate to do. This always gives you a hand up. The power of learning is in your hands; the power to stay on top of your industry is in your library.

7. **Learn to sell your product with pride.** Don't sell, make, or take any product or service to market that you are not proud of or believe in 100

percent. Whether you are selling advertising or life insurance, don't sell it if you don't think it is the best one out there. If you aren't proud of your product, you will not feel good about selling it. You will be shy about it. If a product is so good that you know it is the best one, then selling it is easy. It's also important to learn to sell with pride. Sales is an honorable profession that has been damaged by schemes from people who are less than honorable.

Don't sell to someone in an unscrupulous and deceptive way. Be direct about what it is and what problem your product solves. Tell them what it is capable of and what you want. Being good at sales will make you wealthy, especially when it is done with dignity.

8. **Ask direct questions and challenge your beliefs.** Learn to listen with an open mind that looks for opportunities. Challenge what you know and how you think. This keeps your perspective on life fresh and helps your creative process. Find a millionaire mastermind or think-tank group that will let you participate so that you can explore, bounce around ideas, and create products that are well above consumer expectations.

Be around people who are explorers just like you. Surround yourself with open people who don't think they know it all but want to know it all and aren't afraid to challenge themselves. Be around visionary people, because the people you surround yourself with is what your life becomes. Don't be around toxic people; they will suck the life force right out of you. Let yourself be the explorer and not the know-it-all.

9. **Remember your daily prayer time.** Sometimes, to keep everything in check, especially your ego, you must bend your knees and surrender your heart to something greater than yourself. If you don't, your ego will begin to think it is God, and this is where everything will start to fall apart. When your ego is in the way, you think you are always right and important and everyone else isn't.

Make friends with something else that can guide you into wealth without it becoming destructive for you. You have to remain in contact with this source every day and build an honest alliance with it. If you listen, it will tell you what to do and where to go, and you will always have success when you follow it.

10. **Treat your body like a temple.** Make sure you take care of yourself. Sleep and eat well. Give yourself time to exercise every day, but don't be serious about it. Play, go for a walk on the beach, ride a bike, go dancing, and just make it fun. Some people exercise and stress themselves out because they don't do it to play. Working out has become a serious discipline instead of play. They do it as part of daily chores. If you go to the gym and work out hard, if that's fun for you, then fine. If it's not, then you need to find an exercise that's fun.

11. **If you're married, make sure you pay attention to your marriage.** It needs to have love, intimacy, fun, and support. If you want to succeed together, you need to learn to support each other. Nothing will tear wealth and success down faster than a divorce. It shatters whatever you have built and turns it into dust overnight. The only people who benefit are the attorneys.

    If you're not married, be careful whom you marry. Make sure it is real love and real partnership. Begin with learning to support each other. Find a pastor or counselor to work with from the start. Get to know your fiancé's family. Don't rush into getting married simply because you love them. Create a strong relationship before you enter marriage.

12. **Control your space and protect your hours.** As you become more successful, people will want to waste your time by asking you to help them work out their problems. They will want your help doing it for them and not your answers. Now listen, Vickie, there is a big difference here. It's true that most people do not want your answers on how to be successful. They want you to do it for them. This is not your job.

    When you think it is your job to help them, you are hurting them more than you are helping them. You are enabling them to remain stuck instead of finding help from their inner divine. If you aren't paying attention closely, these people will suck hours and hours, days and days, months and months of your time and will be no better off than they were before.

Don't let these space invaders suck up any of your time. You must protect your most creative hours. If you are more creative in the morning, then you protect those hours and let no one disturb you for any reason. You work on your business in the most creative hours you have. You create your products, services, and other things. It is the same if you are more creative at night. Whatever you do, protect your creative hours and use them wisely. Remember, you are the most important product on your production line. If people want to interrupt your productive hours, you must protect them by saying no or having a do-not-disturb sign on your door. Do your best, most important work in those creative hours.

Control your working space. Don't let anyone into your office when you are working. You have to have a boundary around your productivity. Your family time is your family time, and your working time is your working time. Control your space and don't let your family time roll into your working space; otherwise, you will procrastinate more than you will be productive.

These are the twelve principles that a generous and kind man shared with me. He just talked with me as if we were at a coffee shop, bumped into each other, and struck up a conversation. I only met this man once. I don't even remember his name. It seemed to me that the divine had me go to this conference to meet him specifically so that he could give me these twelve wealth secrets. Sure, you've got to save your money and invest some, but you have to invest in yourself first, and these are the self-investments that create ongoing wealth.

At first this list seemed overwhelming, but then I knew I had to take the time to learn to do what I thought I couldn't. I needed every skillset that he shared with me in order to do so. His core message kept echoing through my head. In fact, it has echoed through me ever since: "Vickie, learn to do what you think you can't."

The interesting thing about this process is that it started to clear up the madness and folly I was experiencing. It helped me learn to focus my attention on what I actually wanted to create. The power of being aware and commanding my focus helped me drill down and hone my skills to develop my craft. This provided huge success.

It didn't happen overnight; it happened over time. I read as many as five books a month and developed certain skillsets—writing, copywriting, marketing, website development, business strategizing. I practiced and failed, then succeeded, then failed, then succeeded. The amount of freedom this has given me is amazing.

The addiction to convenience has made many people learn to avoid any challenges and this has robbed them of their freedom. Often convenience helps us avoid learning what we think we can't. This runs rampant in our world; it is a major marketing ploy to say the words "free, simple, and easy." We buy based on the promise that some simple system will get fantastic results. This is the biggest lie ever.

Fantastic results don't come from free, simple, and easy until you have learned what you think you can't. Success in any activity, role, or relationship requires specific skills that are learned, developed, and maintained in order for things to become simple and easy. The sooner you embrace any learning curve as a lifestyle, the more freedom you will have. If not, you will fall for the free, simple, and easy conveniences that are robbing you of your freedom faster than you can think about them.

PART THREE

Always bear in mind that your own resolution to succeed is more important than any other.

—Abraham Lincoln

Chapter 12

Disruption 2.0

What light is to the eyes-what air is to the lungs-what love is to the heart,
liberty is to the soul of man
—Robert Green Ingersoll

A t first it appeared as if it happened all at once. Millions and millions of people all over the world were displaced. There were haters that judged them and blamed them, saying, "This is your fault; if you had just paid your bills . . ." But the truth is, it was much subtler than that. People didn't see it coming. Otherwise they would have prepared for it.

Instead it crept in unexpectedly, like a thief in the night, while we all celebrated its birth and rejoiced in its capabilities. We had created something that could connect us to each other. Some say it was made to survive a nuclear attack in order to help us rebuild our structures, if that had happened.

Whatever. We had finally achieved our goal. We had birthed the Internet.

We marveled over it without considering what it actually meant. We didn't anticipate being caught in its clutches. Nor did we anticipate its infiltration into every aspect of our lives.

It felt as if it sneaked up on us without exposing its potential for destroying our privacy and our freedom. Its message to humanity? "This is convenient, easy, and free. It will make your life simple. Tasks will become automated. You will have more time to do what you like."

But the truth is it didn't just kill a few jobs or companies; it decimated some of the oldest industries, steeped in the most archaic traditions. In the blink of an eye, it destroyed businesses that families depended on for income. This devastation was so widespread that many people fell into poverty and didn't know what to do. They lost everything; houses, jobs, and families were destroyed by this new god and monster. The Internet caused disruption at every turn. Technology is now calling this past transition Disruption 1.0.

Bill Gates warned of its power to shatter and destroy every living system that people relied on, but not many people believed it would, so they simply ignored the message. He now says, "Big changes are coming to the labor market that people and governments aren't prepared for."

In Disruption 1.0 many people ignored the signs and warnings and were completely caught off guard when its power finally affected them. When the shock of being clobbered by this new technology happened, they looked around, dazed by the speed and devastation of it.

Many confused people still didn't know what hit them and learned too late the consequences of ignoring new advances in technology. This innovation was beginning to upset the status quo. At the same time, it was being applauded for its ability to make things easier and more convenient.

Entrepreneurs were creating online businesses, and venture capitalists were pouring money into what was being called a tech bubble. Many businesses tanked, but many grew into huge companies that are now household names. Amazon and eBay led the pack of Disruption 1.0 as they changed how we shopped for goods. We enjoyed the freedom, convenience, and ease of clicking a button and having our order delivered to our home. This new technology seemed great, until we began to notice wages falling because software had made workers and their skills irrelevant.

All over the world society felt the unusual power and speed of technological Disruption 1.0. There was a pervasive sense that as things were becoming faster, cheaper, and more convenient, they were also becoming uncertain and often perplexing. This is the power and these are the hazards that innovation brings. In Disruption 1.0, the world invited globalization, which produced both winners and losers, but they were controlled, calculated winners and losers—meaning these were strategic moves that helped one area but decimated another.

According to *U.S. News & World Report*, "From 2001 to 2013 outsourcing to China cost the U.S. 3.2 million jobs." This data does not include outsourcing to India or the Philippines. As jobs were shipped overseas, millions of people moved out of poverty in developing countries, producing a new middle class that would work for a much cheaper wage than people in many Western countries.

That left millions of people in Western societies devastated by lost careers and lowered standards of living, losing their middle-class status and moving many of them into poverty. Many of these families could no longer pay their bills and began using debt to maintain their middle-class lifestyles. They thought it was a temporary setback. They did not see that Disruption 1.0 brought on permanent change. Statistics from bankruptcyaction.com show that from 1980 to about 2006, consumer bankruptcies skyrocketed to one out of every fifty-five households in Western countries because two out of three people had lost their jobs. This was a result of large corporations valuing technology over the expense of a human labor force.

We invited robotics into manufacturing plants and assembly lines, replacing human workers. This forced the underdogs of this disruption (humans) to rethink and reinvent their lives and find new careers that often didn't pay as well or offer the same benefits that their former jobs did. Disruption 1.0 created a pattern of technological advancement, automation, and globalization that created changes in how we work, live, and play.

Some of these changes benefited us, but many didn't. Many of them were painful. Even so, many of these disruptions created a level playing field where the small guy could finally compete with a big company without being crushed by an unethical CEO. We loved this change. At first most big companies laughed at the small garage companies. We watched as a tiny company like Amazon became a global giant, taking out larger companies that treated workers like crap. With Disruption 1.0, a person's dreams and creativity were no longer being held under someone else's thumb. Because of the power of this new technology, you could become very rich and free of someone else's control.

We fell in love with this new concept and the underdogs who would take out unethical and abusive corporations. We laughed at the ingenuity used to out-create and eliminate the evil companies. We didn't understand what the underdog's intentions were; we just liked how they disrupted the system and stuck it to the man.

In his book *Future Crimes: Inside the Digital Underground and the Battle for Our Connected World*, Marc Goodman writes, "When Google was founded, it projected itself as the underdog, the little guy battling evil Microsoft. In fact, Google would tell its users that it was so benevolent that it decided to make 'Don't be evil' its official company motto. To allay any lingering doubts, Google's icons and graphics were created to be so cute and nonthreatening that surely they could be trusted."

Google offered their products free to us, and thus we never questioned their motives. We felt aligned to the altruistic appearance they had marketed to us. We believed and continued rooting for the then-small underdog. We loved them and supported their make-believe cause by giving them our loyalty for their free service. We felt free because we now had access, and information was sent to us for free and at speeds that were unheard of. Google had given "free" a new meaning.

In fact, every Google service is free to the user: Gmail, Google Maps and GPS, Google Earth, Google Contacts, Google Drive, Google Plus, YouTube, Google Chrome, Google Docs, Google Voice, all of it empowered users by providing them with free access to tools and information. This looked as if it empowered the individual to create anything they wanted by leveling the playing field, and thus a new revolution began.

The Internet removed the middle man and made gatekeepers irrelevant. Innovators shook up and brought down longtime traditional industries that were steeped in the good ol' boy ways, forcing them to rethink how they operated their businesses. Those that didn't change were simply made irrelevant and went belly-up.

The Internet put power in the consumer's hands, and it held corporations more responsible for how they treated workers, creating fair-trade practices. Because of this new technology, Disruption 1.0 made ours a globally connected world market, where business transactions happened in real time, twenty-four hours a day, seven days a week. But few consumers were asking how Google made its money if everything was given away. They were just grateful for the free tools and noticed Google was selling ads on sites. Google was deemed trustworthy because it was providing services and tools that the public wanted.

Google's ability to provide fast, organized data and free online tools became one of the greatest disruption tools ever produced because it empowered the little guy. This finally meant that if you had guts, you could create glory. Online businesses were making people rich faster than at any other time in history. In Disruption 1.0 things were either failing or exploding with success.

Workers were suddenly free to work from home without the overhead costs of an office. Industries began collapsing as online options became more available. Bank teller jobs were cut following the introduction of ATMs, travel agent jobs were cut, airline ticket counter jobs were cut with self-check-in technology, customer service jobs got shipped out, and manufacturing jobs were shipped overseas. Software eliminated middle-management jobs and replaced the need for bookkeepers and inventory workers, cutting the workforce in half.

This trend also disrupted governments as taxes, including Social Security, paid by employees dropped significantly because the workforce had shrunk so much. Federal, state, and local governments suddenly did not have the working budgets they had before. They too would have to innovate in order to work with less revenue coming in.

This is how the world moved from an industrial economy to a technological economy. We have been through a multitude of changes, both positive and negative, but these changes will be minuscule compared to what Disruption 2.0 will be like. You must plan and be prepared for the next wave of interruptions or you will be caught off guard and not know what hit you. As with the first disruption, the world will be affected by Disruption 2.0, even people who feel safe with their career choices.

We will see miraculous breakthroughs and extreme dangers like we have never seen before. According to the World Economic Forum, "Five million jobs in the world's leading economies could disappear by 2020." Within the next ten years we will likely see more evolution and revolution than in the previous one hundred fifty years. The momentum of this cycle has already begun.

Empowered people are challenging the status quo in ways that were never imaginable before, creating new business models and challenging old beliefs and tyrannies. Disruption 2.0 is in front of you now as it challenges every venue and avenue of past freedom. However, the speed of these disruptions will be faster than ever before.

Freedom has never been stationary. It evolves and grows with the current level of intelligence and consciousness. But the key is that freedom is not convenient or free. It challenges you. In 1955 Rosa Parks was not allowed to use the front seats on the bus because she was black. She went to jail because she refused to give up her seat to a white man. She challenged the status quo in order to create real freedom and equality. Nothing she did to produce this new level of equality was convenient or easy.

Freedom is not something you have or own, which is why you can be born into a free country and still not be free. But you can become free the way Rosa Parks did. Freedom is a state of mind; which is why you can be locked away in a jail cell for twenty-seven years and still be free enough to change the world, as Nelson Mandela did when he became president of South Africa.

As we look at the future, our freedom and how it evolves is at stake. The uprising that is coming will need your discernment and critical thinking to get you through it. We are sensing the beginning of Disruption 2.0. Its full impact is not here yet, which gives you time to rethink and reinvent your life.

This disruption will have good actors and bad actors, and many of the bad actors will be disguised as good guys. You will need strong, unbiased discernment to maneuver yourself through their disguises. There will be both miracles and displacement, just as there was in 1.0.

Right now we are seeing robotic suits that allow paraplegics to walk. We are seeing innovations in cancer treatments that may eradicate cancer. We are seeing teenagers—and even younger children—solving pollution, energy, and disease problems that just a few short years ago our best scientists, professors, and researchers could not solve. We are seeing computer code that's creating new international currency, which I believe over time could become a monetary system. We are also seeing code turn into weapons of mass destruction and legislators taking away freedoms at an accelerated pace.

According to Marc Goodman in *Future Crimes*, "Disruption 2.0 will create a wave that will threaten even the new middle class across the globe and move many back into poverty." People will be challenged by unwelcome disruption and find it hard to find their place in the world or get ahead if they don't challenge their current beliefs and way of living now. Planning—with honest, up-to-date knowledge—data, critical-thinking skills, and discernment are the only tools you will have to get through what will be one of the biggest worldwide disruptions. We have entered the age of "dataveillance" and codification.

Our manmade world is now run by code more than almost anything else. Human skillsets have been and are still being replaced by code. You are losing more and more abilities, freedoms, and privacy to code every day. We don't even notice how much of our lives are run by this code. We are integrated with this code in every part of our lives, whether we are working, shopping, playing, talking, cooking, learning, or dating. It is in our healthcare systems, government systems, regulatory systems, and any other system you can think of. This code was sold to us as a form of connection, opportunity, and advanced freedom, but this is perhaps the most dangerous lie of all.

The most alarming aspect of this is that we have been helping to create our own loss of freedom because we are so in love with the word "free" that we don't see that we are being manipulated by it and have become the product of these big companies. The Internet and its "free code" promised a level of convenience that has allowed for the codification of everything, including your privacy.

Every day you are being coaxed out of more and more freedom not just from your government but mostly by your love of convenience. You are being programmed without your permission and without your knowing it. Much of this comes courtesy of Google.

How is this happening?

In *Future Crimes,* Goodman also notes that in *Code and Other Laws of Cyberspace,* Harvard Law School professor Lawrence Lessig "insightfully demonstrated that the instructions encoded in any software program, app, or platforms shape and constrain the Internet, just as laws and regulations do. Thus, when Facebook and Google unilaterally changes its terms of service to allow your news feeds to become public or your photographs to be used in advertisements against your will, it is as if a new 'law' has been passed. Code is, in effect, law."

Every day we are feeding and adding more and more code to this new use of freedom called the Internet. We share a lot about ourselves on social sites without thinking about why so much on the Internet is free. Facebook is free, YouTube is free, Instagram, Pinterest, Pandora, free downloads, free software, and free apps all make us feel as though our instant manifestations are real, when the reality is you are giving away your freedom to a data surveillance society that Al Gore dubbed the "Stalker Economy." Your freedom is being coded away from you.

These free online features appear in our economy, helping us shop, order, and purchase in both the physical and virtual worlds. It feels freeing to be able to order from the comfort of your office chair. It feels freeing to be able to work from your home or have the information you need at your fingertips. It feels freeing to have the speed of these types of conveniences and instant manifestations. But it disrupts society as it upgrades our systems and lives.

Goodman also writes, "The fact is that we are all contributing to our own digital pollution. Just as in the twentieth century people thought nothing of pouring industrial waste into a river or tossing garbage onto the street, so too do we fail to comprehend the long-term consequences of our digital actions today. The current state of affairs stems from our fundamental misunderstanding of the bargain we have made for so-called free online services."

Our education systems are being moved from school settings to online learning settings. Our GPS and mapping systems are all coded onto virtual templates that are easily accessible. This open unrestricted venue helps soothe our yearning for a feeling of freedom while stealing our real freedom—and we unthinkingly agree to it.

This is happening because most people do not read the terms of service (ToS) agreements when they download that free software service. What is happening today on the Internet is very similar to the housing bubble, in which people did not understand the housing contracts they were signing and did not realize they had signed their lives away. They simply believed the mortgage broker without reading the fine print.

With the codification of all things Internet, we are connected as one human family, but with the many ToS, you are releasing control of your privacy and your friend's privacy, your intellectual property and your friend's, your copyrights and your friend's, as well as your likes and dislikes, history, work, school, friends, choices, and every action you take on the Internet.

You are the raw material these free services need in order to create their real product (data about you) that they sell to their consumers, the big corporations. You are not the consumer using their product; *you are their product,* and this is how they make their money. In order for their business to continue to be profitable and grow, they must know more about you to have something new to sell their clients. Online services are free to you because you're the product and not the client, of big data companies. That's why you get the self-serve software and free use of their data-gathering tools. Data gathering is their real business.

Terms of service agreements are purposely complex and difficult for many people to understand. Most people don't read them and just click "yes." The language is intentionally as complex as our tax code is. The typical ToS manipulates you to give the personal identifiable information that you are not comfortable sharing. You click and create an agreement that is legally binding because you agreed to the terms of service even if you didn't read it.

According to a Carnegie Mellon study, the average American is exposed to 1,462 privacy policies a year with an average length of 2,514 words. According to Goodman, "A study in the *Wall Street Journal* estimated that the completely one-sided language in the ToS policies costs each American household $2,000 a year—for a total of $250 billion annually—money that we are cheated out of as a result of a deck of cards that is entirely stacked against us. Though companies call these policies terms of service, for consumers they would be more aptly described as 'terms of abuse.'"

Further, in *Future Crimes*, author Goodman writes, "Let's just take one example of what it is costing you to use a social media site, in this case, LinkedIn, whose privacy policy states,

You grant LinkedIn a nonexclusive, irrevocable, worldwide, perpetual, unlimited, assignable, sublicenseable, fully paid up and royalty-free right to us to copy, prepare derivative works of, improve, distribute, commercialize, in any way now known or in the future discovered, any information you provide, directly or indirectly to LinkedIn, including, but not limited to, any user generated content, ideas, concepts, techniques and/or data to the service, you submit to LinkedIn, without any further consent, notice and/or compensation to you or to any third parties. Any information you submit to us is at your own risk of loss.

So by using LinkedIn, you are granting it irrevocable and perpetual access (for free) to any information you have ever listed on the site; there's no take backs or do overs."

Privacy settings will not help you either, although they are made to look as if they do. Facebook has more than 50 different privacy settings with more than 170 options. It takes hours of work to adjust the privacy settings, and any updates that Facebook does to their ToS automatically puts all users back to the default settings, which have the maximum settings for openness. Do they inform you of this?

Facebook's privacy policy has grown from a simple 1,004-word document to a 9,300-word document with links to various sub-policies, terms, and conditions. It is unbelievably twice the size of the United States Constitution. PayPal's are said to be the biggest terms of service at 36,275 words.

Apps are no different. They are tools that transmit your private data and read your text messages and follow you everywhere. You may not think privacy is that important to you and you have nothing to hide, so it is all right with you because you enjoy your cellphone—that is until it records how many drinks you had and from which bars, if you are having an affair, if you have purchased and downloaded porn, if you have a sexually transmitted disease, if you've gone to see the gynecologist, if you've purchased sex or a sex toy, if you've purchased illegal drugs, or where you plan on going for vacation. It makes a digital imprint of your life and codes it into data that can be sold to any advertiser or can be used as evidence against you. So why not download that app and play another game?

Goodman further writes, "When you use Google's ToS anybody who enjoys using Google Docs or uploads their work to this free online tool automatically grants ownership of the document to Google. That's according to the ToS. It says, 'When you upload or otherwise submit content to our services, you give Google (**and those we work with**) a worldwide license to use, host, store, reproduce, modify and create derivative works, such as those resulting from translations, adaptations or other changes and license to communicate, publish, publicly perform, publically display and distribute such content.'"

And while we are overthrowing oppressive regimes, empowering women and girls, and balancing the power you have to claim more freedom and build the life you dream of having, you are also destroying your options, giving your intellectual property away and your rights to privacy simply because you are using a free online tool or paid app. You are helping to create a surveillance state that is controlled by the ToS and a privileged few who gather your information and sell it to the highest bidder while claiming ownership of all of your work.

Have you noticed how many software companies are moving to subscription-based services? Intuit's QuickBooks has moved to an online service. Microsoft now offers Office 365 in addition to downloadable software. Adobe Premiere Pro CC is a subscription service. So many software applications that were once downloadable to your PC or Mac now have the same type of ToS that we have been discussing.

These ToS agreements grant the companies the right to read your texts, track your location, and own your work, ideas, and creativity or whatever they want. That cellphone you have has now become a tracking device that provides a continuous stream of data about you. According to a 2012 *Wall Street Journal* study, among the fastest-growing businesses today are those that spy on Internet users.

I can't help but wonder if we are quietly building a one-world government. The disturbing aspect of this is that Big Brother is not doing this to us; we are doing it to ourselves. Your freedom is being coded for sale, and you will receive no remuneration for any of your personal, private, and intellectual assets. Those vacation pictures that you place on Instagram now become Instagram's intellectual property. They can sell them and use them as advertising, and you get nothing. You no longer have the right to your photos the second you place them on the site to share them with friends.

While everyone was shocked at the NSA's surveillance program exposed by Edward Snowden, a lot of the information was obtained from the Internet. The government didn't set up and build the NSA from scratch. It purchased that data from the data brokers who sold the information to them. This reflected your tax dollars at work. Data brokers get that information from our Internet service providers. Everything you buy, do, poke, play, watch, or download is captured by an Internet service provider and sold to a data broker, who sells it to whoever wants to buy it. This is how our surveillance economy is making money—by stealing your freedom from you without your aware permission.

According to Goodman, "What data of yours the government doesn't subpoena, it just buys." And all of this is completely unregulated. If the information is incorrect, there is no correcting it. Unlike our Fair Credit Reporting Act, if inaccurate online data is sold and it affects your life or finances, no one is required to correct it because there is no regulatory or governing body over the Internet.

Because of this, there will be new threats that you will have to look out for and new ways of creating income that you will have to embrace. In his book *Industries of the Future,* Alec Ross writes, "with robotics automating labor that is cognitive and non-manual, the kind of job my father made a 50-year-long career of—practicing real estate law—would be a bad bet for someone graduating from law school today. Tomorrow's labor market will be increasingly characterized by competition between humans and robots. In tomorrow's workplace, either the human is telling you what to do or the robot is telling the human what to do."

The momentum of the Internet and other technological advances has gained traction, and it is not going away. If you try to stop it, ignore it, or argue against it, you will either be run over by it or left behind. If you are addicted to it, depend on it too much, or don't understand it, you will be vulnerable to its destructive nature and devastating outcomes.

These things will either create freedom for you or destroy your freedom because you are ignoring it and refuse to see it coming. Disruption 2.0 will see the global economy undergo a revolution brought on by artificial intelligence that will replace more jobs and careers than at any other time in history.

How you choose to move forward with it will determine your future and your level of freedom. You will benefit most if you are open to seeing both sides of the story. We will experience major advances in science that will slow down aging, we will enjoy longer and healthier lives than ever before—and we will be exposed to threats never seen before.

Disruption 2.0-1 Robotics

In the twenty-first century, the robot will take the place which slave labor occupied in ancient civilization.
—Nikola Tesla

The restaurant never closed. It was an all-night cafeteria where you could get breakfast twenty-four hours a day. It was super busy because the breakfast cook always prepared meals perfectly—piping hot and delicious. The wait staff was friendly, efficient, and well-mannered. This restaurant ran like clockwork, all the time.

The owner never had to go into work because everything ran so well. The staff never left; in fact, the staff worked twenty-four hours a day, seven days a week, for no pay and with no need for rest or sleep. The owner didn't have to feed the staff. They never got tired, didn't steal money out of the register, and were never rude to customers. The staff could do all the ordering and bookkeeping as well. The owner didn't have to provide healthcare or any other benefits. He did not have to pay Social Security taxes and did not have to give anyone a day off, ever!

Welcome to the world of robotics, coming to a job near you and eliminating the need for you. The robots we saw in *The Jetsons* and other cartoons in the 1960s are expected to be a reality by 2020. Robotics will be released into the mainstream, at first to the wealthy. But like any other technology, robots will get cheaper over time. Just go to YouTube and type in "robotics" to see what comes up.

These robots are designed to serve humanity in healthcare, therapy, education, customer service, and other applications. If you own a business and robots run your business for you, you will be free to do more of the things you enjoy doing. However, if the robot replaces your job, you will not be quite as excited about this innovation. But the robotics age is here and has been since the 1970s, when robots replaced thousands of auto assembly-line workers. Disruption 1.0 targeted what is called the unskilled labor force; Disruption 2.0 robots will target professionals. Entrepreneurship will be the new freedom, with robots running many businesses and not many people working jobs.

Robotics have been introduced into surgery, replacing skilled surgeons. This has lowered the number of mistakes made in surgeries that require a great deal of precision. Robots are encroaching on jobs in the service sector that require personalized skills, jobs that were largely thought to be safe from job loss. These robots are made to look human by using silicone and spider silk.

The private sector and many entrepreneurs are investing in robotics and artificial intelligence in order to create new robot designs that serve more industries. Our coding has advanced to the point where we have taught computers to think in much the same way humans do, using algorithms. Robots can add a layer of security to your business.

The fictional restaurant described earlier would never be robbed because the robots have cameras and systems that would alert law enforcement personnel right away and record the whole incident.

The question you may want to ask yourself is this: What side of robotics do I want to be on? In the words of Spock from *Star Trek*, "Computers make excellent and efficient servants, but I have no wish to serve under them."

In *The Industries of the Future*, Alec Ross writes, "More than 2.3 million people are currently employed as wait staff in just the United States. There is a potential for robots to replace many of these wait staff jobs over time. It is already happening in trial forms in many restaurants around the world. The Hajime restaurant in Bangkok solely uses robot waiters to take orders and serve customers, and bus tables."

Disruption 2.0-2 The Driverless Car

One of the biggest disruptions to watch for will be the driverless car. This has the potential to create upheaval in the automotive industry and all its offshoots. Google is leading this disruption. When Google or another company has perfected the driverless car, we will move to the driverless taxi, bus, ambulance, airplane, trains, cruise ships, trucks—every mode of transportation.

Transportation jobs will be eliminated over time. How susceptible are these jobs to computerization? About 2.5 million people in just the United States make their living as bus and truck drivers and could be displaced by self-driving vehicles. A study from the Oxford Martin Program on the Impacts of Future Technology suggests that "nearly half of all US jobs could be susceptible to computerization over the next two decades." We will experience widespread technological unemployment.

In his book *The End of Jobs*, Taylor Pearson writes, "It's the work of understanding and operating in the complex and chaotic systems—*entrepreneurship*—that's increasingly in demand. Despite being more credentialed than ever, the US economy has gone from adding 2.5 million jobs per year between 1960 and 2000 to shedding jobs at a rate of 100,000 in the first decade of the 21st century. Growth hasn't just slowed—it's reversed. We aren't going through a global recession— we're transitioning between two distinct economic periods."

"Forty-seven percent of American jobs are at high risk for robot takeover, and another 19 percent face a medium level of risk. In the greatest peril are the 60 percent of the US workforce whose main job function is to aggregate and apply information," writes Alec Ross in his book *The Industries of the Future*.

According to the World Economic Forum, "The scale of the employment challenge is vast. The International Labor Organization estimates that more than 61 million jobs have been lost since the start of the global economic crisis in 2008, leaving more than 200 million people unemployed globally." Having a job for income is dying. You will benefit most by becoming an entrepreneur or having a small business. This will provide you with the most freedom.

Disruption 2.0-3 The Share Economy

In every new disruption and development, some people will win and some will lose. The share economy was born out of technology and a new social consciousness where people participate in what is being called "collaborative consumption." It is a form of sharing the consumption of goods and services, an example of which is the Uber ride-sharing service.

Its motivation is to do good around the world and cause less harm to the earth. It has exploded and been adopted quickly as a new income source. I have not read its ToS, but they have a page dedicated to it: https://www.uber.com/legal/usa/terms. Services like Uber have created the opportunity for the independent worker to create income by leveraging things they own and are willing to share with others.

In a 2015 paper by Princeton's Alan Krueger, former chairman of President Barack Obama's Council of Economic Advisers, Uber's internal data finds clear benefits for "driver-partners" and notes the new financial opportunities created for tens of thousands of displaced workers. This is also true with Airbnb, which is another online community built on sharing that allows people to create income by renting rooms from their homes.

Just two of these new "share economy" apps have decimated long-standing traditions and industries. According to the *USA Today*, "Taxi medallion prices are plummeting because ride shares like Uber have taken off." Taxi drivers are seeing their income drop as much as 30 percent and have to stretch their driving day to 15 hours in order to make up the difference. Taxi services are a regulated industry where just getting the medallion you need to transport passengers costs into seven figures. The share economy will continue to disrupt similar industries and businesses well into the future.

It will also bypass old regulations and laws that need to be revamped. Disruption 2.0 will bring many governments to their knees. Things will be chaotic and uncertain for governments as they learn to rebuild their systems around this newly disrupted world. Employee tax revenues will hit an all-time low simply because there will be fewer workers. All governments depend on income taxes, and if they shrink at the rate that is expected, we could see many governmental services cut.

Disruption 2.0-4 3D Printing

Dr. Ray Kurzweil, inventor, pioneering computer scientist, and director of engineering at Google says, "By 2025, 3D printers will print clothing at very low cost. There will be many free open-source designs, but people will still spend money to download clothing files from the latest hot designer just as people spend money today for eBooks, music and movies despite all of the free material available."

These 3D printers will print human organs using modified stem cells, with the patient's own DNA providing an inexhaustible supply of organs and no rejection issues. We will also be able to repair damaged organs with reprogrammed stem cells such as a heart damaged from a heart attack. Some 3D printers will print inexpensive modules to snap together a house or an office building, and Lego-style contractors and builders will be found everywhere, but skilled workers will lose their jobs.

These disruption examples are just a tiny look at the power of Disruption 2.0 and living in a world where code is king. Codification has disrupted every old belief and method and will continue to do so well into the future. Codification has been programming you and predicting your habits, then selling that data to big companies. We will see both dramatic advances and complete chaos as jobs disappear and unprepared people wonder about their future. The future and freedom will belong to the entrepreneur. Learning to run a business again will be the most powerful form of freedom you can embrace. It was the way for our forefathers, and it still is today.

Like everything else, it will benefit you most when you want your freedom and understand that it is encoded into your being. This is what I believe they are hoping to remove from us. We have been seduced by convenience in our decision-making process, and it will benefit us most to seek authentic freedom with critical thinking. This allows you to look objectively and discern how you want to move forward through this next wave of disruption.

The human experience is also an evolution in code. We grow inwardly in a way that is similar to how we grow outwardly. Our very DNA is nothing more than a form of code. Our experiences and actions can actually modify a significant part of our innate genetic code. Called epigenetics, this science suggests that what we do as children, what we eat, the environment we grow up in, even the decisions we make as adults—all can have an effect on our genetic makeup and the eventual shape of our DNA. Fancy that! We can change ourselves—at the cellular level—by the actions we take. As consciousness shifts within us, we evolve. This causes major inner disruptions and shifts that promote more freedom within our being. The Ultimate Freedom is within us, and it is what created us; it's what surrounds us.

Our genetic code begins to create itself in the union of sperm and egg, and our physical and mental potential follows along. However, what we do with them is our responsibility. Each of us has innate, inborn capabilities—but only we, as individuals, can decide how to use those capabilities.

Our bodies and minds are a storehouse of codes and information that can be disrupted just like the Disruption 2.0 that we are entering. The freedom we want to create in the world is the same freedom we want to create in our inner world. We are coded with the information to look for and find our Ultimate Freedom, but the truth is that real freedom comes from within our inner world and not some free software tool.

The data stored within us is ultimately more powerful than any manmade data. Accessing authentic freedom means using the code within you. How much information is stored in a human genome? How many megabytes of code are stored in the human body? According to Yevgeniy Grigoryev from bitesizebio. com, who has calculated that data, it is, "1.5 Gbytes x 100 trillion cells = 150 trillion Gbytes or 150×10^{12} x 10^9 bytes = 150 Zettabytes (10^{21})!!!" (That was for our techie readers!)

Your entire being is coded to grow past your current lifestyle, limitation, flexible beliefs, and circumstances, and create advances in your life. You can claim, explore, and create your Ultimate Freedom. You can choose to disrupt any aspect of your life and create a new code that will bring you more inner or outer freedom anytime you want.

Chapter 13

Maybe You've Heard? The System Is Rigged

People feel like the system is rigged against them, and here is the painful part, they're right. The system is rigged.

—Senator Elizabeth Warren

Many people believe that our political and economic systems are rigged to help a few elite Wall Street billionaires at the expense of everyone else. We vilify them but fail to realize that a billionaire in any industry is part of the financial elite—which means online billionaires are doing things that are as dangerous as what Wall Streeters did, if not more so.

Wall Streeters are not the entire cause of the imbalance we are feeling; our media likes to focus on them because they had such a big hand in the 2008 crash. They are an easy and obvious target.

The media has access to our online information just as data brokers do. They create news that feeds us our current opinions. Because social media allows them to see what we are talking about, it looks as if our perceptions and pronouncements are reasonable instead of unfounded. This is where our discernment begins to disintegrate because people love to be right more than they love to know the truth.

The media has divided us into two factions, Democrats and Republicans, even though independents make up more than a third of the electorate. Then they have sub-niched us into religions: Christian, Muslim, Jewish, and others. Then they have provided us with our media entertainment that validates our opinion. None of this helps us think clearly. It only helps us think that our opinion and pronouncements are right, and thus we can't see the truth of what is happening.

Most often, we watch or listen to the news that leans towards our beliefs and think we are discerning. As long as we are being fed our current opinion, we feel well-informed. Thus, the media and online media are divided into factions that are bent towards a position that a group of people hold; Fox News or CNN lean more conservative, while MSNBC is considered more liberal. Online news sources do this too. Bloomberg News is conservative and the Huffington Post is liberal.

Distractions can create tunnel vision. Policies and regulations help perpetuate a cycle of control, dependency, and poverty in the world from many multi-billion-dollar industries, not just Wall Street. These problems are complicated by the fact that we do not want to see our involvement in them. The truth is that it is not the government's or billionaires' fault alone.

Many regulatory agencies offer handouts, mandates, subsidies, and other forms of largesse to the wealthy and well-connected. We call it corporate welfare, and it doesn't favor us. I understand that, but we need to recognize how we participate in that system.

Many people think that our American heritage has moved from being a country of mutually beneficial opportunities for everyone to a tiered society that values the wealthy. The truth is that we have always valued affluence and influence. That has never changed. Would you take a job at a company that was broke and couldn't pay you? Of course you wouldn't. Would you sell your products or services to someone who could not pay for them? Of course not. Would you work for a company that has an important CEO, like Oprah Winfrey or Richard Branson? Most people would like working for influential CEOs. This is an example of how we value affluence and influence.

The issue is that we have also participated in the building of a tiered society that values wealth over anything else. We see people as our politicians do but cannot admit it to ourselves. Seeing people as more than, less than, or equal to us has empowered our flexible belief in a fixed-belief tiered system. Now we are angry because we don't appear where we want to on that tiered system.

So now we have policymaking that is dominated by powerful business organizations and a small number of affluent Americans. Our being a democratic society has become threatened by this behavior. The Constitution and the American dream were designed to create a level playing field that promised that if you work hard and focus on your dream, you can achieve it.

I still believe in our American heritage. But the truth is that this heritage is eroding because "We the People" are not safeguarding it as our forefathers did. "We the People" are being medicated with convenience and other myths and lies about freedom. We are not paying attention while our freedoms are being coded away from us.

With this in mind, we must be willing to rethink and reinvent our future by understanding how these systems have become rigged and what our involvement in it is. Only when we understand how we are involved can we unhook ourselves from them and produce a life that allows us to pursue our happiness and freedom.

We must stand together and decide to either support or oppose ToS policies and privacy invasions that are not in our best interests. We need to begin looking at how we can stop becoming the product and become "We the People" again.

It's time to stop struggling to get ahead and become free of systems that are not designed to let you advance. Remember, results, not intentions, are what matter. If you read this and do nothing, you are only fooling yourself, and Disruption 2.0 will most likely knock you out.

Right now you may be feeling unsure about what to do. If you've made it this far in the book, you are certainly more awake to our world than many other people are. You may want to tell your friends and family what you have discovered and warn them about what is happening in today's world, as well as what is shaping our future.

People know that something is not quite right. They know there is a lack of transparency and an abundance of nondisclosures agreements that keep them in the dark, uneducated, and feeling taken advantage of because they *are* being taken advantage of. They can feel that things are not rigged in their favor but don't necessarily know how it is engineered against them because so much is written in complex terms.

They know that the Constitution was designed to create safeguards for our nation and its people, but somehow this is not working. People understand that their freedoms don't look anything like they have in the past. They do not know how to pursue their happiness or liberty within these rigged rules. It may feel as if being free and achieving wealth is a pipe dream. We live in an era of legalized corruption and manipulation and have had some of our freedoms taken away by unethical politicians and online shenanigans.

The truth is, you weren't made to win in this new system. Instead, you were made to blindly follow and become financially drained by this system. But in order to unlock your Ultimate Freedom, you need to understand exactly how things are being engineered against you.

The better you understand the system, the more discernment you will have as you create the Ultimate Freedom. This means living in a free society, and that includes equality before the law, free speech, and free markets that are not manipulated by Wall Street, online ToS, or lobbyists. It means treating people with respect and tolerance and pursuing your happiness without judging another person's happiness.

There are ten freedom areas of our system that are being manipulated and engineered. What we mean by "engineered" is that law and government policies are set up in ways that make upward mobility much more difficult now, while those same policies protect companies that have a lot of money. There are certainly more ways in which the systems are engineered, but I will go over the main ways our policies do not benefit you or future generations.

Most of you have likely heard the phrase "working the system." Right now, it has both a negative and positive connotation, depending on how you use it. In order to achieve real freedom, you must know what in our system is rigged and what or how these systems can be worked. This is the section where you get a full understanding of how the system is manipulating you. Later, we will look at how to unhook from or work the system.

The Banking Systems Manipulation

The first way the system is being manipulated against us is through our banking systems. These systems are engineered to keep you constantly in debt. When you participate in using debt instruments you are making the banks rich. Interest rates, when you borrow, keep growing, and hidden fees continue to allow the banks to take more of your money. When you participate in this system, you are helping them keep you enslaved to their fixed system. The banking system is one big scam and has been since 1913.

Most of our system is run by the Federal Reserve Bank, which has nothing to do with our government. Yet, it is considered by most to be the central banking system for the United States. But in reality, it is a privately member owned bank, one that was founded in 1913. This bank was named so as to mislead and deceive the public. It has succeeded in that.

It operates to make profits for its owners; "We the People" are not its owners. How did this happen? President Woodrow Wilson met with a group of the wealthiest private bankers who made him a proposition he couldn't refuse. The deal was that, in exchange for political and financial support from the Rockefeller and Morgan bankers, Wilson would support their banking proposal as well as push for the first-ever progressive income tax. Wilson agreed to the deal. Once Wilson was elected, he followed through and enacted unprecedented changes to our Constitution.

On December 23, 1913, President Wilson signed the Federal Reserve Act and the Revenue Act of 1913, rigging the system by binding all future Americans to the dual dreads of the FRB and the IRS. He knew that what he did was wrong. He would later lament in his diary: "I am a most unhappy man. I have unwittingly ruined my country. A great industrial nation is controlled by its system of credit; all our activities are in the hands of a few men. We have come to be one of the worst ruled, one of the most completely controlled and dominated Governments in the civilized world, no longer a Government by free opinion, no longer a Government by conviction and the vote of the majority, but a

Government by the opinion and duress of a small group of dominant men." This is how our banking system became rigged.

The IRS Systems Manipulation

The second way our system is engineered against us is of course through taxes. The IRS code is extremely and strangely complicated. It was designed to be so complex that the average person will find it impossible to understand. Nothing shifts the playing field in favor of big corporations, the wealthy, and economic elites like the ever-changing IRS tax code that provides big loopholes for them.

These complications create unnecessary incompetence, adds massive operational costs to the system, slows everything down (which adds more costs), and actually works to *increase* the rate of error. This complexity usually means that the government gets more of your money in fees for errors. But there is no compelling reason for the complexity of our tax code.

The complexity is intentional, and this is how the system is rigged. It's similar to the ToS on sites that are looking to manipulate data from you. A flat tax across the board would simplify the whole process. The reason we don't have this is because it is not advantageous to corporations. So instead, big companies use costly lawyers, accountants, and lobbyists to circumnavigate and exploit our tax code and burden the middle class by taking more money from them. This raises the question, "Why don't politicians vote to change the system and protect their constituents?" The reason is that it doesn't serve their self-interests to do so. Their client is not, "We the People," their client is the wealthy donor to their reelection campaign.

The Political Systems Manipulation

The third way our system is engineered against us is politically. Our system has powerful lobbyists, corporations, and rich people that use a legal form of bribery to exercise a large amount of control over how our politicians vote.

Unfortunately, our political system has taken a turn down Bribery Avenue. We've become a country where political integrity can be sold off to the highest bidder. Politicians now represent the affluent and influential, and not their average constituents. Policies are now formed more by corporations and special-interest groups than by politicians representing the will of the people.

Because of this, politicians are rewarded not for their ability to lead or govern but for their ability to fundraise. That is why instead of listening to their constituents, they pander to multinational corporations. This creates an environment where policy is shaped not by the needs of the people but by the corporations that finance politicians' campaigns.

We now live in a world where huge, multinational corporations can make unlimited donations to campaigns through super PACs, which do not have to report the source of their funds—most often from wealthy individuals, large corporations, labor unions, and powerful organizations. This is how the system is engineered. However, the person they are hoping to get the attention of is you. What is the super PAC's money used for? Influencing an election. Political advertising. They can spend unlimited money running political ads as long as they are not telling you whom to vote for or what to vote against, but they are trying to influence your vote.

The Media Systems Manipulation

The fourth way our system is engineered against us is through the media. I remember a time when our news was unbiased and ethical. Now our media works to control what you watch, programs your mind, and shapes public opinion. It's interesting to note how much of the media is owned by our ruling elite.

The media has been working in cooperation with our government to hide the truth in many situations by giving you something else to focus on. NSA spying comes to mind. The media chooses which news stories are worthy and which aren't, often in order to mislead viewers. A lot of corruption exists because the media allows it. Journalist Lee Stranahan says, "The ugly reality is that corruption exists because the media doesn't want to piss off the people in power. But understand that when I talk about power that I'm not just talking about politicians. I'm talking about other people in the media."

If you ask any media whistleblower, you will find that this is true. When you are a journalist, your greatest power is access. You don't want to jeopardize your ability to get the powerful to talk with you. The powerful are not just well-known people but also editors and publishers along with major media outlets. The "just give it to me straight" news died long ago, and the rigged system today invites corruption because journalists who uncover the real story can't publicize it without jeopardizing their life and careers.

The Agricultural System Manipulation

The fifth way our system is engineered against us is with regard to our food. Although we are seeing an organic food revolution, most of the world's food systems are still dominated by Monsanto. Most of our food issues stem from a single problem—the focus of power, land, wealth, and political influence in the hands of a few large players, mainly Monsanto, who have rigged the system to their advantage.

Most of Monsanto's seed and food control is based on corrupting regulatory practices implemented by lobbying politicians to oppose health reforms, manipulate science and research results, destroy farmland, and deceive the public. There is a well-documented correlation between Monsanto employees becoming officials inside the US government regulatory system, mainly inside the Food and Drug Administration.

This has helped Monsanto to bypass the regulatory process. They have received marketing consent in the United States for their products and technologies with minimal safety checks, resulting in what has become known as Frankenfood—genetically modified food as frightening as Frankenstein's monster.

The Healthcare Systems Manipulation

The sixth way our system is engineered against us is in our healthcare. In America, healthcare is now all about money. Our food is deliberately engineered with things that can make you ill and keep you ill. While our healthcare system has become as complex as our tax system.

Rates for healthcare services are pulled out of a hat and guessed at. The pharmaceutical and health insurance companies have funded billions of dollars with powerful lobbyists to buy politicians, influence the media, and mislead the public. Dangerous drugs are pushed through the systems, and this makes the public a lab room full of guinea pigs who are overcharged and under informed.

Healthcare professionals are buried in paperwork regarding constant changes to the Medicaid and Medicare systems. Doctors must deal with rising malpractice insurance costs. Nurses are overwhelmed and underpaid, and hospitals are understaffed, leaving many patients with marginal care. All this so that the CEO's and shareholders can reap huge financial rewards.

The Energy Systems Manipulation

The seventh way the system is engineered against us is through energy. The energy game is rigged in favor of fossil fuels because we ignore the environmental and health costs of burning coal, oil, and natural gas. Lobbyists for the energy industry keep fossil fuels expensive.

OPEC (the Organization of the Petroleum Exporting Countries), the US Department of Energy, and the media specializing in energy issues ultimately determine how much we pay for a gallon of gas or for a month's worth of electricity.

Subsidies manipulate the game even further. According to conservative estimates from the Global Subsidies Initiative and the International Energy Agency (IEA), governments around the world spent more than $620 billion to subsidize fossil-fuel energy in 2011—some $100 billion for production and $523 billion for consumption.

Although we are becoming a greener country, we are still having lobbyists push for policies that don't benefit our environment. This transition to greener energy will take some time.

The Government Systems Manipulation

The eighth way the system is engineered against us is through our government. The day our government regulators slapped corporate executives on the hand after they broke the law and earned the biggest bailout in history, we knew our system of government was rigged. Senator Elizabeth Warren has said, "If justice means a prison sentence for a teenager who steals a car, but it means nothing more than a sideways glance at a CEO who quietly engineers the theft of billions of dollars, then the promise of equal justice under the law has turned into a lie."

When we look at how Homeland Security handled Hurricane Katrina, we can see how our government is failing to respond in ways that help people. Many of our governmental systems have very little accountability; they are old and slow to respond in an emergency. To rely on our government is to rely on a newborn baby to save the day during an earthquake.

The Terms of Service Manipulation

The ninth way our system is engineered against us is the terms of service (ToS) for free online services and the sale of our privacy. This is the newest way the system is taking away our freedom. ToS are mainly used for legal purposes by websites and Internet service providers that store or use personal data. The terms are legally binding and may be subject to change.

It is in the privacy-policy section where they outline the use of personal data. Then in the disclaimer section, they assert release of legal liability for any damages you may incur by using their site. Hidden inside these ToS are several sections that give them the right to your privacy, your intellectual property, and the profitability of your work that is sold to other companies. The ToS code is now creating global laws because of its Internet-based and legally binding contracts.

The Water Systems Manipulation

The tenth way our system is engineered against us is through our water supply. Most people know that there is a shortage of clean, safe drinking water. A global water crisis is imminent. According to the United Nations, 1.3 billion people in the world today lack access to clean water, while 2.5 billion do not have adequate sewage and sanitation. No less than thirty-one countries are considered to be in water-stressed areas.

Worldwide demand for water doubles every twenty years, twice the rate of population growth. By the year 2025, demand for fresh water is expected to outstrip the global supply by 56 percent. Because water is becoming scarce, corporations like Veolia and Suez and all their subsidiaries are seeking to profit by managing local water.

According to the Polaris Institute, "To date, there have been at least three models of water privatization: (1) the complete sell off by governments of public water delivery and treatment systems to private corporations (which took place in Britain); (2) the granting of long term leases or concessions allowing corporations to take over the delivery of water services and the collection of revenues (which has been the French model); and (3) the more restricted approach where corporations are contracted by governments to manage water services for an administration fee."

Ishmael Serageldin, former vice president of the World Bank, once forecast: "The wars of the 21st century will be fought over water." Our water is now becoming corporate-driven, as we see sales of bottled water rise and privatization and commercialization grow.

You can't beat these systems unless you take a different approach. You will either be enmeshed with these systems or become more self-reliant; those are your only choices. Those who choose to remain more enmeshed with these systems will be controlled and victimized by them.

Those of you who choose to become more self-reliant will create more freedom and security for yourself. Self-reliance is how you grow more of the Ultimate Freedom. You are less influenced by outside forces that are rigged. It means becoming a person who can think for yourself, a leader who does not want to be shielded from unpleasant tasks simply because you think you can't do it. People who value critical-thinking skills and want to be authentic are those who become more self-reliant.

This will mean letting go of unnecessary dependencies on certain things that hold you and your real wealth captive. Don't be suckered into a rigged American dream full of schemes that were never intended to benefit you. It will mean challenging yourself to learn, overcome, and produce better results than you ever thought possible.

The truth is, your greatest asset and primary sense of security and freedom comes from your ability to produce results. That's what self-reliance is all about. You will benefit more from taking action right now and educating yourself on how to start and grow a business and become free of debt. This will provide you with a strong foundation on which you can grow more freedom. It will benefit you most when you become self-reliant in all six of the Ultimate Freedom areas. This often means going back to basics.

Chapter 14

The Greatest Scam Ever Pulled

And he provides that no one will be able to buy or to sell, except the one who has the mark, either the name of the beast or the number of his name.
—Revelation 13:17 (NAS)

In the 1980s when I was in college, I would go home for lunch. One day, I was running late. I pulled up in the car, locked it, and ran into my apartment to make a quick sandwich. I must have been in the house for about forty-five minutes when I noticed it was time to go back to class. I walked out to the car and saw that the passenger-side window had been broken. My purse was gone.

My purse contained my driver's license, exactly $2, forty-nine blank checks, and my Social Security card because I had needed it for a job application. After the police report was filed and the car was fixed, I began to get calls regarding bounced checks, but I had already closed the account and reopened another at the suggestion of the police officer.

These forty-nine stolen checks were being cashed all over God's green earth, in states I did not live in. Over time, I began to receive phone calls from collection companies for loans and bills in my name in places I did not live nor had ever gone to. I would give them the case number, but the bill collectors would not stop. For years they chased me for bills and loans in my name that were not mine. I even received hospital bills for a pregnancy and baby I did not have.

This destroyed my credit score for a long time because it was not easy to clean it up. At that time there were three major credit reporting companies: Experian, Equifax, and Transunion. This credit score nightmare went on for years. I couldn't get a loan for anything. The person who stole my purse and all its contents went to another state, assumed my identity, and had a heyday with my credit. Back then bill collectors would yell and curse, believing that I was lying all the time. The harassing calls came all day long. At night, I would just leave the phone off the hook.

I had to keep the same phone number I had because my credit score was so trashed I did not qualify to open a new account with a new number. I did not qualify for a new apartment lease, so I stayed at my then current apartment longer than I had planned. The horrible way I was treated, even though I had a case number and a police report, made me realize how awful it is to have debt and poor credit.

It took me forever to repair the damage done to my credit. Then, the pendulum swung the other way. Credit card companies would mail credit cards that at one time offered me a total of $20,000. At first this made me feel good—until I started receiving two or three cards a month. Then I worried about them being stolen and having to go through all that hassle again. I had all the credit I wanted at my fingertips. Either I had access to credit and lots of it, or no access at all.

Credit card companies don't want you to know the truth about their biggest scam, one that is going on right now. This one scam is a flexible belief that affects our daily lives, including our homes, rentals, loans, cellphone service, bank accounts, credit cards, job applications, insurance rates, shopping, and utility accounts. The scam? Your credit score.

Your credit score is completely worthless. It's a lie that banks sell John Q. Public as an important aspect to your overall financial well-being, but this is a crock. Banks would lose billions in fees if people knew about this and its dangers are significant. Because everything has been codified, your credit history and all its private details have been turned into code and sold—or stolen.

A digital representation of you and your complete financial history is stored with the three credit-reporting agencies mentioned earlier. Your data has been sold by these companies to fraudsters who have resold your data numerous times. How many aliases of you are there? Remember, the burden of proof will always be on you.

In October 2013, Experian mistakenly sold personal data to an online ID theft service posing as a private investigation firm, allowing access to some 200 million consumer records. That's nearly two-thirds of all Americans. That data was sold to an organized crime ring in Vietnam. Experian actually sold these identities to fraudsters—did you get that? These thieves had all the data they needed in these reports to max out credit cards and take loans in any of the victims' names.

The irony is that Experian sells data breach resources to customers. This is from their site, "When a data breach hits, one wrong maneuver can put you in the path of fines, litigation, customer turnover and brand erosion. Experian Data Breach Resolution is here to steer you through the storm." Are you kidding me? You sold our data to fraudsters and didn't even know you were doing it!

According to author Marc Goodman, the personal data Experian mistakenly sold to an organized crime ring in turn went up for sale quickly. He says, "That stolen data went up for sale on dozens of hacker websites, including SuperSet. info and FindGet.me, selling for just sixteen to twenty-five cents a record, with payments accepted only via untraceable currency such as Liberty Reserve and Web-Money.com."

Experian only learned of their involvement in the sale when they were contacted by the Secret Service, which discovered the data being sold on the hackers' websites. So if the Secret Service didn't find it, would Experian have ever found out what had happened? This is how your freedom is being coded and sold without concern for you, your safety, or your privacy. Experian's data was breached again in 2015, when 15 million consumers' Social Security numbers and other data from people who applied for T-Mobile financing were stolen.

Equifax's AnnualCreditReport.com website was hacked by Russian hackers who wanted to show their skills by stealing celebrity, political, and law enforcement records and posting them online for everyone to see. Marc Goodman says, "Their Social Security number, dates of birth, every address they had ever used, personal phone numbers, legal judgments against them and other personal and revealing information such as how much they charged every month on their AMEX Black cards. The credit reports of those affected were viewed nearly one million times before the sites were eventually taken down." Some of the victims were Bill Gates, Sean Combs, Lady Gaga, Beyoncé, First Lady Michelle Obama, Joe Biden, Kim Kardashian, and Ashton Kutcher, in addition to many more.

Also, according to the Federal Trade Commission, about 25 percent of all consumer credit reports contain errors, and data brokers such as Acxiom have admitted that 30 percent of the data they maintain on you is most likely inaccurate. That means about 50 million Americans are affected by these errors, and it makes getting a mortgage or applying for a job difficult and challenging. And as always, the burden of proof is on you, even though the inaccuracies issue stems from their inability to protect your data. With just this information, it's fairly obvious that a credit report is nothing more than a scam that allows companies to unfairly charge you higher fees and interest rates.

As long as there are places that sell your data, like banks and credit reporting agencies and hackers that are breaching or scamming these systems, protecting your data becomes an expense to these agencies. They charge you for a service but can't really deliver an assurance that you will be protected despite your paying for that service.

As you can see, most good hackers can get into any data broker's site, steal your data, and then sell your data to crime organizations that will do illegal things in your good name. Could you mistakenly be put on a terrorist watch list because your data had been stolen and used in an illegal way without you knowing it? I think this is certainly possible. Errors in data can affect your life and your liberty.

Credit isn't actually a concrete "thing"—it's an idea, a manmade concept that banks and others use to make more money from you.

When credit decisions made the banks and Wall Streeters billions of dollars, they didn't give a crap what your credit score was. Banks sold you a mortgage instantly, no matter how poor your credit score was. That's why it was called the sub-prime (bad credit) mortgage debacle. Then they bundled sub-prime mortgages with poor credit ratings together with A- rating mortgages and sold them as investments, listing them as grade A investments.

No financial institutions cared about credit scores when credit was making them billions. They don't care now, either. They only care about how it benefits their bottom line. They want to use credit to charge you more in fees or interest. When it involves a thirty-year mortgage, that translates into a lot of money. It is a bogus concept that drains money out of people's pockets.

Again, the actual product is your private data. Having a credit score allows them to legally monitor everything about you. You are the product and not the customer. Your personal information, which can be used to charge you more or assume your identity—that's the real product. And that is the hidden scheme. Remember, in the data game, you are always the product, and someone can purchase or steal your identity and become you overnight.

You may think you are safe with credit monitoring, that is just another marketing platform to sell you more services. Credit monitoring companies' systems can be breached at any time. And in order to take advantage of the free "Protect My ID" credit monitoring program offered by Experian, you have to provide them with your credit card information. Why would you give them your credit card information if they couldn't protect your credit report in the first place?

Do you know that the Social Security Administration uses Experian to authenticate your identity? What if two or three of you try to collect on your Social Security? You are paying to use credit monitoring, and yet these systems can be breached and your data sold to criminal organizations anyway. Credit monitoring has too many issues to be a valid, reliable solution.

The real issue is that pieces of data are being used to identify a particular human. Authentication requires secret data that can be stolen. But this is how they will introduce more codification of your freedom. They will institute retinal scans and fingerprint technology along the way. Can you see how your freedom is being sold out from under you? You may be wondering what you can do about this, but if Experian can be tricked into selling your data to a criminal organization, so can just about everybody.

According to CNN, 47 percent of adults in the United States had their personal information exposed by hackers in just one year. It's not a matter of if; it is a matter of when they get hold of your data—if not this year, maybe next.

Systems that many think are important are not, and in fact, they become dangerous to your freedom. According to Marc Goodman in *Future Crimes*, "Tens of millions of electronic medical records contain incorrect information." Medical record errors are at an all-time high because we are rushing to digitize patient records and store them online. The consequence of this means higher costs to you, as well as the risk of your personal medical records being stolen by hackers and sold on the open market, along with your financial data.

Your credit score only becomes important when you depend on debt instruments. Being wealthy or living within your means negates the need for credit. People have become so dependent on debt that they have lost the fundamental skills of money management and wealth creation.

Spending your money to protect an imaginary credit score in exchange for all your personal data—which still does not guarantee your safety from hackers—does not make sense to me. Shakespeare had it right: "Neither a borrower nor a lender be." Benjamin Franklin put it this way: "Creditors have better memories than debtors." Today, I would say that differently: "Hackers have better memories than debtors."

Chapter 15

Back and Forward to Basics

Bad habits are made in good times, and good habits are made in tough times.

—Unknown

There are basic building blocks to almost everything we do, and that's what we build freedom and success with. These skills are necessary to master in order to create a strong foundation that will provide us with a lifetime of future success. For example, reading, writing, and math are the building blocks for our educational system. Mastering these foundational skills means you will be more resourceful throughout your life and enjoy more success.

Using math, your brain calculates by adding, subtracting, multiplying, or dividing. It learns to give change back by calculating it in your head, and then with practice and over time, you acquire speed with these skills. Suddenly, it does not matter whether you have a calculator in your hands or not; you can do basic math easily because you have mastered basic math skills. There isn't a shortcut to having these skills. You must learn and practice them in order to master them. Most people spend at least twelve years of their life learning math, to varying degrees.

Let's imagine that the only foundational skill you had mastery over was math. Can you see how that might hinder your life, no matter how good you are at it? Can you see that without the ability to read and write, having math skills would not be enough? Even if you applied for an accounting job, you wouldn't be able to fill out the job application because you wouldn't be able to read it. You wouldn't be able to solve a math word problem because you couldn't read the problem.

Building blocks do just that—they build on each other and provide a well-rounded set of skills and capabilities that are often dependent on each other and necessary in order to achieve a lifetime of success. And in order to enjoy this level of success you must be well-versed in all three foundational building blocks because they depend on each other in order for you to enjoy the ultimate understanding and use of them. This is why the six key areas of freedom are so important. They depend on each other and build on each other. They are the foundational building blocks to having and claiming your Ultimate Freedom. They are the primary skill sets, and they're interdependent.

When you have mastery over them, you can apply them to anything you wish in order to produce the Ultimate Freedom. To our misfortune, we have been outsourcing these key skill sets instead of mastering them, and thus many people are easily manipulated and are struggling instead of thriving. Often, people have mastery over only one of these skill sets; because of this, they are limited in what they can do. They don't realize that in order to produce the Ultimate Freedom, they must have all these skill sets at their fingertips and have a level of mastery over them.

Marketers will attempt to sell you shortcuts to these skills, but there are no shortcuts to learning them. Shortcuts may only work when you have mastery over the basic skill. For example, you must learn your ABCs before you can learn to read. There is no shortcut to learning the alphabet; you must memorize it and master it by learning how the letters sound in combination with each other in order to form words and phrases.

In order to unlock your Ultimate Freedom you must understand that it is the transfer of ideas and knowledge that will bring you money and not your learning of the ABCs. It's essential to success to realize that mastery is developed with experience over time and there's no shortcut to this process. If you continue looking for a shortcut to this process, you will be looking for convenience and not real freedom.

Unfortunately, we have given many of these freedom building blocks away by labeling them as "old school," which now means pre-computers. Our reliance on computers has replaced reliance on ourselves and abilities, on our perceptions and inner knowings. These key building blocks are what provide the Ultimate Freedom, but many people are letting them atrophy, which results in a life of struggle. Instead of mastering them, many people are hoping technology will help them get around these foundational building blocks.

Because of this, we are becoming slaves to devices; we can't seem to leave home without them. Our reliance on technology has turned our freedoms into code and has made our world dependent on systems. The use of software and technology has dumbed us down and replaced our inner awareness, critical-thinking skills, basic knowledge, natural inquisitiveness, and discernment. These are the old-school building blocks to authentic freedom, but they still apply today. Without these fundamentals as our sustainable foundation, we have nothing but counterfeit freedom and dependency on systems that are not stable and have proven to be easily penetrable and collapsible.

This is why our electrical grid is a key target for hackers from all over the world, including Russia, Iran, and China. They know if they can take out our electrical grid, they will take out every critical system that depends on electricity, including the Internet. They know our basic skills have been eroded and replaced with a dependency on devices and other computer technologies. This means most Americans are vulnerable and unprepared.

However, as long as our electrical grid is up, technology is here to stay. In order to find a healthy balance with it, we must move forward with the basics and include some "back to basics" in order to fully integrate this new world we are creating. It may appear as if disconnecting from the Internet would make your life more secure, but this is not true because there is already a digital representation of you out there, and it is better for you to be able to monitor it than disconnect from it completely.

Just being aware that we have begun Disruption 2.0 will help you make better decisions. It will not be easy to build a sustainable future with our dependency on the convenience of technology, simply because the Internet was not built to do all that it is doing now. We have turned critical systems into code and placed them on the Internet, where they become vulnerable and susceptible to sabotage by hackers.

The Internet was designed to create open access—and it does. It was not designed for security, which means there are some vulnerabilities that hackers can take advantage of. If you go to http://map.norsecorp.com/#/ you will see in real time the cyber-attacks that are happening on a global scale and how relentless these attacks are. This is our war zone now. The weapons are not bombs and bullets; the weapon is code.

Because our society seems to embrace a new motto—"In Code We Trust"— we work, play, date, shop, see friends, and get advice, directions, and guidance from our computers and other devices. Every time you create a post or use a web search tool, your every move is coded and placed on the Internet to help it keep track of you. Some people can't even eat a meal without snapping a picture of it, turning it into code, and placing it on Facebook or Instagram. We can't shop without going online first and reading other people's opinions and reviews—and believing in them as fact.

A Nielsen study found that 70 percent of people trust reviews they read online as much as a recommendation from a friend. Yet, according to the New York State attorney general, 25 percent of the reviews on Yelp are fake. In September of 2014, a federal appeals court ruled that it was legal for Yelp to manipulate its ratings based on which companies advertised on the site.

You can buy reviews on eBay and Amazon and pay for as many five-star reviews as you want. You can even kill a competitor's product using reviews. There is a technique called "review bombing" through which you can sabotage a competitor's company and its products by purchasing bad reviews and placing them on your competitor's Amazon or eBay product site. Consumers read these poor reviews and buy your products instead of your competitor's.

We seem to have forgotten how to form our own opinions and instead trust the opinions of strangers.

This technique works because many people believe whatever they read online. We don't really think for ourselves anymore because we enjoy the convenience of letting others think for us and provide feedback to us. This is more than dangerous because most of that data can now be faked, bought, or altered in a second. This is so unfortunate because reviews used to be a kind of fair consumer reporting that provided product information to the buyer.

In his book *Future Crimes*, author Marc Goodman writes, "In California, a computer glitch led to the release of 450 dangerous criminals after a system error directed the prison guards to set some of the state's most violent offenders free. Gang members, rapists, armed robbers, and inmates classified as having a 'high risk' for violence walked out of prison statewide because officials accepted the information on their screens as the truth." Maybe our motto is, "In Computers and Devices We Trust."

This is how blindly we trust the code and data coming from our computers. Algorithms, marketers, terms of service, advertisers, censorship, cookies, hackers, scammers, data manipulators, review bombers, and human error make this the perfect storm. Our dependence on these systems will test the world in the coming years as hackers continue to try to knock out our critical systems. This is not a matter of if; it is a matter of when they will succeed.

Governments around the world are not ready for the aftermath of a critical-systems cyber-attack. Author and journalist Ted Koppel writes in his book *Lights Out*: "The American public needs to be convinced that the threat is real. Virtually all of our civilian critical infrastructure—including telecommunications, water, sanitation, transportation, and healthcare—depends on the electric grid. The grid is extremely vulnerable to disruption by a cyber- or other attack. Our adversaries already have the capability to carry out such an attack. The consequences of a large-scale attack on the US grid would be catastrophic for our national security and economy."

With Disruption 2.0 we face challenges that will compromise our freedom if we don't create a more sustainable type of freedom for ourselves. Whether you know it or not, like it or not, a new world is at hand, and because we have chosen to become dependent on code, technology, and data, it will be a complicated world—especially if any one of those systems is compromised in any way.

You may be feeling a bit nervous and fearful right now, wondering how you can trust anyone or anything. This is where it will benefit you most to go back to the fundamentals and begin to put into place the systems in the six key freedom areas that will support you in creating the Ultimate Freedom.

The basics are now being neglected, and the danger is that we think we can move forward without them. This is not true. Human interaction skills are being replaced by Facebook and texting. Learning to work well in groups is being replaced by working alone from home and in coffee shops, pretending that you can do it all; you just need to put your head down, use your new software, and work faster and harder. We do this because we believe in shortcuts and think that speed equals success.

Working fast and furious, wherever you do so, has become the norm. Many people may not even see the issue with being like this. Because of technology, we've become so accustomed to an accelerated pace of living and the idea that we must constantly do more and be more that we are blinded to how it is not serving our best interests but rather killing our fundamental freedom.

When we slow down, we have access to more of our true selves and our inner intelligence. When we blend our passion, purpose, and prosperity with our inner intelligence, we claim our freedom and success. Rather than looking outward, we can tune in to our internal field of knowing and seek a wiser and healthier solution. This always results in greater clarity and success because we have stopped confusing success with speed.

Many people believe they can get rich quick because they believe success comes from working harder and faster than they did the day before. We are sold this lie by marketers who want us to buy their product—and if we do it *now*, they will give us their "fast action" bonus. They tell us how they made $100,000 in seven days and how you can too, with their system. We are sold the concept that a shortcut plus speed equals success. And because the Internet has become fast at delivering data, we think we can shortcut even that process.

The truth is that you get rich by mastery of something, not by the speed of something. Only after you have gone through the process of mastering something can you develop speed and accuracy. Even the fastest racecar has to have an experienced master driver in the driver's seat to win the race. An amateur in the driver's seat will probably spin out of control and hit a wall. For many people, speeding toward a shortcut to achievement, instead of mastering something, is why their lives are spinning out of control and they hit the wall.

Many people join a multilevel marketing (MLM) group and expect to make millions of dollars fast, without first learning to build a business and then mastering how to build a downline—MLM jargon for the new distributors they recruit. This is why a lot of people quit. They want success to be easy and fast. When it doesn't happen fast enough for them, they become disillusioned and frustrated and abandon their dream.

Many people believed the Internet would give them the speedy path to riches by sidestepping everything they felt was hard to do, but this proved not to be true. You still must learn and master the skillsets that will create wealth for you. The Internet has made access to learning available to you, and you still will have to gain mastery before success happens.

In his book *Mastery* Robert Greene writes, "In the process leading to mastery we can identify three distinct phases and levels. The first is the Apprenticeship; the second is the creative Active; the third, Mastery. In the first phase, we stand on the outside of our field, learning as much as we can of the basic elements and rules. In the second phase, through much practice and immersion, we see into the inside of the machinery, how things connect with one another, and thus gain a more comprehensive understanding of the subject. With this comes a new power—the ability to experiment and creatively play with the elements involved. In the third phase, our degree of knowledge, experience, and focus is so deep that we can now see the whole picture with complete clarity. We have access to the heart of life—to human nature and natural phenomena. That is why the artwork of Masters touches us to the core."

In order to have mastery, you need to develop awareness and a deep connection with your inner skills and heart. I've seen people suddenly feel better emotionally and physically, and more connected to themselves, by simply taking a few breaths and checking in with their internal state. When we are on the fast train and living in overdrive, we mostly tend to the outer matters of running errands, getting on the conference calls with China, and finishing the next proposal.

It's not that those matters are not important; it's that we are ignoring our inner worlds completely, but that's where our mastery, discernment, power, and true knowing lies. When we stop rushing and make time for visiting our neighbor, or noticing a red bud blooming, we are more aware and available to connection with ourselves, others, and the natural world.

When we take the time to notice ourselves and our world, it gives us a healthier mental state. It helps us live in our true power, not some programmed and codified version of what we think we ought to do or be. We are more resourced and our creativity can flow. We have time and energy to be with our loved ones, time that can only come when we are not speeding around frenetically with the quiet hope of some human connection. Connection comes in a moment of presence and attention, not speed.

This requires slowing down and paying attention to what is happening inside yourself and around you too. This is a lost skillset that once recovered will bring you more joy, freedom, and connection with what matters most to you. Speed separates you from knowing what you truly want and need. Living in speed and overdrive tricks us into following along and automatically surrendering our discernment.

We are missing the value of living at a slower, more aware, and better connected pace where we engage more with our natural inner intelligence and our world, which over time gives us mastery. The neurotic speed at which many have chosen to live has kept them from slowing down enough to even read the Terms of Service agreements. Instead we just click "okay" because we don't have the time or energy to read it. We live in a fast-speed mindset where we often tell ourselves that we have no time for something. We outsource our decision-making process to a code, online review, or system.

Go now and visit http://www.theultimatefreedombook.com/lower-stress and discover a powerful technique that will show you how you can become instantly more peaceful, discerning and connected with your inner genius.

When you routinely live at this speed, you lose discernment and awareness skills simply by the nature of how fast your life is moving. This is what marketers,

ToS, and those who rig the systems want. They want you to lose your ability to discern. They don't want you to notice, be aware, or be present. This is how you get tripped up when you live at this speed. You cannot properly attend to everything, and thus you lose awareness and your human relations suffer greatly. In order to keep up with the speed, we can be manipulated and pressured into an unhealthy decision-making process such as using social proof.

Remember, technology promised us fewer working hours and more unfettered free time. Instead it has sped us up, dumbed us down, and kept us preoccupied with an abundance of data. We are often working the job of three people. This creates dysfunction in our life experiences and makes it hard for us to work with groups in a healthy way, whether it's a family group or a working group.

We have become numb to living at this speed and living in overdrive because we have been doing it for a few decades now. This addiction to instant manifestation and living at top speed and in overdrive is not freedom, and it will rarely produce success. Authentic mastery and achievement require all of your integrity, inner creativity, and intuition.

Without living from your inner compass, you may lack integrity and the connection to claim the success that naturally dwells inside you—a success that is specific to your divinity, personal mission, and calling in this life. Instant gratification and the speed of the Internet were not intended to provide a model for an ideal and rewarding human life.

We have learned to live in and accommodate this insanely neurotic fast pace. It is unhealthy for our bodies, minds, and lives. We have unnecessary stress and pressure because we keep going faster and faster with slower results because the system is rigged against us. You are not meant to win as the system is now set up.

Not so long ago humans—like the rest of the natural world—moved with nature's pace. Our lives were rhythmic and seasonal. We have become disconnected from our natural ways of living. Time poverty is now a recognized psychological and social stress. According to Wikipedia, "Being time-poor is increasingly the only way to stay out of poverty as wages have remained stagnant or been cut and as the price of living expenses have risen. High-paying roles have the longest hours, around 80 and more hours a week while low-paying jobs often less than 35 hours a week so low-earners have to work more than two jobs simultaneously in order to pay for living expenses. Increasingly, overworked people turn to the Internet as a tool to maximize the recreational utility they can get out of scarce leisure time. 'Time poverty' is not restricted to the wealthy, but can occur at all levels of society."

There is no freedom in living and working at this pace. You can't have discernment and clarity when you work this hard, neither can you have peace or happiness. Constantly rushing just to keep up while the system is rigged to have us inevitably fall further behind finds us destroying our health, our lives, and our planet. The danger of this fast-paced life is that our manmade speed and technology blinds us; we don't see how our lives have become engineered and codified into controlling our freedom in so many areas: technology, agriculture, pharmaceuticals, intellectual property, financial, and political. Plus, our time, creativity, and reality have been hijacked without us even noticing.

We have become completely frazzled and out of sync with our deepest selves. Many of us have forgotten how to reconnect with our natural rhythms inside us. The speed of modern living and the rigged systems have created an epidemic of binge drinking, explosive rage, loss of sex drive, indigestion, and heart disease.

According to *The Daily Mail*, "The findings of a survey of nearly 550 adults aged 25 and over highlights the extent to which people are struggling to juggle work commitments with the demands of family and keeping up with friends. The report, called 'Life in the Fast Lane,' found 85 per cent of adults are suffering indigestion, while 62 per cent have a reduced interest in sex." Many people are now too tired to make love.

The power of slowing down means that we finally get to reconnect with ourselves. This means we stop rushing through life so fast that we lose track of ourselves and what's important to us. We reconnect with our natural rhythms and that inner voice that guides us to freedom. Without these two fundamental skillsets, we don't make good, healthy decisions. If we are going to have the Ultimate Freedom, we will benefit most when we are in sync with our inner pulse.

When your inner pulse is honored, you become more aware and don't rush to the pace of someone else. You do things at the right speed for you. You cook a meal, work, and play with a level of passion and clarity because your brain is not foggy from the overexertion you feel from the speed at which you had been living.

When we honor our natural rhythms, we don't try to do everything at once. Multitasking is an invention of our rigged system and the sped-up life. When we honor ourselves, we become mindful and present. We move our focus to whatever we have in front of us and give it our full attention. We don't split ourselves by doing two things at once.

When we slow down, we become more resourceful. The problem is that slowing down often becomes confused with laziness. This is not true. Slowing down is inviting the art of precision and care into your life. You still have commitment, drive, eagerness, and excitement when you slow down, and you will have greater endurance because you are caring for yourself. You will either choose to slow down or live with the illness of living too fast. Freedom isn't about the constant speed of chasing some illusory success. It's a masterful state of being that doesn't engage with manifest destiny. What exactly is manifest destiny, you may ask? That's the topic of our next chapter.

Chapter 16

The Addiction to Manifest Destiny

Our manifest destiny is to overspread the continent allotted by Providence for the free development of our yearly multiplying millions.
—John S. O'Sullivan

Despite the fact that I am a female and we were living in Montana at the time, my father would often say to me, "Go west, young man!" This has often reminded me of a college history lesson on manifest destiny. Whether or not you are familiar with the phrase "Go west, young man!" you know that the United States started on the East Coast and over time spread to the West as far as it could.

Pioneers crossed rivers and mountains in covered wagons. Many stories tell of the trials and tribulations of these brave discoverers who settled along the way or kept moving west, looking for opportunity, gold, and other trades in order to stake their claim and create great wealth. We called these people expansionists.

While this westward movement was at the time a move across thousands of miles of land, over time we mistakenly internalized this notion to the point where we believe we are still expansionists and can conquer more and more, and that the possibilities are endless. We have never reached a point of satiation and have yet to be truly, deeply satisfied.

We have created a kind of insanity and madness around striving. We are always moving toward achievement and success because we have confused it with our heritage and birthright. This madness has now become our country's way of thinking, passed down from parents to their children: "If you get good grades and a degree, you can strive to get ahead in life." But this striving has depleted a huge percentage of our planet's resources, destroyed our real national heritage, and polluted our skies—and our minds—with an unhealthy addiction to material possessions.

When you deconstruct the scene of a crime, you can piece together the clues about what happened, and this can bring about healing, closure, discernment, peace, happiness, and freedom. This is a critical point to understand because we were once a very free world when we lived in balance with nature, and now our freedom is in jeopardy because we are codifying it and selling it to big companies that want to profit from it.

As we look to the future and the codification of our infrastructures, we can see that they do not bring balance to us; instead they bring an unhealthy dependency, manipulation, control, and dominance. These are all threats to freedom even if they look like innovations. Authentic freedom does not suffer from greed or manipulation. True freedom honors the flow, rhythms, and seasons because it is how we connect and collaborate with divine timing. Right now we live like pirates on the earth, trying to overthrow and control its natural rhythms to fit our striving and our need for achievement.

We spray the earth with poisonous chemicals; frack its skin; strip its forests; mine it for fuels, gems, and gold; pollute its skies; and dump plastic and other trash on it without considering how this will affect the earth's balance and rhythm. We do all of this in the name of striving and convenience. Our madness is so great that much of humanity doesn't even notice the earth's pain. People notice their coded device more than they notice what is going on around them. In fact, many think their device *is* what's going on around them.

In the 1800s this idea of American expansion was introduced into our national psyche as not just a possibility but also a right of divine providence. It was used as the logic to secure the Oregon Territory, California, and Mexican land in the Southwest. However, this feeling of divine providence gave these pioneering men the attitude that they had authority over the land and the rights of the indigenous people. If those people did not cooperate with their mission, they killed them. Thus they committed genocide, decimating the native people who had been living on the land—many of them peacefully. Bison nearly became extinct because pioneers thought they had dominion over the bison and did not live in balance with them slaughtering them for profits.

We are still suffering from this madness in our psyche. Manifest destiny has quietly been stamped into all of us. In the past, we crossed valleys and mountains to get to the promise of the next vista. With no more land to conquer, we're pressed to secure more of the Internet because it is the new world. We cannot see that we are killing our golden goose—the earth—in the name of progress. Some people think saving the earth is someone else's calling. We didn't understand that "Go west, young man!" was just the meme of the time and not our national heritage or motto.

The hope of what manifest destiny could offer in jobs and land was the reason people left their native countries to come to America, where the streets were supposedly paved with gold. We became the land of opportunity and still are considered this today. Now, however, this expansionist mentality has created an addiction to acquisition and materialism, which is harming the planet and us, simply because we have confused acquisition with the true meaning of being an expansionist.

At first, the Homestead Act provided the opportunity to put your stake in the ground and build your freedom and wealth, because owning land and homesteading created wealth. You handed this now established and working land to the next generation as their inheritance. The next generation worked the land and added to its value and care, leaving it better for the next generation that inherited the family legacy and repeated the cycle.

Safety and security were tied to the land and how people worked and cared for it. They were nurtured by the land and nurtured it in return. They lived in the rhythms and flows of the land and were connected with it. They were not trying to control the land for profit; instead they worked in collaboration with it, the land and the people giving mutually and beneficially. The people didn't take more than they needed and prided themselves on having respect for nature's processes and timing.

In America, putting your stake in the ground meant that you were provided with an amazing opportunity to create and leave a legacy. But now we have taken this out of context; to us, success means striving, conquering, and expanding. Caring and nurturing are no longer important principles. In the past, by working their farm and taking care of their animals, people learned the importance of caring and nurturing. Helping a goat give birth or tending to the needs of their orchards and chickens was how people understood the importance of those values.

Author and farmer Dr. Joel Salatin has said, "As a culture, we view life as fundamentally mechanical; we're asking 'How do we grow the pig faster, fatter, bigger, cheaper?' And that's all that matters . . . . Our side asks, 'How do we make the pig happier, more piggy, and more expressive of its pigness?' We recognize the fundamental honor and sacredness of that life form or that being, if you will. That's the fundamental difference." This is living in harmony and an awareness of what *is* instead of living in a world of trying to conquer and change what is.

Salatin says, "This striving to grow it faster, fatter, bigger, cheaper has made our food unhealthy to consume." This is part of the madness of the striving to achieve instead of striving to be in communion, connection, or collaboration with all things. There are other ways of being an expansionist that are healthy and more freeing, but we have forgotten it—or never learned it—because we have yet to give up our unhealthy expansionist mentality.

Now we've traded farms in the valley for companies in the cities. While the land was being conquered, raped, and poisoned, we didn't even notice that we were killing our golden goose; we only seemed to notice what else we could conquer that could provide us with trinkets and a false sense of self-esteem.

With the Internet as the new world, the launch of some companies is akin to Columbus landing on a Caribbean island. In the modern version, the Internet landscape is used to purchase domains and stake a claim because the urge to acquire has never stopped. We are out of land to take over, so now the Internet has become the place where you "go west, young man."

We think that we are experiencing progress and liberty until we read those ToS agreements and realize we are not. It's a corruption of divine providence. They want us to believe (and have convinced many of us) that they are offering a sort of freedom.

With the ToS creating new global laws, you will see this is not the creation of liberty. It is dominance and control of humanity and the critical infrastructures of food, water, air, land, and freedom. Humanity is now the indigenous people of the Internet world who were once living freely and peacefully but now have their freedoms threatened.

In the same way the indigenous people of the earthly New World were tricked into signing treaties and selling their precious land and belongings for beads, you too are clicking on the ToS without knowing what they really mean and selling your life for a Facebook like. Hackers will steal your identity, just as the land was stolen from the indigenous people.

Online companies are trying to conquer and expand by getting us to accept their ToS agreements, and this is making them global law. The attacks are different but the result is the same. A massive hack at Anthem Insurance exposed the private information of eighty million Americans, including names, birth dates, Social Security numbers, email addresses, and everything else an identity thief could use to ruin your life.

Even if you decided to drop off the grid this moment, closing your Google Gmail, Facebook, and online banking accounts, it wouldn't make a difference because your data and information is now stored indefinitely. We will be living on in cyberspace for generations to come.

If you look for a job, many companies send you to their website rather than meet with you in person. When you find a position, the application is often online. Your new job requires an email address. Whether you shop in a brick-and-mortar store or online store, your credit card information is stored in their computers. Many health centers have an electronic platform with every patient's entire medical history on it. There is no escape from this. These companies believe it is their right to this expansion on the Internet.

Is it convenient for people to shop, access medical and financial records, do searches, play games, watch movies, and chat with friends online? Absolutely. Our lives are much more convenient because of this technology. But the law of unintended consequences also applies to the Internet, and what is convenient for us is also convenient for thieves and hackers. They can topple governments, corporations, and the little guy in seconds.

Because America sets the tone for much of the world, this right of divine providence is becoming the standard by which the rest of the world measures its success or wealth. We have passed this "dis-ease" to other countries, and they are now looking to us as they strive to have as much as we have. The world sees America as the "haves" and the rest of the world as the "have-nots."

One question you may want to explore is, would you rob the rich or would you rob the poor? Do you practice being accessible online? Then you are exposing yourself to the new dangers of manifest destiny. Do you have your paycheck electronically deposited into your bank account? Do you pay bills online? Can you view your retirement funds online? Do you send and receive money via PayPal? Do you use debit cards? Do you have real cash reserves or only digital cash reserves? If you have digital cash only, you are vulnerable. If all you have are online riches, you are in a weak position—because if anything happened to jeopardize your accounts, you could end up broke. Something as simple as an electrical grid outage or as complex as a massive hacker attack could put your online funds at risk. How would you recover from this if it were to happen?

As in the 1960s and 1970s, recently people have been "going back to the land"—abandoning urban life in favor of buying a small farm and growing food on a small-scale basis, for themselves and others. This "modern homesteading" movement is a reaction to things like climate change and the alarming increase in GMO food, and a desire to grow and eat organic food, while returning to the balance of being self-sufficient and therefore freer.

The power in creating this option is what Henry David Thoreau wrote about: "I went to the woods because I wished to live deliberately, to front only the essential facts of life and see if I could not learn what it had to teach and not when I came to die, discover that I had not lived." For the past few decades ours has been a solidly urban, consumerist, and technology-addicted society. The idea of living simply and well seemed passé and almost laughable as we strived to achieve more.

As climate change, obesity, and food-safety issues began to emerge, we opened our eyes to how out of balance we have been in chasing our addiction to manifest destiny. Then with the 2008 recession, many people began to realize how sped up and disconnected their lives were from the natural world. People started to reevaluate and rethink the modern definition of the American dream and remembered their American heritage. Soon many people embraced concepts like intentional living, sustainable living, urban farming, downshifting, downsizing, simple living, and slow living.

Tim Kasser, a psychologist at Knox College, studies this kind of downshifting. According to his research, about a quarter of Americans have at some point voluntarily simplified their lives by taking a pay cut or cutting household spending, while perhaps 10 to 15 percent of the population practices hard-core types of voluntary simplicity such as homesteading. Another study, this one in Australia, showed that nearly a quarter of Aussies have downshifted, defined as those people who make a voluntary, long-term lifestyle change that involves consuming less.

The glimmer of hope in this modern homesteading movement is that we can let go of our addiction to manifest destiny and the right of divine providence, and humanity can experience harmony by bringing balance back to the expansionists and supporting them in finding the joy and happiness in simplicity, communion, connection, and collaboration with the natural order of things.

Having a modern homestead is a fantastic backup plan for surviving a future cyberattack, an electrical grid attack, Disruption 2.0, and robotics job loss, as well as lowering our stress levels and learning to slow down.

In some states homeowners can take advantage of a homestead exemption. Essentially this allows a homeowner to protect the value of their principal residence—this is key—from creditors and property taxes, and in the event of death it can protect the surviving spouse.

When it comes to homesteading, a portion of the home's value is generally shielded from property taxes. A typical homesteading benefit is that the first

$50,000 or $75,000 of a home's assessed value is exempt from taxes. Property taxes are levied only on the remaining assessed value.

Another great reason to have a homestead is that your home is shielded from a forced sale to satisfy certain creditors. For instance, if you defaulted on a loan for a recreational vehicle, the lender financing your RV can't force the sale of your homestead to cover your default. But homestead exemptions will not protect you from mortgage foreclosures or defaulted property taxes. Laws on homesteading vary from state to state; however, under most homestead laws, after the death of a spouse the surviving spouse usually retains the homestead rights as long as he or she continues living on the land.

The power and freedom in having a modern homestead and being more self-sufficient are the major factors leading people into this lifestyle. They want freedom from our centralized food supply and electrical grid systems. Whether there is a small emergency or a big crisis, most homesteaders have learned survival skills that many people either never knew or have forgotten. While the rest of the world is suffering from a lack of personal preparedness, they will be able to weather the storm.

You may be thinking that you can't afford the cost of homesteading. Then you will be happy to know that our government is helping this back-to-the-land movement by providing grants to homesteaders and farmers. Start2Farm. gov is a government site dedicated to providing resources and programs to beginning farmers and ranchers in the United States, with funding provided by the Department of Agriculture. To qualify, you must have less than ten years of experience in farming or ranching.

The importance of releasing yourself from the madness of manifest destiny and divine providence is that it will assist you in building your personal critical infrastructure as well as help you reconnect with what is important to you. You will have more discernment and will make better decisions when you slow down enough to read the road map before your vehicle spins out of control and hits the wall.

Time magazine posted an article on the top ten risks to the world in 2016, and number six is the rise of technologists. "A variety of highly influential non-state actors from the world of technology are entering the realm of politics with unprecedented assertiveness. These newly politically ambitious technologists are numerous and diverse, with profiles ranging from Silicon Valley corporations to hacker groups and retired tech philanthropists. The political rise of these actors will generate pushback from governments and citizens, generating both policy and market volatility."

Chapter 17

Financial Freedom

Rather go to bed without dinner than to rise in debt.
—Benjamin Franklin

I sat at a couple's kitchen table going over their financial needs analysis. Their house was valued at half a million dollars. Lovely pictures of international trips with friends and exotic excursions they had taken together graced their home. It was clear that they loved going on amazing vacations together, and it was a major factor in their lifestyle.

This was an adventurous and athletic couple with no kids. They had pictures of them ascending huge mountains, skydiving, on a boat on the Yangtze River, on safari in Africa, and on mountain bikes after a ride. They had BMWs and Range Rovers and every luxury you could want. Both were in private practice—the wife was a physician, the husband an ophthalmologist, which meant they owned two successful businesses.

By the looks of it, this happily married couple was the epitome of success. I was there to help them refinance their home. They wanted to take all their debt and roll it into the house and then have only one house payment. This sounded reasonable and smart to me, as I was confident that they had plenty of money.

Yet, after doing my research, I felt nervous as I sat in their home. I didn't even make half of what they made together, but I had way more money than they did. They were about to lose their home because they could not afford their debt payments and the house payments. This couple had racked up more than half a million dollars in debt. Even if I refinanced their home, I could not fit all of their personal debt into the refinance.

When I broke the bad news to them, the shock on their faces left the room silent. My mind was racing, trying to think of something kind or uplifting to say, but the reality was that even though they made half a million per year, they were dead broke by more than half a million dollars in debt—apart from their mortgage.

I regrouped and tried to relieve the tension in the situation by talking about a debt-stacking plan. They were both stunned but listened to me as I told them that a debt-stacking plan would require a huge shift in their lifestyle and way of thinking. They would have to sell their expensive cars, sell their home, and take no vacations to exotic places for at least five years. No more going out to dinner every night with friends. No stops for lattes in the morning. No extra spending whatsoever. They would have to shift to what they thought was emergency mode to rescue themselves from their dire financial situation.

The husband looked at me and asked, "Are you sure this is the only option? We really don't qualify for a loan? We make a half million a year. We can afford a loan."

I told him, "I understand you make a lot of money, but do you understand that you have as much debt, even without your mortgage, as you both make in a year? In fact, your debt payments are large and growing, and you only make the minimum payments. At this rate, if you continue on this path, you will lose everything. Your choices are either to lose everything or create new habits now. That still doesn't guarantee you won't lose everything."

They both looked as if they didn't know how this had happened, wondering how they could make so much money but be broke.

The husband looked embarrassed and said something I will never forget. "When you go to medical school, they teach you how to be a doctor; they don't teach you how to own a business or what to do with the money you'll make."

That comment has stayed with me ever since. In college you learn what you need to earn you the degree you want, but you won't learn life skills. Most parents don't educate their kids on how to make money other than to get a job or start mowing lawns. Most kids learn the debt structures their parents have used for years.

Your profession helps you earn money, but it doesn't tell you what to do with that money once you have earned it. Unfortunately, this is why the myth of financial freedom as a marketing tool can take your money from you, especially if you don't have healthy self-esteem and good money practices. Debt has always been the killer of wealth, and it is sold to everyone in a very seducing way.

Financial freedom and wealth building are often marketed and sold as convenient materialistic experiences. The car you drive, the house you live in, the neighborhood you reside in, the designer clothes and jewelry you wear, the career you have, the type of credit card you have (gold, platinum, or black)—these are supposed to be signs of financial freedom, wealth, and success. They are designed to make you look successful and feel good. However, the truth is that these are the counterfeit wealth tools of instant gratification.

They are marketed as something that will give you a sense of pseudo respect in the world. Many people still believe they will be valued more by their peers if they are wrapped in the trinkets of fashion and success. The truth is, it's just marketed to us in this form. This hierarchy of importance based on wealth has been marketed to us for eons as a fixed belief. This is why many people still think they are more important because of the wealth trinkets, career, and success they have achieved.

But more important than what? More important than your fellow man or the earth, air, water, and animals? You may be saying "no" in your head, but isn't that what happened on *Titanic*? Didn't thousands of people die because they were not among the wealthy who were allowed on the lifeboats? Today this is expressed in our use of first-class seating, service, airline flights, and so forth. And if we are honest, most of us, including me, want the good life. However, wanting it in hopes that you will feel more important or more confident is a sign of poor self-esteem.

Authentic self-esteem is born from an appreciation of yourself because you have spent the time to lovingly evaluate and meet yourself, not because you have the most expensive trinkets or eat in the finest restaurants. If you are using debt instruments when buying these trinkets in order to feel important, you are using counterfeit wealth to buy counterfeit self-esteem. When you exhibit this behavior in front of your kids, you are teaching them that their value is based on trinkets and approval from others.

Benjamin Franklin knew how insidious debt is and believed that it was better to cut expenses severely rather than incur debt. Yet now we are sold the opposite and told that living above our means is a normal and acceptable lifestyle. People often accept this without understanding how it is robbing them of their freedom. If you want authentic financial freedom, you will have to let go of this flexible belief that you can buy wealth with debt.

For real financial freedom, it will benefit you to take a good look at the possibility that you are addicted to convenience and instant gratification. For me, this was not easy. I have an "I want what I want, when I want it" personality. I changed that personality because I want real freedom more than any trinket.

The shift in your point of view has to come from inside you. You must know that it is a flexible belief to have trinkets of success purchased with debt. This is where discernment is important because you will always be offered instant gratification and access to counterfeit financial freedom. You need to recognize the difference between the two in order to create real financial freedom. Ask yourself if you are using counterfeit money or real money. If you're addicted to counterfeit wealth tools, then when that credit card comes in, you need to cut it up or turn down that offer. At first it may feel the way an alcoholic does when he's trying to muster the strength to turn down a drink.

I don't think this system of using counterfeit wealth is going to change soon, so you need to know the difference between real and counterfeit money. Real money gets you access; debt does not. Unlocking the Ultimate Freedom means knowing that real financial freedom tools provide you with actual assets, access, or opportunity. Credit cards don't provide you with any of those things. They are counterfeit wealth tools because they're a debt instrument pretending to be a wealth tool disguised as access, but it's really instant gratification and instant debt that creates instant servitude, not access. Debt is never an opportunity.

The difference between access and instant gratification is that financial access is planned and grown, while instant gratification is a strong, immediate, and unhealthy desire for some trinket or result. Debt instruments give you counterfeit access as they wrap and strap your future in servitude to that debt. To build financial freedom, you must understand what gives you access to more freedom and opportunity, not what gives you access to more pseudo respect from your peers and servitude to debt.

People use debt to access money because they confuse pseudo self-esteem and respect from others with instant gratification and the trinkets of success. We have lost our understanding of what real respect and success look like.

Claiming your financial freedom starts with a deep conversation about what you think financial freedom is. Most often we are sold someone else's picture of financial freedom—as a marketing ploy—in order for us to buy their version of counterfeit financial freedom.

On the Fourth of July we celebrate our nation's freedom with parades, barbecues, and fireworks displays. But at the end of the day, many people go home to lives they hate because they are strapped in debt and tied to a job they don't like. They continue in this misery so they can make the payments on the debt they acquired. This is not freedom. This is living a life of imprisonment and servitude and emotional pain. Strapping yourself to this kind of liability decimates your options.

Prior to 1950, Americans lived without credit cards and did just fine. We had layaway plans that allowed us to live within our means. We said no to our kids, and it was okay for them to feel their disappointment until their parents could buy what they wanted with cash.

Back then children were not given instant gratification, which would have put the family in financial peril. Instead parents focused on teaching children how to earn the money to afford what they wanted. Shoveling snow, babysitting, and mowing lawns were typical ways kids earned money. You need to ask yourself if you believe that credit card companies benefit from your fixed belief that they are a necessity—and if you think they want you to *believe* they are a necessity.

Having debt is not smart. It is being sold to our kids as a way of life. If you want to have an education, either the student or their parents will be taking on an average of $35,000 worth of debt (plus interest), without the assurance of a job at the end. And by the time some degrees are earned, the education they reflect will not be up-to-date with the industry. As we head deeper into Disruption 2.0, getting a college degree in some fields will not be a smart move.

In Disruption 2.0, it will be more than devastating to have any kind of debt, especially if you have a job, because the continued eradication of jobs will be swift and relentless. If your obligations meet or exceed your income, you need to make some changes now. As this disruption begins to gain momentum, you will not be able to afford a life of revolving debt, no job or reduced wages. More importantly, recovering from that job loss will be much harder than it has been in the past because, just like the jobs of auto workers, those jobs aren't coming back.

Our society has been programmed to accept debt as a standard way of life. It is a societal norm to live all your life strapped and stressed over debt. It is not freedom when you are drowning in student debt, with a thirty-year mortgage, a car loan, credit card debt, healthcare costs, and monthly bills on top of all that. Yet this is the form of freedom many of us have been sold. We have been sold the American dream of owning a home that takes thirty years to pay off, *if* you don't refinance within those thirty years. If you do, it will take you longer.

We are sold the lie that financial convenience is freedom. But like all codification, it is not freedom; it is surveillance. Every purchase is cataloged, coded, and stored for generations. Then we are sold the lie through marketing slogans that claim that freedom is the ability to buy what you want, when you want; all you have to do is use your credit card to purchase responsibly, because you have earned the right to have credit.

Remember that many people's "method" is usually the most convenient way and has nothing to do with the result. There is no "responsible purchasing" when you are addicted to the convenience of debt. Disruption 2.0 will take out high-earning professionals who may now believe that their careers and earning potentials are bulletproof.

Using a credit card to shop responsibly doesn't make sense. When you use a credit card, you are often living above your means, and this is not responsible buying. But we are sold the ridiculous idea that credit is something we earn and not the truth—that the purchase of debt comes with a high interest rate. In fact, this is the perfect way to look at how debt is marketed to you as a convenience.

When I was younger, they actually called a credit card by a different name. They called it a "charge card." So at least your mind knew the truth that it was charging instead of buying. Charge cards were not such a hit with adults who remembered the World War II era. Charging anything was not considered normal or smart to do.

In his book *Once Upon a Time the Way America Was*, author Eric Sloane writes, "Once upon a time, believe it or not, America was frugal. Waste, which was once-upon-a-time deplorable, has now become fashionable as a national habit. We often waste more in one month than the average old-timer saved during his lifetime. Waste was once considered bad manners, the mark of a fool and something quite un-American. Some of us have been fooled into the theory that the more we waste, the more we need to buy and so waste therefore aids the national economy."

Abraham Lincoln said, "You cannot bring about prosperity by discouraging thrift." Back in the day, people took pride in their ability to save and create wealth. In fact, there was no such thing as garbage as we know it today. Old dictionaries defined the word "garbage" as the entrails of animals. There was also no such thing as "junk" as we now know it. In old dictionaries it was defined as odds and ends of rope.

Americans used to take pride in their financially fiscal mindset; you were a responsible adult if you followed good money-management practices. What happened? Have we lost our American heritage? Shakespeare wrote, "Neither a borrower nor a lender be, for loan oft loses both itself and friend, and borrowing dulls the edge of husbandry." Our grandparents understood how damaging debt was to living a free life.

Banks changed the name from charge cards to credit cards because the new name was more attractive to unsuspecting people. Credit was marketed as something you earned that made your ego feel important and responsible. It provided a false sense of self-esteem by giving access to money, which made you feel and look important and financially responsible.

It allowed you to borrow more money because you were credit worthy, which helped you feel more important than those who did not qualify. Qualifying began to look like a rite of financial passage. I know—I fell for it too! This ploy sold way more debt to unsuspecting people with low self-esteem (including me) than trying to sell a charge card to someone who did not believe in racking up debt.

What Shakespeare understood is that borrowing dulls the edge of husbandry. His reasoning was that lending money to a friend is dangerous because attaching debt to a personal relationship often causes bitterness and, with the possibility of that friend not paying it back, will lose the lender both his money and his friend. Borrowing invites more risk for both parties. It replaces saving and domestic thrift (husbandry), which in Shakespeare's eyes was an important value.

This is what happened to the two doctors trying to refinance their home. Even though they were in the 1 percent of income earners, they were broke because they kept borrowing on credit cards. This dulled their senses of the cost of the money they were borrowing and how much money they actually had until they were the richest dead-broke people I had ever encountered.

By the way, in the days when Hamlet was first staged, borrowing had become widespread among the upper class, who sometimes neglected saving and husbandry to the point where they were selling off their estates bit by bit to maintain a pretentious lifestyle in London. We are still doing this today because of the amount of debt people take on to support a pretentious lifestyle and ego.

It's hard to get out of a deep addiction to convenience and instant gratification, mostly because you can't see that you are addicted. Many people don't realize this is an unhealthy addiction to desiring. They don't see that they are unable to say no to themselves or to their family and stop the addiction to desiring things.

To truly have financial freedom, you need to give up the addiction to putting things on credit and paying them in the future. It will be like quitting smoking at first; you will feel the want to charge and will have to stop yourself and ask if you're having an "I want it now" moment.

When you have real wealth, you don't need to purchase with credit because you have access. Having financial freedom means discovering what real wealth is and how to protect it. This means understanding the system and having all the information you need so you will know how best to move forward.

Mindset and Financial Wealth

She was a single mom who had just left an abusive relationship. She and her young son had just moved into a tiny apartment. She was a dear friend of my parents and was at their house for dinner one night telling them about how she and her son were adjusting to their new life. She was uplifted and happy, but things were tight until payday because she had just leased a new apartment.

She said, "If I just had fifty bucks for food for the week, we'd be okay."

Before she finished the sentence, I said, "I can lend you that."

I popped up out of my seat at the dinner table to go into my backpack to get her the money. My stepfather popped up out of his chair too; I thought he was going to the kitchen to get something.

Instead he came down the hallway to have a word with me.

"Vickie, I don't lend money to people ever. So if you are going to do anything with that money, don't lend it; give it to her without expectation of it being returned. You don't have to tell her that. Just don't hold out for it to be returned to you; otherwise you may be disappointed. People don't usually pay back money."

I realized what he was telling me was important. I didn't think about whether I could do without that money or not. I just wanted to be helpful. From that moment on, I decided that I would never lend money. Either I would give it or not. I returned with $50 and handed it to her without saying anything. To her credit, she returned it to me in a week, after she had received her paycheck.

I don't lend money to anyone, but I do invest in businesses and projects that I like and think will be a benefit, but lending is out of the question. Financial freedom is hard earned. It is a strong shift in thinking and the code of ethics that you live by. Your mindset around wealth and how you handle it is as important as how you create it. It becomes part of your attractor field. Your attractor field shifts because you do something different, not because you think something different.

For example, when it comes to building wealth, the traditional view is to have a job. However, jobs are no longer a secure way of producing income, simply because jobs are being shipped overseas or are being innovated, disrupted, and transformed. The reality is that your mindset around keeping a job may be stationary. However, we are seeing huge changes in how we make a living. Eventually your job will likely be disrupted.

Only one form of wealth creation has never been disrupted, and that is to start and grow a business. Owning a business and learning to run it well shifts your mindset and attractor field because you are taking a different action. It raises your resonance and creates a powerful momentum that changes your opportunities and outcomes. You have more freedom because you have more options. During Disruption 2.0, it will be important to shift your mindset from that of employee to business owner.

From as far back as Jesus' time, people owned businesses. Creating and selling value is how you can become wealthy. Having a business has been building prosperity for thousands of years. However, how you run a business is very different today than in past eras. Author Eric Sloane in his book *Our Vanishing Landscape* writes, "A hundred or more years ago, whether you were a blacksmith, a butcher, a carpenter, a politician, or a banker, you were also a farmer. If you were retired, you were a 'gentleman farmer.'"

In the 1700s Benjamin Franklin noted that everyone had at least two businesses. The one common business was that everyone was a farmer. Even our first president, George Washington, was a farmer. There was no class system back then because everyone was a farmer and everyone understood the necessity of another's skills. The second business was a trade of some sort, as Eric Sloane said.

In early America everyone in Congress was a farmer as their first business and a congressman second. Benjamin Franklin felt that farming was a necessary part of common education. He always referred to it as a way of life and complete philosophy for existence. Having two businesses supported generations of people who would inherit the family business and the family farm. This is how families grew their wealth.

By the time these businesses were handed off, they were paid for, systems were set up, and their client base was already established. This is how the next generation would continue to do better than the previous generation—they were handed the legacy of two successful debt-free businesses. Jobs do not provide you or your lineage with that kind of wealth creation. Most graduates won't have jobs as Disruption 2.0 grows, and neither will you.

Today, nearly every household has two jobs instead of two businesses. If this describes your household, then this may be what needs to change in your financial freedom area. In his book *The End of Jobs*, author Taylor Pearson writes, "Software is eating the world." Jobs and businesses are being eaten up by software that is replacing human ability. Also, a job limits the amount of money you can make; a business does not.

The cycle of having jobs to support your lifestyle is being greatly reduced in America. A new entrepreneurial revolution is happening even as we are experiencing the end of jobs. However, we are mistakenly using debt instruments to help us get through this transition, and it is melting our freedoms and bankrupting families at an alarming rate.

In the past when you opened a business, you could pass it to the next generation. It wasn't going to be disrupted by software or some other technology. Your business served a local community and did not compete with the world. Supply chains were local and not overseas. When you made a bid for a job, you were competing with local talent, not overseas labor markets with such low wages that it was advantageous for owners to outsource the job overseas.

Today, these are the obstacles that workers and business owners are dealing with all over the world. To top that off, we have had financial tools and market manipulators create markets that are volatile and unstable. All that said, owning a business is still the best way to create financial freedom because even though the terrain is transforming, the benefits afforded business owners are not changing. Governments support business no matter where you go in the world. You may have to change and become more agile with your mindset, but the opportunities are plenty for business owners.

When you have a business, your mindset shifts because you begin to attract money instead of chasing or begging for it as you do with a job. If you have a business, you will attract people whose sole purpose is to give you money for your product or service. If you have a job, you will attract more work because your sole purpose is to work for money. Having a business shifts your focus and mindset because instead of focusing on debt and chasing money, you're focused on solving people's problems. You begin to solve the needs of others, and it will in turn solve your own need for income.

Your mindset is where you put your attention and attitude, and it creates your results and point of view. Perception is everything. The way you view anything is important. Why? Because that is what triggers our reactions and thus our actions. The biggest problem people have is listening to their own mind and not challenging it.

They believe that the voice in their head is true and accurate. They don't realize it is the voice of the past, stuff they learned years ago that is most likely not relevant now. We either empower or impair ourselves with the perceptions that create our abilities and experiences. When you own a business, it forces your mindset to move from a reactive view to a proactive view.

You will challenge yourself more when you have a business than when you have a job. If you remain in a reactive mindset, your business will go belly-up and so will your wealth. However, if you begin to move into a proactive mindset, you will have greater wealth abilities and outcomes. If you want it badly enough, you will figure it out. You will remove the obstacles and go through the barrier to move beyond any reactive belief. Disruption 2.0 will force you to think differently.

Your mindset will either help you take the right actions or leave you in your past. Using the Ultimate Freedom and becoming wealthy is not about wishing or visualizing wealth falling from the sky. It's not about soaking in a feeling of wealth and waiting for its arrival. According to figures from the Federal Reserve, US household wealth fell by about $16.4 trillion of net worth from its peak in spring 2007, about six months before the start of the recession, to when things hit bottom in the first quarter of 2009.

According to CNN, "One reason that the U.S. economy still struggles to achieve sustained growth is that Americans are a long way from recovering the trillions of dollars of household wealth lost during the Great Recession. While a rebound in the stock market, and improved savings rate and consumer steps to reduce debt resulted in net worth gains since 2009, only a little more than half of that lost wealth—$8.7 trillion—is back on household balance sheets. That leaves American household wealth $7.7 trillion less than it was before the recession."

Disruption 2.0 will be more chaotic than the 2008 crash because there will be even fewer jobs. People are still financially vulnerable because they have not completely recovered from Disruption 1.0. It will benefit you most if you have two or more businesses instead of two or more jobs. This will mean taking an action now to secure your future.

I use the tools of copywriting, speaking, and consulting on how to develop business and freedom. However, I still have brick-and-mortar businesses where I make and serve ice cream, at the Crestone Creamery http://www. crestonecreamery.com/. Obviously I am also an author. I have a consulting firm that sells products and services to other businesses and helps people learn what they think they can't do. I also have a small homestead where I have an orchard of fruit trees and gardens that produce food for me. I don't have debt outside of my tiny mortgage, and I invest in growing businesses that create income streams for me. In Disruption 2.0, having only one source of income will not be smart. It will be dangerous.

I looked at what our forefathers did and built my businesses in that manner. Interestingly, many others are doing this as well. According to the USDA, sales of organic farms are up 72 percent. Also, Wall Street investors are buying up farmland. A recent report by the Oakland Institute documents a new trend: "Corporations are starting to buy up U.S. farmland, especially in areas dominated by industrial-scale agriculture, like Iowa and California's Central Valley. But the land-grabbing companies aren't agribusinesses like Monsanto and Cargill. Instead, they're financial firms: investment arms of insurance companies, banks, pension funds, and the like. In short, Wall Street sees money potentials in those fields of greens."

Why are Wall Streeters plowing cash into such an inherently risky business with such seemingly low profit potential? The Oakland Institute noted, "Over the last 50 years, the amount of global arable land per capita shrank by roughly 45 percent, and it is expected to continue declining, albeit more moderately, going toward 2050."

Where are they investing and why? What do they know that you don't? With Disruption 2.0 beginning, one of the smartest actions you can take is to own a farm or homestead. There is a lot of freedom in just being able to grow your own food. According to *Mother Jones*, "Wall Street's move onto farms comes at a time of severe ecological flux that will be exacerbated by climate change. On top of deepening water woes in California—where half of U.S.-grown fresh produce comes from—there's a slow-motion, largely invisible soil crisis brewing in the Midwestern grain belt."

If Wall Street is shifting their mindset from their normal investment strategy into urgently investing in something new, then they are rethinking and reinventing something. Usually Wall Streeters operate under pressure to deliver short-term profits to investors. This is their modus operandi. Food production must be an issue that will create a supply-and-demand imbalance they can profit from. Otherwise they would invest in something different and not pursue this avenue for profitability.

I have built my freedom into my world so that I have some control over what is happening. But at one time I had huge debt, super low self-esteem, and a bad, disempowering attitude. I had created madness and folly for myself. I worked jobs that I hated and did not know how to manage money well. I had paralyzing credit card debt and felt stuck as if there was no way out.

At first I did not see that our forefathers had left us clues on how to live and be in freedom. I did not feel confident enough to learn what I thought I couldn't do. I just thought that I couldn't do it. I was super focused on what other people thought of me and how I fit in. I spent my money in a way that would help me feel as if others approved of me. I had platinum credit cards, appropriate clothing and cars, an education, and a job that made me look successful, but I was broke, miserable, and clueless as to what to do.

Like an alcoholic, I had to hit rock bottom with this horrible addiction before I decided to do something else. I had suffered enough, and I was willing to turn my life around, come hell or high water. When you hit this place, success becomes your only option, so take heart. The first thing I did was update my library card and read financial books as well as business books. I didn't just read the books; I implemented the advice they offered.

I took the drastic measures they told me to take. I made a budget and began saving money while I was paying down my debt. I cut in half two credit cards, with a total credit line of $40,000, and closed those accounts. I bought a used, beat-up car for cash. I lived in a trailer instead of buying a house until I had paid everything down to zero and built a savings account that would keep me from ever going back in debt.

I shut off the TV to protect my mind and have not watched TV since. In order to repair the damage I had done, I worked two jobs while I learned how to create a website and learned to write. I didn't go out with friends. I became a hermit for about five years because I was saving every last dime I could, as well as reading, studying, and practicing.

I practiced writing every day, completing at least five articles a night and ten articles a day on my days off. I learned to sell by selling insurance, mortgages, hard assets, and other investments. I began to make a sizable amount of money, but mostly I began to get a sizable amount of confidence and self-respect, which I had not planned on.

Financial freedom began with my shift in mindset when I learned the power of saying no to myself and my unhealthy behaviors around spending, instant manifestation, and living above my means. At first it hurt, and I felt disappointed sometimes, but then it felt empowering as I saw my cash flow grow.

I started asking questions of myself like *Do I really need a brand-new car for people to like and respect me? Do I really need to have people see that I am successful, or can it be a secret just between me and me?* I saw how others were trapped without financial freedom because of their unhealthy flexible beliefs around money and success, so I just kept my secret to myself, and I liked blending in.

This was my first step to creating financial freedom. The second step I took was to get a financial education so I knew how money worked. The third step I took was to implement that advice. I liked Robert Kiyosaki's advice about saving money to start a business, so I did it. I highly recommend reading *Rich Dad, Poor Dad* by Kiyosaki. He explains the cash-flow quadrant and how important it is to understand the power of business ownership.

Not every business I started was a success, but I never lost my shirt in business because I had used my business savings cash and not credit cards or investors. I could recover quickly because I had no debt. When you have no debt, it only takes one good business to help you lift off the ground and help you invest in another business. Over time I began to understand more of what I thought I couldn't learn, and I realized that I was capable of learning what I thought I couldn't. This new confidence helped me take command of my financial freedom.

I still read voraciously about business and the world because it is important for me to stay on top of my industry. We have new threats to our financial freedom that have never been here before—cybercrimes and cyber terrorism. To combat this, I have both online and offline income streams. You will have to educate yourself as to how you wish to protect yourself from cybercrime. I have backup plans in place so if one income stream is interrupted, another is there working for me.

I am a big believer in businesses because they help you enhance the skills of husbandry, and you become thrifty with your money. Starting a business with a credit card is not financially sound, and it is super risky. Bootstrapping (in general parlance, bootstrapping usually refers to a self-starting process that is supposed to proceed without external input) helps you learn what you think you can't do, and you suddenly find out that what you first thought was impossible suddenly becomes possible.

Saving and Financial Freedom

In his 1911 book *The Eight Pillars of Prosperity*, James Allen writes, "While writing this, I pause, and turn to look through my study window, and there, a hundred yards away, is a tall tree in the top of which some enterprising rook from a rookery hard by, has, for the first time, built its nest.

"A strong, north-east wind is blowing, so that the top of the tree is swayed violently to and fro by the onset of the blast; yet there is no danger to that frail thing of sticks and hair, and the mother bird, sitting upon her eggs, has no fear of the storm. Why is this? It is because the bird has instinctively built her nest in harmony with principles which ensure the maximum strength and security.

"First, a fork is chosen as the foundation for the nest, and not a space between two separate branches, so that, however great may be the swaying of the tree top, the position of the nest is not altered, nor its structure disturbed; then the nest is built on a circular plan so as to offer the greatest resistance to any external pressure, as well as to obtain more perfect compactness within, in accordance with its purpose; and so, however the tempest may rage, the birds rest in comfort and security.

"This is a very simple and familiar object, and yet, in the strict obedience of its structure to mathematical law, it becomes, to the wise, a parable of enlightenment, teaching them that only by ordering one's deeds in accordance with fixed principles is perfect surety, perfect security, and perfect peace obtained amid the uncertainty of events and the turbulent tempests of life.

"Business and all human enterprises are not exempt from the eternal order, but can only stand securely by the observance of fixed laws. Prosperity, to be stable and enduring, must rest on a solid foundation of moral principle, and be supported by the adamantine pillars of sterling character and moral worth. In the attempt to run a business in defiance of moral principles, disaster, of one kind or another, is inevitable. The permanently prosperous men in any community are not its tricksters and deceivers, but its reliable and upright men. Prosperity, like a house, is a roof over a man's head, affording him protection and comfort."

Today, saving is marketed and sold to us as a shortcut to something—saving time, saving money, saving coupons. It is not sold to us as a way of having discernment and building your nest in harmony with principles that ensure maximum strength and security. When James Allen wrote about these principles, it was because he observed something in the natural world and not in our electronically created world.

He wrote, "Individuals, families, nations grow and prosper in harmony with their growth in moral strength and knowledge; they fall and fail in accordance with their moral decadence." But what is moral decadence? This is a very personal question. For me, it is an unhealthy level of self-indulgence that throws you out of harmony with yourself and the natural laws of the universe.

Benjamin Franklin wrote, "Think What You Do When You Run in Debt: You Give to Another Power over Your Liberty." As of this writing, America's national debt is nearing $20 trillion. Our government is addicted to debt just as much as many of its citizens are. This amount of money is so large that it is hard to conceptualize, but let's see if we can put it in perspective.

Let's say that I gave you a million dollars a day to spend. Great, right? Well, let's say I started giving you that million dollars a day from the time Jesus was born, some two thousand years ago. A million dollars a day for two thousand years is only three-quarters of a trillion dollars. We wouldn't even be through one trillion dollars yet.

Do you know how much of that $20 trillion in national debt you owe? According to *Forbes* magazine, it is more than $155,000 and growing. Now multiply that number times the number of people in your family. This level of debt has thrown us out of harmony with the natural laws of the universe. It is hard to conceptualize how self-indulgent and out of balance we have become as a nation based on our government's spending. How can we see how harmful it is if *they* don't see how harmful it is?

In 2015 more than half of all US households were running a deficit. Were you? The mean American household was able to save roughly $4,900 last year. Almost half of Americans would not be able to cover an unexpected expense of $100 or less. An estimated 22.9 percent of men and 22.7 percent of women say they don't have at least $100 in their emergency fund.

We have not built our nest in a stable place because we have not instinctively built our nest in harmony with principles that ensure the maximum strength and security. A strong Disruption 2.0 wind is beginning to blow; the top of the tree will sway violently by the onset of the blast. Because saving is now sold to us as a shortcut instead of the harmonious alignment with principles that ensure maximum strength and security, we don't value the universal principle of our American heritage of thrift. Instead we value manifest destiny, which we turned into instant manifestation.

We see saving as something we do with money. We set aside money into a savings account and save for a rainy day. Some think of saving as not trusting the universe to have our backs and provide for us, but this is not what saving is. Saving is about respecting and honoring the natural rhythms of lifecycles—respecting and honoring the value of ourselves and the earth.

When we fail to see saving as a way of honoring ourselves, we lose the harmonious balance and principle of maximum strength. We don't value ourselves, and the world is a reflection of that loss of value. The world becomes a reflection of our imbalance; we are unwilling to save not just money but also our water, relationships, and earth, sky, animals, and fish. Piles of trash pollute the land, water, and air. Our abilities and desire for instant manifestation and convenience are deemed more valuable and important than our ability to honor ourselves and our natural lifecycles.

When we save, we honor, appreciate, and savor the gift, and its history, craftsmanship, and sacrifice. One day while walking through the rural mountain town where I live, I met a ninety-eight-year-old man who had lived in this tiny town all his life. We struck up a conversation about his apple tree, whose limbs were bent under the full load of apples.

"Do you want some apples?" he asked. "I got plenty of apples; let me get you some apples from this tree."

His generosity melted my heart, and this man became excited to have some company, someone to talk to, and someone to share the apples with. I figured I would make an apple pie and take it to him. He gave me enough apples to make two pies. I could see his pride in the apples on his tree.

I thanked him, went home, and made the pies. When I delivered them, he was clearly pleased and invited me to have a slice of pie with him. As we were eating, he asked if I knew how old his apple trees were. Of course, I didn't.

"These apple trees are almost one hundred years old," he told me. "My family planted them when I was a little boy. One day the train came to town and it was loaded with fruit trees, and the conductor of the train said we could have as many trees as we wanted as long as we planted them within the first couple of days. So all these fruit trees you see around here were planted from the day that train came to town."

This was unusual for this mountain town because it is located 8,100 feet up in the Rocky Mountains of Colorado. Pinyon pine trees dominate these areas, not apple, plum, and apricot trees.

He smiled as he took a bite of pie. With a satisfied look, he said, "Yep, these trees have been feeding us for almost a hundred years now. Rabbits, bear, deer eat from these trees. If you want to leave a legacy, plant an apple tree. It'll feed you for a hundred years."

I finished my short visit with him and left him with the rest of the pie. He died a short time later. But I had learned a valuable lesson about what leaving a legacy actually means—it means leaving something that generations can enjoy. This is the power of saving. It's not a shortcut; it's a legacy.

On my property I have planted an orchard in remembrance of him. I have four kinds of apple trees. I have three kinds of apricots and four kinds of plum trees. Can you see how this is saving for future generations and living within the rhythm and life force of *real* wealth? Can you see how planting a simple tree is a form of saving and respecting the future?

This is the power of saving money for your future. It doesn't matter how much you save; just start saving and it will grow. Saving and honoring ourselves shifts our resonance and character. It helps you grow authentic self-esteem and wealth.

In our history, having a profitable business was like planting an apple tree. It was a form of wealth and savings, and it left a legacy that fed you and your future generations.

Having a savings program is the first step in planting, honoring, and respecting your future. In my house respecting our heritage means buying things that last—things that reflect the quality craftsmanship we are interested in. I have three savings accounts. One is for contingencies, one is for business investments, and the third is for fun.

None of this happened overnight for me. I spent nearly nine years paying off the debt I had. At first, when I failed at business and took a few lumps, I never lost my shirt because I planted more than one tree. If that tree died, I simply replaced it and tended to my other trees. Saving is an accountability that allows me to feel responsible, abundant, and discerning. I can turn down work if I don't like it. I can donate or surprise someone with a gift because I have money tucked away.

But the most important thing that happened was that savings unleashed my creativity. It allows me to feel safe to explore and experiment without being afraid of losing it all. I will always have money in case everything falls apart and I have to start all over again.

To me, money is like seed. If you save seeds and you have a bad crop, you can plant again. This is respecting the rhythm and lifecycles of the unknown, and it's a habit that builds confidence and harmony in your life. Unlocking the Ultimate Freedom means planting seeds that bear fruit now and in the future. Debt does neither of these things.

So—how many savings trees have you planted? Savings trees are income streams that provide you with control of your choices, income, and freedom and create harmony in your life.

If you don't have any, you will want to plant those trees right now before Disruption 2.0 starts to move faster. Savings does not just mean money in the bank. It means saving your income by planting more income streams. It means having or starting a business and learning to make it profitable. It means being able to say no to your unhealthy desire to charge things while saying yes to your Ultimate Freedom.

Author and commodities genius Jim Rogers, who co-founded and administered with George Soros an investment fund named Quantum that returned more than 4,000 percent in ten years, said in an interview for the Brazilian magazine *Veja*, "People working with agriculture will be the world's next billionaires! Wealth will come from farms. Farmers will be the owners of Lamborghinis in the future, not the smart guys working in finance."

Many celebrities have implemented this form of business design. Actress Reese Witherspoon has a ranch. Musician Jason Mraz and actor Tom Selleck have avocado farms. Actor Mark Ruffalo has a dairy farm. Roseanne Barr has a macadamia nut farm. Nicole Kidman and Keith Urban have a farm in the United States and a cattle ranch in Australia. Martha Stewart has a farm and greenhouses. Russell Crowe has a cattle farm. Ted Turner has some fifteen ranches throughout America. Oprah Winfrey has a farm on Maui where she grows fruits and vegetables. There are many others.

Billionaires, Wall Streeters, celebrities, and even insurance companies are buying farms. My point is that they have two businesses, just as many of our forefathers did. They are farmers and have another income source, such as acting, music, finance, or media. Making the move from having two jobs to building business income streams will help you get through Disruption 2.0.

Your Business 2.0

As we move deeper into Disruption 2.0, having a business will be important to your overall wealth and freedom. Our business world has shifted into an innovative working platform. The world is more connected, so our partners can be based all over the world. We have moved from hierarchy and bureaucratic leadership to collaborative and cooperative business leadership. Top-down business leadership will move into business groups. We are moving from a top-down leadership style to a think-tank group leadership style because our future requires flexibility, agility, and creativity.

Business leaders will get more work done through collaborative and creative efforts because it will help them manage all the unknowns that businesses will face. Groups and teams will have more than one business together so they can use the speed that will be necessary to enter a market. Because of this, companies will become communities. Once your team is put together, you will be able to use online systems to connect, create, and grow a business.

Small and midsize businesses will still account for more than 99 percent of all businesses in developed economies and 40 to 70 percent of value added to the economy. Companies will continue moving toward having home offices instead of having a downtown office. The digital lifestyle will provide that a community or family business can happen while everyone lives in a different place. Family and couple-run businesses will make a big comeback because people will want to do business with them instead of with a big company. According to SAP, more than 70 percent of customers believe small businesses understand them better than large companies and provide a more personal customer experience.

Family businesses grew America. Husband and wife teams worked together, and as their children became able, they worked the family business and learned the trade. The business was handed from generation to generation. Families worked together—until our country provided more options than to simply inherit the family business. Now only 30 percent of these businesses survive into the second generation, and a meager 12 percent make it to the third generation.

However, those families that work together well have built some of the strongest, longest-running companies in America, including Walmart, Cargill, Berkshire Hathaway, Ford, and Comcast, which have become household names. The family unit is an important way to start a business when you are preparing for the future.

Families will start working together because jobs will be scarce. Money and credit for small business startups is shrinking, and families will begin to bootstrap their income sources. Some families will be forced into this; others will cooperate, and success will be easier for them.

If you can run a business out of your home, that's best. If you can run a family business and learn to work together, your business has a better chance of surviving instead of having business partners that are not family members. Here's why:

Speed: With a family working together, you can talk about something over the dinner table and implement it the next day. The family is a natural team, and when you need to get something to market quickly, hustle is everything.

Tax benefits: According to *Entrepreneur* magazine, "When done correctly a family business can also create tax savings. When you hire a family member your business can take a deduction for reasonable compensation, which reduces the amount of taxable business income. As a business owner you are responsible to pay Federal Income Contributions Act (FICA) and Federal Unemployment Tax Act (FUTA) of employees, wages paid to family members are subject to withholding of certain taxes in some states. Typically, the payment of these taxes will be a deductible business expense for tax purposes. But if you hire a family member—a child, spouse, or parent—to work for your business, you may not have to pay FICA and FUTA taxes.

"For instance, you don't have to pay FUTA taxes for services performed by a child under 21 years old. And you don't have to pay FICA taxes for a child under 18 who works in your trade or business or a partnership owned solely by you and your spouse. For family members under age 18, you don't have to withhold for FICA, Medicare, FUTA, or SUTA. If your spouse is employed, you don't have to withhold for FUTA and SUTA but must withhold for FICA and Medicare."

Trust: This is a key ingredient to any business. If you have a patentable idea, intellectual property, or software or trade secret, most often your family will have a very high level of loyalty and be naturally protective of the family's secrets.

Solidarity: When a family works together in a business, their goal is to win and have a successful outcome. But business partners may have their own agenda, and this can sabotage the business. However, in a family business, if there is a problem, family does not usually leave. Instead they join forces to look at how they can solve the problem. Suddenly you see your kids and parents as allies. You have youthful ingenuity and the wisdom and experience of age to help solve the problem.

Obviously some families fight and argue; many are dysfunctional and working together is a "no way" proposition. But those families that can work together—or learn to work together—will have a much better likelihood of success and degree of freedom. Sure, it has its challenges, but family members will work harder for you than employees will, for longer than employees will.

The key to family business success is starting out correctly. This means having a system to work out family conflict and governance by creating a succession plan and a family charter that spells out your family's long-term vision. You need to determine what kind of structure to build so the business can be handed to the third generation and beyond. What model of mediation will you have in place when family conflicts arise? How will you balance the personal and the professional? These considerations will need professional expertise and ongoing support. However, once you have them in place, you can build a strong legacy that survives the unknown future.

If your family is too dysfunctional to work together, it will be important for you to find or build a working community with the right team of people. Then you can pick the businesses you would like to build. According to World Bank

Jobs Report, "Right now more than 3 billion people are working, but nearly half of them work in farming, small home-based businesses, or seasonal day labor."

What You Need to Know 2.0

1. In order to manage Disruption 2.0 the best you can, start where you are. If you have debt, begin paying it off now. Debt will be crippling as Disruption 2.0 becomes stronger.

2. Begin to save as you pay your debt down. Savings will give you future options and access to opportunities, and protect you from things that you may not see right now.

3. Create businesses and make or join a business community or family that can work together collaboratively.

4. Learn how to produce food in your home or backyard. Food shortages and prices will be skyrocketing over the years as climate change, water issues, and energy become more controlled and costly. Consider having a homestead or farm.

5. Begin to move from being in a job to becoming a business owner. Having at least two businesses will help you have income safety. An online business as well as a local business can help you create some stability over time.

Chapter 18

Emotional Freedom

There are no broken people; it's just that they are operating from hurt and broken ideas.

—Robert G. Smith

M ost people try to avoid emotional pain. Isn't that one reason we like Star Trek's Spock? He's half human and half Vulcan, and Vulcans have no feelings. They purge emotions from their being, so they only use logic. We loved this concept of not being ruled by emotions and having supreme intelligence because we value academic intelligence over everything. The issue is that instead of seeing feelings as an important aspect of our human experience, we often see emotions as painful and unnecessary.

Until we began to watch *Star Trek: The Next Generation*. In this series we met another form of intelligence through the character of Deanna Troi. We loved her personality so much that she became one of the best-liked characters of the series. Deanna Troi was the ship's counselor, and her job was to use her emotional intelligence to sense the well-being of the crew or the emotional dynamics of a particular situation.

This emotional sensing is another powerful form of intelligence that does not use the brain/mind and its thinking process to make decisions. Instead it uses the intuitive heart and body/mind in order to connect at a heart level. This was Deanna Troi's secret. She was deeply in touch with her inner intuitive and emotional intelligence and reported her findings to the captain, as well as helped the crew with their emotional issues.

Captain Picard counted on Troi more than anyone else to give it to him straight by telling him the things he needed to hear. Then she would reassure him that he could overcome any doubts or fears. Deanna Troi was not just the emotional balance of the ship; she was also the inner intelligence ambassador who went along on missions to help the captain understand their subject's emotional state. What were their subject's intentions and fears? She could empathically feel what others wouldn't admit to, and this made her a valuable asset.

When Deanna Troi used her emotional intelligence skills, there was less confusion and violence. She could create a field of inclusiveness and compassion during negotiations with the subject because she developed a heartfelt connection with them. She also helped foster an emotional connection between the subject and Captain Picard that resulted in trust and honesty, which opened communications and understanding.

The secret to using and understanding emotional freedom is to know that it is a language and an intelligence all its own. Star Trek's Counselor Troi was a breakthrough character on a TV show because she was the first character that allowed the world to see the power of raw emotion as a form of intelligence.

Emotional freedom is a form of inner balance, but it is also a powerful skill that allows you to evaluate, explore, and read intentions and options. It is hard to lie to a person who is emotionally intelligent because they can sense their inner intelligence raising a red flag. They don't have to know what the lie is; they just have to be willing to sense the red flag go up. Being out of balance emotionally will destroy almost anything—your career, your relationships, your life, and especially your freedom.

During Disruption 2.0 having emotional intelligence will provide you with more options, but more importantly it will protect your freedom more than money or a gun will. It will give you more credibility and influence than any other skill. Emotional freedom is an often ignored form of intelligence that will be in greater and greater demand in our future.

The world will continue to be in turmoil, and those who have emotional intelligence will be better prepared and freer than the average person. People will want to work with them because they will have greater discernment and make better decisions. Without this gift of emotional intelligence, you are not free. Academic intelligence without emotional intelligence will not give you happiness or freedom.

When you think about becoming an effective leader, what characteristics come to mind? Chances are you'll want to know when to trust your intuition and listen to gut feelings. You'll want to be someone who is a good listener and stays cool under pressure. You'll want to be able to feel the fear and do it anyway. You'll want to know that you will not be run over by your emotions, but you'll be able to understand them by listening to the data they are providing. You'll want to understand how your inner world works and how it can take care of you by helping you identify your true feelings.

People who have mastered these skills are highly valued and have a strong degree of freedom and success. They have learned to recognize emotions in themselves and others. They understand feelings and notice how they affect the people around them. They are good motivators and positive people. Not only do they know their internal state, they also have an awareness of other people's emotions. They can encourage others to share their insights and what they are feeling. This allows them to notice where other people are coming from and helps them avoid potential conflicts. They manage relationships better.

Emotional freedom is a learnable skill. The most important aspect of mastering this is getting to know and understand yourself. Here are five elements that define emotional intelligence as described by Daniel Goleman in his book *Emotional Intelligence*:

1. **Self-awareness:** When you're self-aware, you understand how your feelings affect your abilities and how they are affecting people around you.
2. **Self-regulation:** This is the ability to control your emotions and actions. It's the ability to get over yourself or determine if you need boundaries. You must know what your values are and hold yourself accountable when you make a mistake.
3. **Motivation:** Putting off short-term rewards for long-term success involves understanding what your intentions are and the intentions of the people around you.
4. **Empathy:** This is the ability to identify with other people and understand their wants, needs, and viewpoints.
5. **Social skills:** These help you work in a positive way with other people and manage conflict effectively.

Having emotional intelligence is not just a skill but also a type of currency that will provide you with more access and opportunity, especially in Disruption 2.0. Our misunderstanding of emotional freedom stems from thinking that leadership means not feeling anything as Spock does instead of acknowledging emotions as Troi does. Growing up, boys didn't cry and were called sissies if they did; instead they were taught to suck it up and walk it off.

True power involves feeling the movement of emotion through you without judging it or acting it out but instead listening inwardly while reporting on it as Troi does. This helps you gather the data these emotions are conveying. When you have learned this skill, you will have authentic, grounded well-being while things are shifting or falling apart.

Some people confuse emotional freedom with emotional intelligence. One is an aspect of good leadership. It doesn't require you to engage with freedom. It is just a necessary tool. However, emotional freedom is being free of fear or being controlled by your emotions. We are willing to explore them moment to moment.

Our feelings are our inner intelligence, giving us data that will benefit us when we pay attention to it. It feeds us valuable information about the present moment, but what we have been taught is to purge, avoid, react, dramatize, or drown that information instead of reading the data from it. Emotional freedom is the ability to read that data and extract its meaning.

When we don't connect with this inner guide, things can fall apart. We can't find our way and begin to feel overwhelmed or fearful. When we don't have emotional freedom, we often ignore our feelings and needs, ridicule ourselves, or allow our lack of self-esteem to crush our dreams. We can feel empty and alone because we are simply ignoring our self.

Emotional freedom is the continued gentle conversation with our inner being. It is meeting oneself and learning how to support our inner well-being. It is giving ourselves permission to experience a wide range of emotions, both negative and positive, without belittling or judging ourselves but instead exploring ourselves. It's learning to express and communicate our emotions in a healthy manner.

Why is this important? So many people live in fear, anger, guilt, and shame, and they don't know how to stop being controlled by these emotions. They are so ruled by these emotions that they don't see themselves as living in an abnormal environment; they just live a life that seems constricted, meaningless, or boring.

Being ruled by these negative feelings is how we can be manipulated by our outer world. We can keep ourselves so busy or addicted that we never deal with our unhappiness. Maybe we spend our life following someone else's beliefs or wishes instead of our own. Can you see how this would rob you of a life of freedom?

We can be rich and miserable at the same time when we only know how to create financial freedom and not how to create emotional freedom. Money does not make you happy. Having emotional freedom makes you happy and more discerning with your money and your life experience. Emotional freedom helps creativity and productivity giving you more success.

Just imagine what it might feel like to live without being controlled by guilt, anger, anxiety, or shame—no more chronic anger or complaining. This is emotional freedom. It's the ability to liberate yourself from the emotional patterns that no longer serve your freedom. If you don't have strong, healthy emotional freedom, you are more likely to be in debt, battle with addiction, and have unhealthy relationships, as well as be easily manipulated.

We live in a time of unprecedented options. Thanks to online life and growing consumerism, we've got more choices than ever about what we eat, how we spend our time, and where to go. Unless we live in the wilderness, we are brimming over with multiple demands for our attention.

When I was a child, we had only one choice for school lunch or for school at all, for that matter, with fewer private school options than we have today. After-school activities operated similarly; either join the seasonal sport or do nothing. This made it pretty easy to decide because our choices were few. Beginning from a very young age, today we are presented with the widest range of choices in pretty much every department.

In many ways this puts the emphasis on the external world rather than what is going on inside us. With the abundance of options, many of us feel pressured to choose the right one. We are overwhelmed and uncertain. Some may realize that they are responding to being overwhelmed, but others are out of touch with their response.

To be healthy emotionally, we must know the internal state that for decades we've been taught to ignore. We've got to be able to check in with ourselves and truly know the answer to "How are you?" We do so with our physical body; we can see the usefulness of being able to sense when we are hungry, tired, or energized. It's just as important to be able to do this with our emotions. Take a moment now and ask yourself how you are doing. Can you identify your feelings and state of mind? If you answered "I am fine," what does that mean? Can you identify the emotion you are feeling when you are in a "fine" state?

In order to be responsible not only to our world but also to our families and friends, we must know the state of our inner feelings. If we are not aware of our feelings, we are going to behave in ways that are not in line with our best and freest selves. You may snap at a colleague or walk off in a huff after hearing news you don't like. This is not good human interaction. It is an unconscious acting out of the emotional state that can all too easily land you in an unpleasant situation.

A place to start is by learning to identify emotions. To make it easy, consider these broad categories: mad, glad, sad, scared. That pretty much covers it, in a simplistic manner. It's not unusual for people to have a limited vocabulary for their feelings. I never got this information in my formal education and most likely neither did most people.

When I teach beginning therapists who are graduate students in a counseling program, I hand them two sheets of paper. The first has about seventy small faces with a range of expressions and a one-word description below them to give an idea of what is depicted. Troubled, hesitant, satisfied, or jubilant are suddenly evident by seeing the picture and the word together.

The next handout on emotions is a list that is organized under broad categories like these: delighted, relaxed, scared, frustrated, nervous, and content. Underneath each heading is a list of more nuanced expressions. For example, the subset of "delighted" includes joyful, happy, amused, adventurous, blissful, and elated. You can find something similar by doing a search online, and we've included one of the handouts in the secret bonus room online for this book. I highly recommend them. Even my emotionally and psychologically inclined friends have found these tools to be of help, which suggests that whether you are an expert or a beginner, you likely have more to learn about feelings.

Knowing who and how we are on the inside, including the feeling state, is so critical to unlocking the Ultimate Freedom because it allows us to unleash our discernment. There is a great deal of external information and manipulation. When you can tune in to your internal sense, you can receive up-to-the-minute information that is accurate without being biased by outside messages. This allows for better choices and decisions that are suited to your freedom rather than some pre-programmed idea of how things should be.

Daniel Goleman, a leading science journalist and psychologist, says, "Emotional self-regulation and empathy may be more salient skills than purely cognitive abilities. As it happens, some of these circumscribed realms are of major importance in our lives. One that comes to mind is health, to the extent that disturbing emotions and toxic relationships have been identified as risk factors in disease. Those who can manage their emotional lives with more calm and self-awareness seem to have a distinct and measurable health advantage, as has now been confirmed by many studies." Additionally, we know that relationships of every type, from business to personal, improve when people are in touch with their emotions.

Disruption 2.0 will create more job losses in Western countries. As a result, people and communities will emerge and begin the process of developing small businesses. Usually there will be more than one project on the table, and it will be a more stressful environment because of the speed and learning curve it will take to bootstrap a business. Under this kind of pressure, people will use their past learned habits and strategies for dealing with this new stress. Many will become defensive, judgmental, protective, and competitive. This will no longer work in Disruption 2.0. In fact, it will be dangerous because if a company goes belly-up, it will be harder for a contentious group to start a new one.

Working groups are the future of business. They will bring their skillsets together and create value and products that produce income for the group. This means the concentration is not going to be on what business to start but who your partners are. For example, if you are in a band and each bandmate plays an instrument well, loves their bandmates, feels valued, alive, and included, and is honest and respectful of all the other bandmates, then it doesn't matter whether they play jazz, rock, blues, country, R&B, or hip-hop.

It is the bandmates who matter; the music they choose to play is secondary. Bandmates work at bringing synergy to the band. When they are onstage together, synergy will be what people sense and notice. If they become a group that is inclusive, compassionate, and alive, the audience will feel that and engage with them. They will have more fans. If the bandmates dislike each other and argue nonstop, the audience will feel that vibe as well.

The band lives, travels, and works together as a community, from startup to success. They work and practice in this community long-term. They create products that promote the freedom and well-being of the whole group. Songs, music videos, concerts, and private parties are income sources for them, and in order to achieve success they must all work together harmoniously. This is how the band becomes a living organism, and its success or death depends solely on the health of the organism.

Emotional health will create the most creativity, productivity, and money. Lack of it will kill it. This will be the future of working groups. It is not the project; it is the team, whether it is a team of two or a team of ten. The emotional success of your living organism will be its outer success.

This means having a conscious co-creative and interconnected team of leaders who work like a band and know how to succeed long-term. This is what robotics can't do. They can't create a sense of belonging that invites more creativity. They can't create authentic relationships. They can't generate a sense of aliveness and inclusiveness. They can't be innovative. They can only do what they are programmed to do. The rest is exclusively in the human realm.

When you create heartfelt relationships, you can build networks of partnerships that collaborate and access income sources. You will be able to address complex problems and face the world more effectively when you are part of an integrated team. No burden becomes too heavy if everyone lifts and works well together.

This is a learning curve and training involved in a new type of leadership. Groups of people become cohesive and functional so they can work and live with much more productivity, creativity, and happiness. People learn how to become a vibrant living system. In the natural world, the birds, bugs, trees, and foxes know how to work together, something many humans have forgotten. However, by looking at and studying the science of how nature functions, we can apply those principles to having fulfilling human interactions.

Through reconnecting these skillsets, we learn how to work together in a way that is mutually rewarding and beneficial to the group. After two decades of supporting and training groups to be healthy and functional, I've learned that people enter groups in two main ways.

Some are excited and happy about doing so. This suggests that they've had positive experiences with groups in the past, and they are interested in learning more. Other people are scared, put off, and hurt by their past groups—and apprehensive about joining another one. They need to feel welcomed and included in a safe manner.

This means that you will want to get the most and best out of yourself and all the other members of the group. The days of antagonistic and combative styles of working together are long gone. Working collectively can be an excellent support system.

By initially focusing on creating safety and a sense of belonging, people learn that collaboration in a group setting can be enriching and productive. This is applicable for any setting, from our family life to whatever work we do. As a teacher, I use the tactics we teach in group trainings in my classroom. Simple exercises allow people to immediately get connected to themselves and each other in a way that allows for greater learning and effectiveness.

Thanks to our caveman ancestry, our brains are constantly scanning for safety, and naturally we do this in any new setting. When we learn how to inform ourselves that in fact we are safe and well through simple activities that promote inclusion of everyone, we know we are safe and can get down to the business at hand. That may mean making a meal together or creating a product launch; it doesn't matter. When we become better at working with each other, we get better results and feel more satisfied. We become freer.

What You Need to Know 2.0

1. Emotional freedom is an inner intelligence that builds discernment.
2. It will be in great demand in our future as we head deeper into Disruption 2.0.
3. It is a leadership tool that helps productivity and creativity in working groups.
4. It is the ability to no longer be controlled by negative feelings.
5. It helps strengthen relationships and safety in working groups.

Chapter 19

Spiritual Freedom

Jerry: Which of the world's religions is the closest to the divine truth?
God: The divine truth is not in a building or a book or a story. Put down
that the heart is the temple wherein all truth resides.
—From the movie ***Oh, God!***

Becoming spiritually free by using your mind is an impossible task, because spiritual growth is a process of the inner soul awakening and not mental awakening. Spiritual freedom is the raising of your soul's consciousness beyond its ordinary existence into universal truth. Explaining what it's like in words is not easy. But the outcome of expanding in this way gives you a vast amount of happiness, joy, opportunity, and success.

Freedom has a multilayered aspect to it that produces the life of your dreams. In order to create the life of your dreams, you address all aspects of freedom and find out, in each area, where you would like to claim more freedom. As you grow in the six areas of freedom, your being becomes more awake and the divinity within you creates the Ultimate Freedom.

We can see Oprah Winfrey's journey to creating her best life and note that her spiritual development was a core principle in getting her to live her best life. She understood deeply that she was a developing soul and that ultimately she is an evolving soul. The deepest form of freedom comes from the soul. It does not come from material possessions or mental acquisitions. When you die, what has evolved is your soul, not your mental learnings.

This is the key to embracing spiritual freedom. When we understand that we are a developing soul, we can begin where we are by meeting our soul and the divine within it. You cannot be free without recognizing your own soul's being. The inner soul has needs just as the body does. When you feed your soul, you are creating connection and expanding your consciousness.

Oprah didn't start out being as spiritually conscious as she is now, but over time she has grown in her spiritual wakefulness and consciousness, and it has guided and grown her success. Her show also helped many people grow their level of spiritual freedom. She was the first TV personality who embraced the importance of feeding the soul daily as an essential aspect of wholeness. She knew we are spirit first and humans second. She knew that spirit is where she came from and would return to.

She grew her consciousness and spiritual freedom just as she grew her emotional and financial freedom. This unlocked her passion, purpose, and prosperity, giving her the best life and Ultimate Freedom. If we understand that living a human existence offers the opportunity to expand and grow in consciousness, then we can begin to see how important spiritual freedom is to all-around well-being. It is foundational to all other freedoms.

However, people often confuse the heart and the soul, and although they often work in unison, when you are deeply in soul, you feel no emotions. You are awake and observing. Soul has a pure level of resonance and awareness that bathes you in stillness and love. There is a sound like a cosmic hum when you are resting in soul. There is no conversation and no emotional roller coaster when you are in soul; you are in quiet awareness. Your soul is the director of your attention and where you place it. Your heart and its feelings jump in along with your mind and make a commentary, and this triggers an emotion or feeling.

For example, when you see a sunset and you feel joyful or sad that the day is ending and how beautiful the sunset is, this is your heart and mind; the soul only notices that the sun is setting, and all is perfect in each and every moment. Your soul will observe and notice, and your heart and mind will create the story and the array of emotion behind it. However, if the mind does not think and emotions are quiet, the soul will only feel love. Your soul has no negative or toxic emotions—only the mind does.

Soul lives in the sound and hum of your level of resonance or consciousness. It neither judges nor reacts—it just observes and guides the next moment. It can guide your mind to create the next best action. It doesn't create an array of new emotions, only a deeper and greater love. Soul bathes and exists in only the energy and resonance of the "now" and of love. It doesn't know past or future.

When you're in soul, there is no ego. Soul is quiet and undisturbed by human emotions because it lives in raw awareness. Soul is the part of you that is forever a piece of the great divine. It is the nonjudgmental observer that has the answers you need to move forward. But it is often smothered by the thinking mind to the point where we don't give our soul a chance to simply be.

Your spiritual freedom resides in your soul, and so does your current level of consciousness as soul, not mind. Engaging with your spirituality is an individual path, and yet it affects the whole of everything because we are all interconnected. On the one hand, it is a form of wakefulness, being present, and processing information. On the other hand, it is deeply personal between you and the divine. It is a pure state of awareness that has no thinking and no words, but it does guide.

That is why the mind cannot create spiritual freedom for you. It can only entrap you in more thought. It can be a faithful servant, but it will never set you free from thinking or lead you into pure awareness or give you spiritual freedom.

Most people get a glimpse of their soul when the mind no longer has an answer. It is usually something shocking. For me it was when a robber stuck a gun in my stomach. I went into fear and my mind had no answer. This allowed my soul to show up and take charge, which introduced me to what I call the silent intelligence. When soul shows up, it is almost as if everything goes into slow motion. It gives you guidance, and you need to listen to it and surrender to its guidance because it knows the best way.

Meditation and contemplation are how we learn to engage with and hear our soul without shocking our minds with fear or other feelings. Instead we learn to be in the silence and hum of the soul. We begin to notice our mind and our emotions, but we stop believing in them as truth, and this begins to set us free. We learn to notice them instead of believe them. Then we learn to focus our attention.

When we let our soul guide us, we are letting the divine guide us and allowing our minds to assist. Viktor Frankl said, "The highest and greatest of the human freedoms is to choose your attitude in any given set of circumstance, to choose one's own way." And this is the importance of having spiritual freedom, because each path is individual and offers the perfect lessons and awakenings specifically designed for each individual.

Your attitude is meeting the part of your soul power that can choose its own way. It is meeting the power within you to change your current life into what your soul is longing for. Usually our soul is longing for freedom. Viktor Frankl says, "If we don't consciously decide what sort of person we want to be and then work to become that person, our environment and our experience determine both our identity and our destiny for us."

MasterPath's Sri Gary Olsen says, "You will never be able to alter your attitude if you feel that the external environment controls your life. Remember, you are not in the world, but the world is in you. You have the power and the right to transform the outside environment into anything you desire. The outside world is actually dependent on your inside world, which is the play of your attitude and attention."

Spiritual freedom comes when you decide and practice where to place your attention. Will you place your attention on your thoughts, your emotions, or your soul? Meditation and contemplation quiet your mind and your emotions, allowing your soul to lead and having the faith to assist the request of the soul. When you embrace this practice, you begin the process of becoming free and not just feeling free.

Carefrontationally (gently and firmly) guiding and controlling your attitude and attention helps you transform the outside environment with discernment. Your attitude and attention change from your soul, not your mind. Your mind is the habitual action you take. Creating the awareness to take a different action comes from your soul. The mind may assist the action involved, but the leader of the change is your soul.

Contemplation and meditation help the thinking mind relax and become quiet enough to connect with the soul. The thinking mind entraps the soul with its constant discursive thinking. There is no room for soul to make an appearance when the mind is going a mile a minute. Acknowledging your soul even for a second helps you quiet down.

Understanding spiritual freedom does not mean you are behaving strangely or trying to escape from relating and being in this world. Instead it is a way of embracing the responsibility and happiness of being in the world and with yourself. It is also learning to communicate and interact with this silent intelligence by yourself and not through a third party like a channel, psychic, or medium of some sort. It is not using your mind or words either. The mind has nothing to do with your spiritual freedom.

Knowing something does not mean anything if we can't take action or implement it. Humanity loves concepts and platitudes. We put them all over Facebook and share them, and yet we don't see how we are any freer after reading or posting them than we were the day before. Because the mind does not set the soul free, the mind entraps the soul whereas unlocking the soul is how we set ourselves free.

Spiritual freedom is recognition of your soul and its abilities. All freedom comes from the action you take. A free life requires that you take the action of caring for the body, mind, and spirit. Many people confuse their mind as being their soul, because sometimes we must go through the mind to enter the soul. We may read a book and use our mind to help us free ourselves, but our mind is not our soul.

It is much easier to access the soul when you go to your heart. Tibetans point to the heart when they are asked where true knowing is located. They seem to know that it is the direct route to the soul. People love the ease of understanding a spiritual concept, but that is nothing but spiritual convenience. Living from your soul is living from your real heart, and this is authentic spiritual freedom. When it is spiritually free, your authentic heart isn't emotionally charged. It lives in a state of love and knows everything is perfect.

Authentic freedom is cosmic in that it does not rely on human thinking. Often when we go looking for the truth, we use our thinking mind and don't actually find the truth. Instead we find an idea that matches our current beliefs or values. This makes us feel good, but it is not freedom.

We think spiritual growth is the feeling we get when we find an idea or concept that we like better than our last one. So we take it on, thinking we have grown spiritually. We know that if we "change the way we look at things, the things we look at will change." We know that we will "see it when we believe it," as author and speaker Wayne Dyer says. These are fabulous concepts.

We love the notion of these ideas, but spirituality deepens notions, ideas, and concepts by asking questions that transform them into inner soulful tools. Before we can turn these concepts into inner tools, we must have an opportunity to use those concepts and tools. We are bound to this supreme law. It is how we have an individuated path. The opportunities and challenges presented to you on your earthly journey are specifically designed for you by this law. No two people have the same journey. We are like snowflakes in that way.

The tendency to use our mind instead of our soul strengthens our ego, and not in a good way. We become more self-righteous or think we are more realized than we actually are. Spirituality is not the validation of your beliefs. Instead spirituality is surrendering to something cosmic in your soul. It's living with your heart and mind open. It is letting your soul lead the way and allowing your mind to serve it.

Spirituality is individuating and knowing that the "Kingdom of God is within you" (Luke 17:21). I am not using this as biblical Christian doctrine, although it is. I am using this term as spiritual fact. You are from this cosmic place. Wayne Dyer explains it in his quote, "We are not human beings in search of a spiritual experience. We are spiritual beings immersed in a human experience. You are infinite spiritual beings having a temporary human experience."

We are divine beings, not beings looking for divinity. If you are looking for divinity your mind is involved. Spiritual freedom is about letting your divinity out. Your divinity is your soul. Your soul—not your mind or heart—carries your calling. Spiritual freedom is about claiming your divinity and letting it out of you. It is between you and the divine master within you. You cannot learn it; you have to meet it. Realization comes through your own soul and not from another. It is within you—not in a book, not in a teacher, preacher, metaphysical scientist, or other authority. There is no medium that can help introduce you to your soul.

Spiritual freedom is the ultimate surrender to the divine and the ultimate success. It produces history's greatest legends. My favorite "shero" is abolitionist Harriet Tubman because she was led by her spiritual freedom and freed thousands of others. She was a slave and then a conductor on the Underground Railroad.

She believed that God would guide her. That's all she had. She didn't know how to read so she prayed. They nicknamed her "Moses" after the prophet Moses in the Bible, who led his people to freedom. We can see this type of spiritual freedom in Mahatma Gandhi, Mother Teresa, and Nelson Mandela. Gandhi said, "You must be the change you wish to see in the world."

Spiritual freedom comes from the authentic wakefulness of your own soul. And just like these amazing souls, there can be no other authority than the union between your soul and the divine one. This allows your soul and not your mind to lead the way. Only the soul can set you free; your mind can't. Otherwise it would be a very different world.

The issue with the mind is that it likes to control and be controlled. It takes the soul's authority and tries to negate its efficacy so that your mind can be the supreme leader. This is why the human race gives its power away and is being hypnotized by other pseudo gurus: TV, advertisements, marketing, news, social media, and so on.

We have the greatest spiritual freedom when we do not fixate on any one thing but observe all things and take the next step. We stay open to everything without formulating a one-track approach to it. When we are supple and living from our soul, we are able to see limitless possibilities. Without fixation, we can be available to much more of our experience of freedom.

At times your mind will have no answer, and you will need to look for the answers in another part of you. Spiritual freedom means that your heart has no questions and your mind has no answers. You will know what you must do to help yourself when you listen to that part of your soul.

What You Need to Know 2.0

1. Spiritual freedom is the gateway to the Ultimate Freedom.
2. Soul carries your calling. Calling is an aspect of your soul and not your mind or emotions.
3. Soul has the answers that your mind does not.
4. Soul will guide you to your next best step if you listen.
5. Meditation and contemplation help quiet the mind so you can meet your soul.
6. No one can introduce you to your soul except you—no psychic, medium, or channel.
7. When your mind has no answers, your soul does.

Chapter 20

Social Freedom

Leadership is not about a title or a designation. It's about impact, influence, and inspiration. Impact involves getting results, influence is about spreading the passion you have for your work, and you have to inspire teammates and customers.

—Robin S. Sharma

S ocial freedom is important to understand outside the realm of social media. It has the greatest power and influence of all the freedoms and is the most misunderstood freedom of them all. In the case of the Ultimate Freedom, it means being trusted enough to influence actions and policies to make an impact in the world. It is thought leadership at its deepest level. It is the strongest and most delicate form of freedom there is. When it is understood and used in its best form, it creates the greatest well-being, wealth, and change in the world.

Imagine how much influence you would have if you were the president of a country and Oprah Winfrey asked what she could do for you. Say you replied, "Build me a school." So she paid for and built one of the best schools in your country simply because you asked. This is the kind of social freedom we are speaking about.

Most people understand social freedom more as a political type of freedom; the ability to exercise their rights under the laws of their country. But it is not just about supporting free speech, laws, or regulations. It's not about having so much money that you can buy a vote. It's much more powerful than that. Politics is a piece of your life whether you are dealing with office, small-town, church, or boardroom politics. Your actions are what do or do not create social freedom. The key to having this kind of freedom is others must trust you in order for you to grow your influence so you can have an impact.

When right action meets right idea and right relationship, social freedom is generated. The theme and motto of social freedom is "We achieve success together." Whether you are creating a revolution, a company, a family, or a country you cannot do it alone. This is why social freedom can only be supported by "We the People." It is the ability to create honest and ethical influence, inspiration, and impact.

Social freedom is a powerful source of freedom when used for the greater good. What if, because of your request of Oprah, you had changed the history and education of young girls in South Africa for years to come? This is the kind of impact that betters humanity for generations. Because you had the influence to get it done simply by asking, you could change the world. This is the kind of power and influence Nelson Mandela gained over time by his continued right action. It wasn't his money or position but his right action that created this influence and power.

Social freedom will produce the Ultimate Freedom when used with right action. It is the ability to have influence and power while using it for the greater good. This is what Oprah does. She has earned her influence by consistently demonstrating right action (leadership), right relationship (her audience and authenticity with them), and right idea (live your best life). This is the most powerful tool of influence that you can have.

There is no using this power in an unethical way and calling it social freedom. Then it is manipulation. Social freedom is expressed in an ethical manner only. Our world's most powerful leaders have focused on growing their social freedom;

this is how they grew their legacies. We will draw a line in the sand right now and remind you that no matter what has happened in the history of the world, over time people always overthrow a corrupt and negative political agenda. There is always an uprising against tyranny.

The value of people in Disruption 2.0 will be heavily graded on the amount of social freedom they have and how they apply it. Influence and impact are the currency of the future. An app called Klout uses social media analytics to rank its users according to their online social influence, resulting in what is called your Klout score—a number between 1 and 100 that measures the size of your social media network and the interaction with the content you create. When your Klout score is high, you can generate perks in which other companies offer freebies to you, hoping you will write about your experience with them on your social media platforms. They anticipate that this will influence others to try the products.

Social freedom is powerful, but it grows over time. It depends on how people perceive you and how you interact with the world.

That means the video your friends took of you while you were falling down drunk in college, which was placed on Facebook for a laugh, will influence your career. That skin pic you took of yourself and sent privately to your boyfriend or girlfriend isn't private. The video of you in middle school bullying and beating up another student may mean that you won't be able to get the job you want or get into your favorite college. You have been labeled a bully, and that will be a hard stigma to shed when the imprint of you doing this becomes permanent.

Your influence will impact your life, your opportunities, and your success. If it is strong, you will be able to inspire world change. People will want to work with you and join with you on projects. You will be offered more opportunities and access to people and ideas than you can even follow up on. While this all sounds great and wonderful, social freedom is an area where you must have the most discernment.

There are also bottom feeders who will want to manipulate you and who don't care if they harm your social freedom as long as they can further their agenda. Isn't this why we have no respect for politicians who take money from lobbyists who are essentially buying votes? We the people no longer have faith that our representatives will not be influenced by corporate money.

People who have authentic social freedom understand that it is a hard-earned freedom that can be easily destroyed. It will benefit you most when you realize how to earn it and how to protect it. Over time, social freedom will help you have impact on others, on your industry, and on the world. This is how Oprah grew her influence. She is fierce about living it and protecting it.

Oprah is discerning when it comes to her influence. It is often said that when she meets with people who are pitching her an idea for a show, they usually talk about how much money it will make. She tells them, "I already have plenty of money. Tell me how this will help my audience." She says they often get quiet and begin shuffling paper because they have not answered that question. They are only focused on how much money it will bring in. This is not the focus of social freedom. However, for OWN, they know their power relies on social freedom and following the mission of her company 100 percent of the time, and this is why her audience trusts her.

Following the mission of her company has given the Oprah empire its influence, inspiration, and impact. Your company earns social freedom by doing the right thing 100 percent of the time and keeping to your word. Yes, it is part of creating your brand, but it is much deeper than that, because your brand is just a small part of your mission. With social influence, you maintain a strong moral compass. People see it, sense it, and hold you accountable for it.

Newman's Own has this kind of social influence. The company donates 100 percent of its profits to charity. Their company motto is well known: "Shameless Exploitation in Pursuit of the Common Good." Consumers hold them accountable. The company has built its social freedom into their business model. The result is that they have provided more than $300 million to thousands of charities all over the world. This is passion, purpose, and prosperity benefiting humanity. This inspires loyalty from consumers and helps them have a greater impact on society.

Growing social freedom is hard work. You do what you say you're going to do, and you do it with a level of passion, purpose, and prosperity that enables you to set the bar of excellence. You remain humble and kind while you hone your skills and grow your leadership in a way that others admire. You communicate well and practice communicating well. You respect yourself deeply and see the value in all others equally. You give back in ways that benefit humanity and grow more opportunity.

You become the kind of person others want to work for and with—not because you're nice but because you are driven by something greater than yourself. People can see it on you and feel it in your presence because it is who you are. You are neither toxic nor negative. Instead you are authentic and vulnerable and protect your mindset from unhealthy activity. You never stop leading by example. Essentially you want to become the best you that you can be because you want the Ultimate Freedom for everyone. You pursue the greater good with passion, purpose, prosperity, and a willingness to continue exploring a new level of excellence.

You protect your social freedom by understanding and following the principles of "right relationship and right action." It is the practice of understanding and allowing for people's needs as being part of the negotiation and process. It includes kindness, honesty, and integrity in all your dealings, all the time. It is never taking advantage of your position, authority, or influence over another. It's understanding the mission of your company and making sure that every aspect of your company and its leadership follows and honors that mission.

To protect and grow social freedom, you ask yourself and the people you are working with:

- "What's our intention?"
- "Are our actions aligned with our mission?"
- "How can we be of service?"
- "What feels good and right to do now?"
- "What's our next best step?"
- "Does this align with our mission?"
- "How will this benefit our audience or target market?"

This will help you see whether you are in right relationship and right action within your mission and values, doing the work with passion and purpose.

Protecting your social freedom is an ongoing job that even Oprah has had challenges with. James Frey exaggerated and lied about his life in his memoir, *A Million Little Pieces,* a book that attained bestseller status in part because of Oprah's influence. Once his lies were exposed, Oprah confronted him on her show because he jeopardized her influence by his dishonesty.

The importance of social freedom is not just in its influence; it is also in building value, trust, and likability for the greater good. It is having your philosophy and actions in life benefit as many people as possible. This means dreaming bigger and bigger over time. You can start the process by starting locally and growing globally. Oprah Winfrey has said, "You become what you believe, and to believe that you are created by the power that's greater than yourself means anything is possible."

What You Need to Know 2.0

1. Social freedom has the greatest power and influence of all the freedoms.
2. Social freedom means being trusted enough to influence actions and policies to make an impact in the world.
3. It is not following the money but following the mission with right action (leadership), right relationship (never taking advantage of your position), and right idea.
4. Influence and impact are the currency of the future.
5. In Disruption 2.0 nothing you do will be hidden from the world once it is put into the codification system and placed as data somewhere.
6. To protect and grow Social freedom, ask yourself and the people you are working with:
   a. "What's our intention?"
   b. "Are our actions aligned with our mission?"
   c. "How can we be of service?"
   d. "What feels good and right to do now?"
   e. "What's our next best step?"
   f. "Does this align with our mission?"
   g. "How will this benefit our audience?"

Chapter 21

Time Freedom

An hour with a pretty girl on a park bench passes like a minute, but a minute sitting on a hot stove seems like an hour.
—Albert Einstein

Time is one of the greatest illusions ever created. We are conditioned to believe in it. It controls our days and our decision processes. The confusion most people have is thinking that time freedom means having the time and money to do whatever you want, when you want, and with whom you want, in an almost rebellious manner. But the truth is that time freedom is a level of relationship and mindfulness with the silent intelligence that grows your success, faith, and trust in yourself. It is living and interacting with the divine in a collaboration that provides you with the actual freedom you are searching for.

If your time is filled with interesting projects, wonderful relationships, and healthy remuneration then you likely feel fulfilled—purposeful and free. When your time is filled with a job that you hate, a restrictive income that doesn't meet your debt load, and demands on your time, you feel a lack of time freedom because you are living out of sync with what time really is.

For example, the difference in a comedian's success with a punchline is his timing. Whether the food is burned or cooked correctly is timing. The difference between asking your boss for a raise and getting it is timing. Motivational speaker/ author Zig Ziglar said, "Success occurs when opportunity meets preparation." This is an aspect of synchronistic timing. This is time freedom happening inside divine timing, and this is how this time freedom grows. But before either of these two things can enter into the divine timing and mindfulness funnel, a lot of preparations have been made.

You have invested time in honing a skill. A lot of failure and more practice have been put in place. A few crowds have booed at the joke, a few meals have been burnt, and a "no" on your raise questions have happened, and you've continued practicing skills and producing better work. On a deeper level we know that time is an illusion and that really there is no such thing as time.

However, when it comes to the Ultimate Freedom, time freedom is a daring and bold act. It is the courageous pursuit of your dreams. In this case, timing is everything. When timing is divine, we often call it serendipity, synchronicity, being in the right place at the right time, or coincidence, but it is actually a result of growing and honing skills and developing more wakefulness while collaborating with universal timing. It is learning to take care of yourself and filling your time with things that fulfill you.

All dreams have the influence of manmade and divine timing and the lessons that are best and specific for you to acquire. Dreams and goals give us leadership, faith, and action lessons that help us understand more about divine timing, which means that everything happens at its exact right time. This inner timing, which is part of the silent intelligence, will send an inspired thought or some sort of epiphany to you, and you will feel it throughout your whole being and body. It gives you a feeling of purpose and passion, and this is liberating.

These feelings of purpose and passion invite you to enter divine timing and collaborate for your own benefit—and over time, for the benefit of the whole. It will feel great and inspiring. It will feel big at first because it is meant to stretch your reality beyond its current flexible beliefs. Having an idea or an opportunity is an invitation for you to step into divine timing.

You will either think about the idea or engage with the idea. If you have chosen to think about it, you are using your mind, but this will not help you. Thinking about it and wondering what other people think about your idea separates you from the "divine" part of the timing, because you are interested in other people's opinions more than in taking action regarding the dream.

Divine timing doesn't include a lot of thought processes. It is a feeling with an "action steps" process. If you engage the idea, you are using your heart. If your heart says "Yes, let's do this" and you begin your action steps, you are following your heart. You have engaged with divine timing. The heart has no questions about it. It just knows that it has strong resonance with the idea and wants to pursue it. Your mind will have no answers because there are no questions. You will have to ask yourself "What is the next best step?" and then take that step. This will allow you to manage how you use your time each day.

At first you will be honing your skills and making mistakes that will help you hone more of your skills. You may take a class or get a coach. This is not failure; this is the learning curve. Time freedom means being in alignment with the divine and engaging with what creates time happiness, which is what we are truly looking for. Time happiness is a matter of your attitude and attention. During the learning curve and when success is realized it will be the feeling of happiness derived from your achieving what was important to you that will make you feel as if you have time freedom.

The resonance and alignment of taking action steps will create confidence so strong that you will have better discernment. An inner knowing will tell you what your next best step is. This divine timing will become a guide because you will know when it feels right to make the next move. You will check in with yourself, and your next best move will tell you what to do. If you do not take the next best step, one result is an unpleasant feeling, and you become out of balance.

If you are aligned with divine time freedom, then you are more aligned with being in the moment and are more present. This allows the universe to assist you in unfolding the power of your dream and its timing. Singer Sevyn Streeter said, "I've learned over the years to appreciate God's timing, and you can't rush things; it's gonna happen exactly when it's supposed to." Your job is to continue taking the next best step. But the next best step isn't the next easiest step. Don't confuse the two.

Also, this does not mean you should quit or procrastinate, nor does it mean you should stand and wait either. It doesn't mean work yourself to death or keep working in your spare time. It means you need to pay attention to the next best step. If that means you should read a book or learn this software or seek a coach, then do that. When things are not happening as fast as you think they should happen—or that you have done all that you can—it can be easy to get discouraged. However, this is when divine timing is working with you. It helps to pay attention and ask for what you need.

For me this lesson showed up when my business partner died and I was having my meltdown in the middle of nowhere. I decided to ask the universe for the help and assistance I needed, and then I believed in and waited for Mia to show up. In fact, I believed I had been answered so strongly I simply relaxed and forgot that I had made the request. My heart just knew someone would show up, and I knew it would be the perfect person.

When I met Mia, I also knew in my heart that she was the one the universe had sent me to work with. My heart understood divine timing and had the discernment to recognize my answered prayer. My mind would not know this. It would have suffered from analysis paralysis, and I would have overwhelmed myself wondering if I made the right decision.

If you suffer from analysis paralysis, it simply means you have stepped out of divine time freedom and moved into trying to think your way through it. This is how we become a control freak and think we have to know and do everything ourselves. Divine timing gives us lessons in mindfulness, awareness, alignment, discernment, patience, practice, readiness, and faith.

Even your birth and death are acts of divine timing. You are here in the perfect time, in the exact moment the divine wished you to be here. There is no mistake about that, and to think that you are not in relationship with this divine time freedom only creates a power struggle between your ego and the universe.

We live in the era of instant gratification, and we want it now. And when it doesn't instantly show up, we often think something is wrong. We begin to judge ourselves and "should" ourselves into misery. Then we belittle our skills and our idea, and this is how we destroy the dream and disconnect from the divine and its timing.

Divine timing doesn't come through the mind—it comes through the heart. You can see divine timing all over the place, especially if you look in the mirror. Earth is all about time freedom. She is the best example and most necessary part of meeting the divine order of timing. Time freedom is engaging with the moment and allowing it to unfold in its time and knowing how to be with its unfolding. Yes, this takes practice.

This is why our sped-up lives are hurting us so much. Author and lecturer Marianne Williamson says, "This is a self-organizing and self-correcting universe." Divine timing is time freedom when you engage with it. The acorn becomes an oak tree, the bulb becomes a flower, the caterpillar becomes a butterfly. Clearly there is an invisible force, a divine intelligence at work, and it creates the transformation in its divine timing—and it will with you too. This is time freedom. When you are engaged with it, you feel more freedom than you have ever felt before. You feel fulfilled and will have your needs met.

When you love your work, you do your work with love in your heart. Working does not feel like some painful and arduous task. You don't watch the clock waiting to see when you can quit. Instead it feels like playing, and there is nothing better than being in this kind of timing and work. You feel a sense of communion and connection with everything and every part of the project. It gives you more life force and well-being to be engaged with it. You love to talk about it and be in it because it gives you a sense of meaning and purpose.

When we engage with an art form, we begin to feel this divine time freedom because we accept and understand that art forms help us connect with our heart, and we accept the learning curve of an art form. We are learning and enjoying the art, and we know that the more we practice, the better we become at it. We mindfully connect with the space where we create our art and allow our divine timing to enter the space with us and show us what to create. We don't question it or analyze it to death. We think about the process in steps and ask, "What is the next best step?"

We simply begin creating, whether it is through painting, dancing, pottery, design, writing, knitting, or gardening. It is this same principle with life and business. Time freedom is created from this space. You and the divine know what is best for you and how to create the life you want. Your mind can assist you in creating this if you let your heart lead the way. You are an important and integral product and part of divine time and freedom.

Imagine a piano in front of you with a key missing from its keyboard. You can see that the piano is no longer whole. It is missing a key, a note, a sound. You can't play music that requires that key, note, or sound if it's missing that key. In divine timing, that's how important it is for you to be here now. It's as if every person on the planet is a key on the piano keyboard of the divine. Each person represents a key, sound, or note on the chromatic scale of the divine.

Divine timing is so precise that without you here now, the piano would be missing a key, a note, and a sound. It would not be whole. That's how important you are to divine timing and how important it is to you. When we play music on the piano, we don't press all the keys at once. We push the keys down sequentially in a timed fashion that allows for a melody to be created. At the right time we hit the key that is the correct note in that moment that produces the most beneficial sound, in the precise universal time.

Your mind can only think about music; it can't participate in the universal music being created. Your heart knows when to play the note of you at the exact time when it is listening to and engaged with this time freedom. Playing that note and expressing that sound is your greatest joy, happiness, and freedom. This is when timing is everything.

When change happens in your life, do you go to your mind and start complaining, belittling, or scaring yourself or listening in for your next best action? In Disruption 2.0, timing will be one of the most important factors to listen to because the disruption is happening so fast that logic will not work. Your intuitive timing and following the next best step will be important for you to surrender to.

Your inner timing and intelligence will tell you what you can be doing next to build, claim, and protect your freedom. It will tell you whether to take action right now or stay put. It will tell you which opportunities have traction and which don't. It will guide you to the partnerships you can work with and what to do next. The key is that you must be working from the place of inner intelligence and divine timing. Disruption looks like chaos. It is not organized or simple. It can be overwhelming to the mind, but your inner time freedom is what will recognize your next best step. If your mind resists this step, you will begin to struggle.

The future is not as fixed as it has been in the past. Things happen at speeds unheard of before. We have many hurdles and challenges ahead that are going to test humanity to its core. Our freedoms are being eaten alive right now, and it will be up to you to figure out what is best for you and how to move forward with your life. I can tell you what I know for sure. First, it is no accident that you are here now, and second, the timing of you being here is perfect.

Your options for your future can be considered right now. You can ask your inner intelligence to show you options, and you can determine which one to devote your time to. The future is not fixed. It is a flexible, malleable movement. We will be looking at huge challenges, unintended consequences, innovations, and bad actors that will challenge everyone to the core. This means our past time-freedom skills and habits will not work. Your creativity and inner intelligence will be key factors in producing future income and freedom.

What You Need to Know 2.0

1. Time freedom is a daring and bold act that determines how you live your life. It is the courageous pursuit of your dreams.
2. Time freedom or timing is a level of relationship and mindfulness with the silent intelligence that grows your success, faith, and trust in yourself
3. You will have to ask yourself, "What is the next best step?"
4. If you suffer from analysis paralysis, it simply means you have stepped out of divine time freedom and moved into trying to think your way through it.

5. Your birth and your death are acts of divine timing. You are here in the perfect time, in the exact moment the divine wished you to be here.

6. Your inner timing and intelligence will tell you what you can be doing next to build, claim, and protect your freedom.

7. Disruption looks like chaos. It is not organized or simple. It can be overwhelming to the mind, but your inner time freedom is what will recognize your next best step.

Chapter 22

Creative Freedom

A creative man is motivated by the desire to achieve, not by the desire to beat others.

—Ayn Rand

Creative freedom is sacred. It is the ability to be authentically who you are and comfortable in your own skin. It is the ability to follow an idea coming through you until it manifests in the form that is visualized through you. Whether it is a book, business, art form, or theory, creative freedom is the expression of your faith and action toward manifesting it. It is you giving yourself permission and allowing yourself to believe in the impossible. It is allowing yourself to believe that the impossible has called upon you to bring something forward.

Creativity allows us to look at things differently and interact with things with an eye for what else they could become. Without this ability, you have locked up a part of you that is here to create—a life, career, relationship, and happiness. Creativity is something that is specific to you and is an aspect of your individuality. Creativity is an expression of your being. To be creatively free involves you taking the risk of being yourself and engaging with your imagination.

Albert Einstein said, "Logic will get you from A to B. Imagination will take you everywhere." Your future is being reimagined, and creative freedom will be one of the highest forms of value that helps you manifest it.

When you have creative freedom, you are fearless and courageous at allowing yourself to be who you are. For example, when good music plays, your body moves the way it moves to the music, which is usually different from the way another person moves. Allowing your body to move the way the music is moving is engaging with your creative freedom. Allowing yourself to like the type of music that you authentically like is also an expression of your core essence or creative freedom.

Creative freedom is the expression of you that is uniquely you and no one else. If you can't let *you* out, how can you be free? Your creativity is the sound of you playing your note. No two notes are the same note. Expressing your individuality is the power behind creative freedom. Creative freedom asks questions like "How can I ____?" or "What do I want?" Long term or short term, we add to this question to get clear about what it is we are going to create in the moment. It looks like this:

- What do I want—to have?
- What do I want—to do right now?
- What do I want—out of life?
- What do I want—in or from a relationship?
- What do I want—as a career?
- What do I want—to see before I die?
- What do I want—to experience before I die?
- What do I want—to express?
- What do I want—to give?
- What do I want—to be?
- What do I want—to say?
- What do I want—to know?

- What do I want—to ask?
- What do I want—to eat?

These are the questions that only you can answer. Then imagination ignites with the question and sparks possibilities. Without knowing what you want, creativity hangs in the balance waiting to be unearthed. Opportunity and divine timing don't have a way to express themselves through you without you being creatively free and allowing your imagination to know that "if you can dream it you can create it." Financial freedom has no way of creating itself. Emotional freedom cannot happen when we are trying to be like the crowd. Spiritual freedom will have no outlet.

Creative freedom is where we begin to take responsibility for our needs and wants in life. We become curious about ourselves and our own individuality. We stop being emotionally fragile about other people's perception of us, and we embrace who we are with love and kindness toward ourselves. We begin to see others compassionately because we know how tender we felt when we weren't able to express ourselves. Only you can free yourself in the way that best expresses your sense of creative freedom.

Creative freedom invites you to rejoice in you because it unleashes your inner genius. Your money, health, wealth, freedom, and best life sit inside your inner genius. Your inner genius is born of imagination and not scholastic ability. Henry Ford had only a third-grade education. Often when you are too smart, your mind can become dangerous because it wants to talk you out of your imagination. It can compare you to others and tell you that you are not good enough or are not worthy. Creative freedom is raw, pure possibility. It doesn't have or see obstacles. It just feels solutions and possibilities in the form of imagined ideas.

Creative freedom is the expression of letting your inner genius play. It is the aspect of you that wants to get real in order to allow freedom and happiness out of you. You explore and express your specific gifts, and this usually inspires others. Artists, entertainers, writers, and others express their unique inner genius as a form of creative freedom. Your inner genius may have nothing to do with creative arts, and still it will set you free.

Songwriters make wonderful music that not everyone is going to like, and yet their imagination and creativity creates music that many people love, and they are rich because of it. Not every song is going to be a hit, but the practice will allow your creativity to flow and continue creating. Your creative gift can be simple and easy; it doesn't have to be complex in order to be great.

Oprah Winfrey said that she was always talking in class. She would get in trouble for talking, and yet that was her unique gift. She could get anyone to spill the beans about anything. She became the world's most trusted interviewer because she loved to talk. When your creative expression brings to you a feeling of beauty, love, truth, kindness, and authenticity, you are expressing inner genius and creative freedom.

The human experience longs to express authentic self, and this is where language can be limiting. In order to connect with this aspect of creative freedom, we need to quiet our minds. Meditation can help us contact our intuitive, nonverbal, silent intelligence. We know far more than we think we do. Creativity comes in flashes of insight and not logical analysis. This means genius arises in moments of stillness and silence. Creativity needs spaciousness and connection with divine timing. Too much thinking can block creativity.

You can't "busy" your way to creativity and inner genius; you have to meet it and let it out of you. Inside you are the seeds of invention, transformation, vision, and freedom. When we get quiet inside and allow our creative freedom to emerge, we must support it by creating focus. This is the time to ask, "What is the next best step?" This is how we start and how we become responsible for our creations.

Because our minds can be such saboteurs of our creative freedom and all other freedoms, it benefits us to have support. We can learn to explore and invite, appreciate and rejoice, and allow and be seen in a safe place that enables our inner genius and imagination in the room so it can express itself safely.

Creative freedom is not just about making money. It's about you exploring your options because you have a mission, passion, or calling to express something through you. It has ingenuity and originality. Money can be made out of imagination too, but creative freedom is a type of freedom that allows you to manifest and not just money.

What You Need to Know 2.0

1. Creative freedom is raw, pure possibility.
2. Creative freedom releases your inner genius.
3. Creative freedom is the ability to follow an idea coming through you until it manifests in the form that is visualized through you.
4. Creative freedom is allowing yourself to believe that the impossible has called upon you to bring something forward.
5. Creative freedom asks questions like, "How can I _____?" or "What do I want?"
6. Creative freedom allows you to explore and express your unique and specific gifts.

Thank you for joining us on this journey to unlocking the Ultimate Freedom. As you grow more confident with the six key freedoms, they will bring you a life of passion, purpose, and prosperity. This is the expression of living your best life, by introducing you to your best self. Yes, life includes uncertainty and unknowns, but with your imagination and inner genius you can unlock your Ultimate Freedom and live the best expression of you.

In your future, having freedom and mobility will be the strongest forms of freedom you can create. As much as you can free yourself from systems, beliefs, and old patterns, the more freedom you will have. Whenever possible, we need to free ourselves of jobs, credit cards, debt, credit scores, emotional baggage, TV watching, and so forth in order to create real freedom. The more you are freed from, the more freedom you will invite. Remember freedom is something you become.

We want to invite you to go now and get your free bonuses that come with this book as a thank-you for getting this far. Go to http//: www. theultimatefreedombook.com and see the freebies that await you. We want to leave you with a quote from our Ultimate Freedom mentor, Harriet Tubman: "I freed a thousand slaves. I could have freed more, if only they knew they were slaves."

Let your freedom ring.

Vickie Helm and Mia Bolte

About the Authors
& Smart Group Firm

Founded by Vickie Helm and Mia Bolte based in Boulder, Colorado, Smart Group Firm is an independent consulting firm that specializes in bringing research, data, and solutions that create "thriveability." We work side by side to assist you in solving problems and capturing your greatest opportunities. We go deep to unlock unseen potential and drive permanent transformation. Together we work to strengthen the capabilities that will enable lasting success.

Our business is directed by two simple principles:

1. We strive to give our clients the most up-to-date relevant information and systems in a timely manner so they can maximize productivity, create plans, capture opportunities, grow profits, and safeguard their freedom.
2. We are devoted to building strong long-term client relationships; we only provide and publish data, advice, and research from analysts whose advice and strategies we use for our own families and businesses.

We believe in offering a range of views and options: We do not work with a one-size-fits-all mentality. Our experienced team of professionals work with

233

your unique concerns in mind. As a result, we customize options and strategies that fulfill your goals. We provide you with customized solutions and support.

We believe in a long-term methodology: Our business strategy is based on building long-term relationships with our clients. We aim to provide consistently relevant, dependable, actionable, and profitable strategies and advice that focus on having all-around success. As a result, many of our internal marketing efforts are focused on selling instantly accessible memberships, which provide our clients with immediate access to the most current knowledge base at a much lower total cost.

This also guides our business, joint ventures, and strategic alliance partnerships as well as our employee culture. We strive to build a community of thought leaders and business owners dedicated to creating thriveability in our world, and we invite you to join us.

We believe in transparency and accountability: Since trust and goodwill are demonstrated by having consistent, integrity-filled actions, our overall goal in business is to simply and consistently create the best products and services we can and provide our clients with outstanding care. Whether you are a startup, small, or Fortune 500 company, our goal is to support you in achieving strong productivity and profit levels by powering creatively capable teams and cultures. Learn more about us at http://www.smartgroupfirm.com where we look forward to talking and finding out how we can serve you.

Create an abundant future today with success in both your business and personal relationships. With over eighteen years experience and multiple businesses, Vickie Helm has a degree in accounting and graduated from the Barbara Brennan School of Healing. She is also an acclaimed international author and business development strategist.

Whether you're an entrepreneurial couple or in any business partnership, she shows you how to maximize your potential and multiply your results. As a world-class speaker, seminar leader, and trainer, Vickie is regularly sought out by the media to answer business, partnership, and marketing questions. She possesses a unique perspective as both a recognized business development strategist and a leading relationship expert.

As a keynote speaker, Vickie shares her own experience of starting her first business at only ten years old when she became an "accidental entrepreneur" for life. Currently, she is the CEO of two successful companies and a sought-after consultant for others. Discover the invaluable secrets, tips, and tools she offers to empower your partnerships, productivity, and profits. Find out how you can become stronger and more productive by having unstoppable leadership and business partnerships. Attract more money and have more influence by learning how to join forces and build thriving partnerships more effectively and easily than ever before.

Create more prosperity and fulfillment in every area of your life. As a recognized and acclaimed expert in relationships and career development, Mia Bolte has more than eighteen years experience helping people achieve success. Mia holds a Master of Arts in Counseling Psychology from Naropa University, where she now serves as an adjunct faculty member. She has also taught at the University of Minnesota.

Often called compassionate, wise, and gentle while at the same time having profound insight, deep compassion, and impeccable ethics, Mia is a sought-after consultant, coach, and mentor for people who are seriously looking to deepen their leadership skills, improve their productivity, and achieve lasting change.

She knows how to help your team out-perform expectations because she understands the functional dynamics of emotion and behavior and their translation into human performance. She can provide you with spot-on feedback—from the heart—that will guide you forward into the life you dream of having.

As a keynote speaker, seminar leader, and trainer, Mia is engaging and empowering and has the strength and ability to guide you toward a deeper understanding of what will make you succeed, helping you achieve more success than you ever thought possible. Mia will show you how you can get the edge in your career by having stronger leadership, more productivity, and a deeper understanding of your inner dynamics.

A free eBook edition is available with the purchase of this book.

To claim your free eBook edition:

1. Download the Shelfie app.
2. Write your name in upper case in the box.
3. Use the Shelfie app to submit a photo.
4. Download your eBook to any device.

Shelfie

A free eBook edition is available
with the purchase of this print book.

CLEARLY PRINT YOUR NAME ABOVE IN UPPER CASE

Instructions to claim your free eBook edition:
1. Download the Shelfie app for Android or iOS
2. Write your name in **UPPER CASE** above
3. Use the Shelfie app to submit a photo
4. Download your eBook to any device

Print & Digital Together Forever.

Snap a photo   Free eBook   Read anywhere

The Morgan James
Speakers Group

↗ www.TheMorganJamesSpeakersGroup.com

We connect Morgan James published authors with live and online events and audiences whom will benefit from their expertise.

 Morgan James makes all of our titles available
through the Library for All Charity Organizations.

www.LibraryForAll.org

Printed in the USA
CPSIA information can be obtained
at www.ICGtesting.com
JSHW022219140824
68134JS00018B/1151